The Anglo Concertina Music of
WILLIAM KIMBER

The Anglo Concertina Music of
WILLIAM KIMBER

Second Edition

Dan M. Worrall and James J. Branch

With a Foreword by Andy Turner

The Anglo Concertina Music of William Kimber
By Dan M. Worrall and James J. Branch

Second Edition, Copyright © 2024 Dan Michael Worrall and James Jarrett Branch

First Edition, Copyright © 2005 Dan Michael Worrall and
　　　　　　　　　　　　　　The English Folk Dance and Song Society

ISBN: 978-1-953208-21-7

All rights reserved. No part of this book may be reproduced, scanned, transmitted or distributed in any printed or electronic form without the prior permission of the authors, except in the case of brief quotations embodied in articles or reviews.

All music is in the public domain unless otherwise noted.

Music type setting by James J. Branch
Type setting and book design by Dan M. Worrall
Type set in Adobe Garamond Pro

Printed and distributed by Rollston Press
1717 Ala Wai Blvd #1703
Honolulu, HI 96815
USA
info@rollstonpress.com

Front cover: William Kimber, as photographed by John Gay. Courtesy of the Vaughan Williams Memorial Library.

Frontispiece (previous page): Headington Quarry, from an old postcard ca. 1900. Photo courtesy of Stephanie Jenkins, Oxford History website, www.headington.org.uk.

Rear cover: Oxford University Men's Morris dancing on Broad Street, Oxford, May Morning, 1931. William Kimber is playing concertina. Photo courtesy of David Rogers, Chris Sheffield, and the Oxford City Morris.

For Eleanor and Maggie

Table of Contents

Foreword/ xi

Introduction/ xv

Acknowledgments/ xxi

A Note on QR Codes and Audio Files Used in This Book/ xxv

Chapter 1: Headington Quarry and Kimber's Early Years/ 1

Chapter 2: The English Folk Revival and Kimber's Later Years/ 43

Chapter 3. Playing Like Kimber: Style and Technique/ 73

A Note on the Transcriptions of Chapters 4-8/ 107

Chapter 4: The Headington Morris Dance Tunes/ 111

Bacca Pipes: 113, 128
Bean Setting: 114, 130
Blue-Eyed Stranger: 115, 132
Constant Billy: 115, 133
Country Gardens: 116, 134
Double Set Back: 116, 138
Getting Upstairs: 117, 140
Haste to the Wedding: 118, 142
Headington Morris Reel: 118, 274, 292
How D'ye Do, Sir?: 119, 145
Hunting the Squirrel: 119, 146
Jockie to the Fair: 120, 148
Laudnum Bunches: 120, 152
Old Mother Oxford: 121, 154
Old Woman Tossed Up in a Blanket: 121, 158
Rigs o' Marlow: 122, 160
Rodney: 122, 161
Shepherd's Hey: 123, 163
Trunkles: 123, 164
The Twenty-Ninth of May: 124, 166
The Willow Tree: 124, 168

Chapter 5. Other Morris Dance Tunes/ 171

Bonny Green Garters: 171, 178
Brighton Camp (Eynsham): 172, 180
Cock o' the North: 173, 182
The Fool's Jig/Manchester Hornpipe: 173, 274, 288
Morris On: 173, 184
Morris Off: 173, 186

Princess Royal: 174, 188
Swaggering Boney: 174, 191
Young Collins: 175, 193

Chapter 6. Social Dance Part I: Country Dances/ 195

Bonnets So Blue: 199, 206
Double Lead Through: 199, 208
Hilly-go Filly-go: 199, 212
Off She Goes: 200, 215
Pop Goes the Weasel: 200, 216
The Quaker's Wife: 201, 219
The Ribbon Dance: 201, 220
The Triumph: 201, 222

Chapter 7. Social Dance Part II: Quadrilles and Couples Dances/ 225

Bonny Dundee: 234, 242
Donkey Cock Your Tail Up: 234, 245
Father O'Flynn: 234, 246
I Love the Gal with the Blue Frock On: 234, 248
Keel Row: 235, 250
Kitty Come: 235, 252
Little Polly: 235, 254
Mayblossom: 235, 256
Moonlight: 236, 260
Nae Good Luck About the Hoose: 236, 262
Over the Hills to Glory: 237, 264

Chapter 8. In the Taproom: Step Dances and Songs/ 269

The First of May: 273, 283
The Wonder: 273, 284
The Manchester Hornpipe: 274, 288
Soldier's Joy: 274, 290

Song accompaniment:
The Fly Be on the Turmut: 274, 292
The Village Pump: 275, 294

Novelty piece:
The Church Bells: 277, 297

Chapter 9. Epilogue/ 299

Chapter 10. Discography/ 301

Index 308

About the Authors/ 313

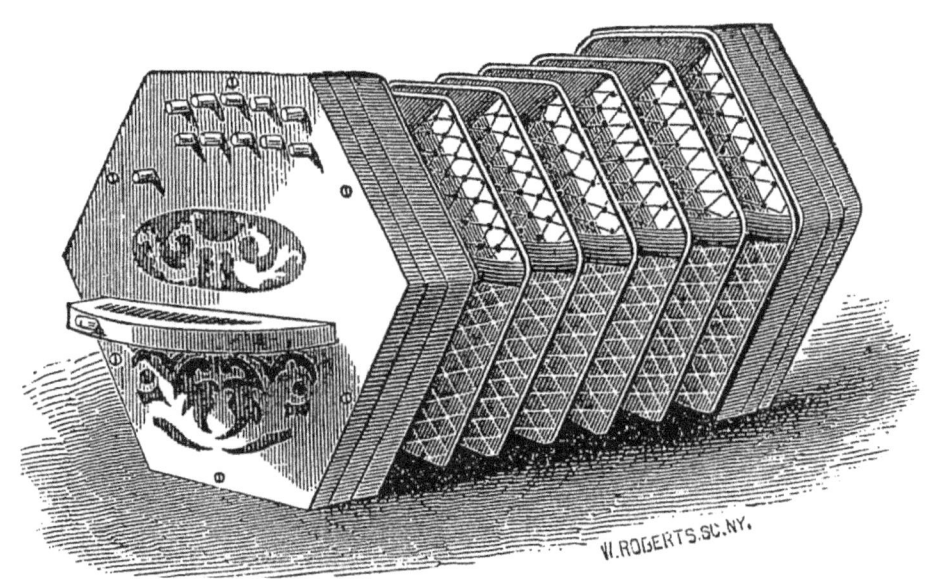

Foreword

In 2017, as part of a series of events commemorating the centenary of the death of Percy Manning, I took part in a recreation of the concert which Manning had organised at the Corn Exchange in Oxford in March 1899. The original concert featured dances from the recently revived Headington Quarry Morris Dancers, interspersed with songs performed by trained vocalists with accompaniment on the pianoforte. The exact same programme of dances and songs was performed at the 2017 recreation, with Headington Quarry putting on a very fine display. The songs were performed by Oxford band Magpie Lane, of which I've been a member these 30-odd years, in a manner more likely to find favour with a 21st century folk audience than the rather polite style in which one imagines they were delivered back in 1899. During the interval, I was unexpectedly asked "Would you mind playing Bill Kimber's concertina?". Well, which Anglo player wouldn't jump at the chance of playing such an iconic instrument? I was pleased to find that the note layout was essentially the same as on my own Anglo, and that the instrument played beautifully – it's nicely responsive, and also really rather loud! Playing 'Laudanum Bunches' on Bill Kimber's Anglo at the start of the second half was a memory that I'll always treasure – my thanks to Julie Kimber-Nicholson, William Kimber's grand-daughter, for trusting me with the precious instrument.

Then in 2022, as HQMD resumed practices after the Covid pandemic, I had a phone call from the side's squire, Dave Townsend. Ill health meant that their veteran musician John Graham was no longer able to play the accordion and Dave asked if I'd be prepared to step into the breach. Now, I'd had no particular inclination to get involved with a Morris side. But I'd been listening to recordings of

William Kimber for decades, and held him in very high esteem as a concertina-player, and as a key figure in the 20th century folk and Morris revivals. And, as I suspect Dave knew full well, the chance of playing Kimber's tunes for Quarry was frankly irresistible. And so it was that I became the musician for Headington Quarry Morris Dancers. Of course, over the years I'd often found myself playing tunes that Kimber had recorded. But playing them for the side to dance to is something else entirely – an honour and a privilege. When John Kirkpatrick heard that I was now the Quarry musician, he simply said "you jammy beggar!".

I came to folk music as a teenager in the mid-1970s, and early influences included the LPs Son of Morris On, The Prospect Before Us, and Plain Capers. Anglo concertinas featured heavily on those records, invariably played by someone called John – John Watcham, John Rodd, John Tams, John Kirkpatrick. So I'd heard quite a lot of Anglo playing by the time – probably around 1979 – that I first got to hear the classic Topic LP *The Art of William Kimber*. Kimber's playing was very striking. It was fast, for one thing – certainly much faster than the contemporary Morris sides I admired, such as Great Western and Old Spot. But it was also so amazingly crisp and rhythmic. And, of course, every now and again (as in the final part of 'Trunkles') you'd get one of those chords that sound surprisingly adventurous – not really what you expect from a traditional musician. Eventually I came to realise – as Dan Worrall has now conclusively demonstrated – that these unexpected chords were in fact the result of Kimber's technique when playing the Anglo, and the mechanics of the instrument itself.

By the time I first heard Kimber's playing I'd already started to play the Anglo myself, but had not yet come close to mastering the trick of playing both hands at once, and didn't yet have an established style of my own. So, when I was able to play a left hand accompaniment, did I try to play like Kimber? Well no, not really. I don't think I've ever tried to replicate exactly what Kimber does. However I've certainly been inspired by his playing – a somewhat sparse left hand, rather than fistfuls of chords, and a definite aspiration to play dance tunes in a crisp rhythmic style, with each note clearly articulated (a lesson I also took from listening to the wonderful Northumbrian mouth organ player, Will Atkinson). And there are certainly times when, without attempting to slavishly copy his playing, I've tried to evoke the spirit of William Kimber.

In this volume, the authors consider the question of why so few Anglo players take Kimber's style as a model for how to play the instrument. Partly, I think, it's the result of a natural inclination to be influenced, and learn from, the performers one sees at folk clubs and festivals – John Kirkpatrick, Cohen Braithwaite-Kilcoyne, Brian Peters, Keith Kendrick et.al. You see the same thing with folk song – far more modern singers learn their songs (and singing style) from Martin Carthy, June Tabor, Jon Boden and so forth, than from recordings of traditional singers like Sam Larner, Phoebe Smith, or Walter Pardon. Given that many of the recordings we have of William Kimber were made in the 1930s and 1940s, the sound quality is actually not at all bad. But, as the authors write, the recordings "might be said to have a certain quaintness, or to sound of a different era". In fact I'd go further. Greil Marcus described the 1920's and '30s recordings on Harry Smith's 1952 *Anthology of American Folk Music* as representing "the old weird America". For many modern listeners I think the recordings we have of traditional musicians such as Bill Kimber, Scan Tester, Stephen Baldwin and Jinky Wells are so far removed from our regular musical experience that they seem like "the old weird England".

However, Kimber's playing of Morris and country dance tunes was simply wonderful, and all Anglo players could benefit from paying careful attention to how he achieved this. This much expanded second edition breaks Kimber's playing down into its component parts, and invites us to try those techniques for ourselves. This should be of interest to players just beginning to add some harmony to their playing – as Dan and Jarrett point out, Kimber's method is actually really quite simple! But also to more experienced players, looking to try a different approach.

Finally, this new edition is invaluable in painting a picture of the social and cultural milieu from which Kimber sprang. Clearly, no musician exists in a vacuum, and an understanding of the world in which he was brought up is crucial to forming a rounded picture of Kimber as a musician, and as a person. The book also considers the vital role which Kimber played in supporting the early 20th century Morris revival; and ensuring that the Morris survived (and, indeed, flourished) in Headington Quarry. It's a fitting tribute to a man who is rightly revered as a key figure in the story of English folk music.

Andy Turner
Didcot, Oxfordshire
October 15, 2024

Chris Kimber-Nicholson dancing the *Shepherd's Hey* jig at the gravesite of his great grandfather, William Kimber, with Andy Turner playing Kimber's Anglo concertina. Photo taken at Holy Trinity churchyard, Headington Quarry, on the centerary of Cecil Sharp's death, June 23, 2024. Photo by Derek Schofield.

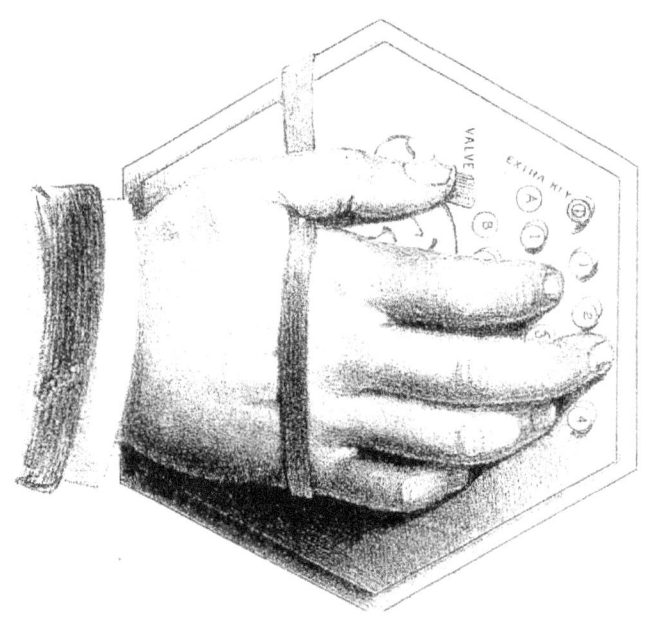

Introduction

This book contains transcriptions of all the known recordings of William Kimber (1872–1961), an iconic figure in the early twentieth-century rediscovery of Morris dance in England, and a renowned and unique musician on the Anglo concertina. An earlier edition of this work, published by the English Folk Dance and Song Society (EFDSS) in 2005, concentrated on his Morris dance music, the great significance of which was recognized by Cecil Sharp, the famed leader of the English folk revival, after he first saw Kimber and the Headington Quarry Morris men dance in the snow at Sandfield Cottage in 1899. This second edition builds upon that earlier work, adding much more of the music that he played for social dances in his village in the waning years of the nineteenth century. To understand better Kimber's earlier years in the rural village of Headington Quarry—the place of origin of his approach to music and dance—a description of his life during those earlier years as well as during later times after he met Sharp has been added, as has a musical analysis of, and tutorial for, his unique style of playing.

While a student in Texas, some fifty years ago, I purchased a concertina from a local music shop, with no idea what to do with it or how to play it. Luckily, a friend introduced me to two recently released record albums of Anglo concertina music. One featured Chris Droney (1922–2020), a Clare farmer and a concertina player of the old school,[1] and the other featured William Kimber (1872–1961), a yet older player from Oxfordshire. The latter LP was *The Art of William Kimber* (Topic Records, 1974). At that time I was in the beginning days of graduate school and, like most of my college friends, was immersed in rock and roll music. Kimber's music was a revelation. I couldn't then put into words its effect on me, but many years later I found an appropriate description written by Mary Neal, who with Cecil Sharp did so much to revive and spread Morris dance and its music throughout England:

> . . . *a little stir of an older life, an older rhythm, an older force, in tune with a simpler life, a sweeter music. . . . [from] a world untouched by machinery and mechanized power but responsive to the vibrant rhythm of sea and wind, earth and stars.*[2]

Kenneth Loveless, Kimber's friend and former concertina pupil, had this to say of his former tutor:

> *His real memorial is in the hundreds of Morris dancers he has taught and influenced, and in the brilliance of his playing which, to my knowledge, was quite unequalled even to within a fortnight of his death. His sense of rhythm, and his wonderful natural ability to use the right chord, and the proper use of the bellows. . . . all these are things that I and many others will long remember.*[3]

How did Kimber come to his memorable and unique style of playing? To answer that, we must first turn to his cultural environment in his formative years.

Most descriptions of William Kimber and his music rightly focus on his "discovery" by Cecil Sharp at the famous meeting in the snow outside Sandfield Cottage on Boxing Day, 1899, and on his role along with Cecil Sharp and others in bringing about the Morris dance revival in England during the ensuing half century. It was an exciting time in the national spotlight, but the essence of his musical style had been set much before that time, during his youth in Headington Quarry. It is to that village, in a time before he became an early twentieth-century celebrity of sorts, that we must first turn our attention (Chapter 1). The Quarry was a distinctive place at that time, one that was perhaps quite unlike the mental image that many of us—especially outsiders—have of leafy and tidy rural English villages of the late Victorian era. Only fragments of the Quarry village remain, because it was overtaken and subsumed by the growing City of Oxford during the early twentieth century. Theodore Chaundy, one of Kimber's several biographers, called the Quarry of Kimber's youth "a corner that was somehow 'different,' the abode of stranger folk and the haunt of gypsies . . . a [place of] rugged and ancient and individual beauty."[4] This "different" place had an impact not only in helping preserve an island of Morris dance in a rapidly industrializing England but, as is discussed in that chapter, it also heavily influenced Kimber's unique musical style.

With a description of the Quarry of Kimber's early life in hand, we then proceed to consider Kimber's life during the beginning years of the twentieth century, in what has become known as the English folk revival (Chapter 2). In its basic elements it is an oft-told story, but the organization and digitization of a wealth of Kimber and Sharp archival materials in the Vaughan Williams Memorial Library in recent years plus the release of several new biographies drawn from that material allow, if nothing else, a certain sharpening of focus in its telling, as well as a better understanding of how the contents of his recorded repertoire were influenced by the revival and its players.

Chapter 3 turns to the main task at hand: a study of the structure, technique, and style of his music, in an analysis that doubles as a tutorial for any students of the Anglo concertina who wish to play in his manner. Kimber's techniques on the twenty-button Anglo concertina are, upon analysis, fairly straightforward although not particularly familiar to most Anglo players today, who play in ways more suited to the much-expanded three-row, thirty-button concertina. Kimber fit all his playing onto the two-row, twenty-button concertina that he began to play in the 1870s. His true artistry lay in how he took a tune and the various technical constraints of the twenty-button keyboard and shaped them to the specific needs of his dancers, both Morris and social.

A brilliant dancer himself, Kimber displayed his long and intimate experience with playing for dance in his formulation of the accompaniment for each tune. Kimber added a left-hand accompaniment, both to help his dancers keep the rhythm and lift their feet as well as to allow the music to be heard in a noisy outdoor setting. Beyond the vitality of the rhythm and the lift inherent in it, his playing has a certain otherworldliness that seems to draw one into an earlier England, or so one might wistfully imagine. Most of this comes from the partial chords that emanate from his left-hand accompaniment. Many of these chords are unusual and surprising to our modern ears. As musicians Dave Townsend and Andy Turner observed in the EFDSS CD compilation in 1999 of Kimber's music:

> [Kimber brings in] *unexpected harmonies at many points. . . . The charm and quaintness of the effect on our ears, accustomed to the usual sequences of western harmony, may not have been apparent to Kimber or to his immediate audience. . . . Kimber's harmonies are nothing like those that anyone trained in western art-music would have produced.*[5]

It is those harmonies that reflect the relative musical isolation of his village upbringing; he seems to have had few preconceived notions on how to produce harmonies on a twenty-button Anglo. Predecessor instruments used in Cotswold Morris, including the pipe and tabor as well as the fiddle, were melodic with essentially no chorded or rhythmic accompaniment (except for the tabor, of course), and there is little in his village background to suggest that he was ever seriously or extensively exposed to the chordal progressions and harmonies of church or classical music. The analysis in Chapter 3 of his playing of these unusual chord choices—ones that do not follow the standard practice of typical chord progressions of western music—show that the chords are not necessarily the results of conscious choices he made, but rather were the result of his particular techniques used in playing the two-row keyboard. In effect, the *instrument* chose many of the chords, especially the "unusual" ones, as a result of the particular way Kimber's fingers travelled across its keyboard.

His manner of playing is different than the playing of many if not most Anglo players in England today. As a rule, the prominent players of the last half century, who began to play well after Kimber had passed away, utilize all the notes that the extended keyboard of a thirty- to forty-button keyboard provides. They tend to apply a deep and intuitive knowledge of chordal music theory—whether obtained from church music or music training or rock and roll—in a search for the "right" chord on the left hand. They then tend to adapt the playing of the right-hand melody to the constraints imposed by the left-hand chord, something that is almost totally absent in Kimber's approach. Modern Anglo playing in England is also strongly influenced by the oom-pah chords of English melodeon music, a style that is not endemic to a two-row concertina.

The effect of all these full chords and chordal progressions on modern Anglo playing, however obtained, is of course often beautiful. But Kimber's simpler, older style of playing is beautiful too. It stands apart as a style less encumbered by modern musical norms and is one not likely to grow again organically from modern roots. A prominent modern player of the Anglo, John Watcham, has observed that he "continue[s] to be surprised that Kimber's lively and often dissonant style has not been more widely adopted by other musicians, particularly bearing in mind his significance in the revival of the Morris."[6] The transcriptions and tutorial of this book attempt to provide tools for those wishing to explore Kimber's ways.

Another reason that aspiring concertina players might wish to take a look at Kimber's playing is the ease of learning it. When modern Anglo musicians roll out those beautiful chords and accordion-like oom-pahs, it comes at a bit of a cost. In accommodating a particular full chord on the left hand, right-hand melody notes often need to be re-routed on the fingerboard to give a bellows direction that is favorable to the desired chord. That re-routing takes muscle memory, plus often an extended keyboard of thirty-eight or forty buttons. Kimber's playing is almost instinctual in the way that it advances across the twenty-button keyboard, and the amount of memory work (and muscle memory) required is significantly less than that of modern three-row styles. And yet, the bounce and vitality of Kimber's playing is second to none.

Kathryn Wheeler, a rare modern-day twenty-button Anglo player who lives in Worcestershire and plays and dances for a local Morris side, notes that "the instrument and the way it's laid out, and how that feels, will [allow one to] come up with opportunities. . . . Twenty buttons feels more than enough. It is good to be working within some limitations and it is somehow more exciting to play with. I don't consciously *think* (although I might have an idea of a mood for a tune), and yet an interesting pattern or sequence will come out."[7] One senses that Kimber would have agreed.

Much of Kimber's playing *techniques* can be reduced to a repeatable pattern of application of a small number of "basic" and "finishing" steps, explained in the tutorial. His artistry—his *style*—lies in how he variously applied these steps to fashion an accompaniment, and then shaped the notes, rhythm and dynamics of the finished product to fit the needs of the dancers at hand.

Chapters 4–8 contain the largest segment of the book: note-for-note transcriptions for all his recorded work, including some fifty-four tunes organized by dance type, as well as a discussion of their sources. The detailed transcriptions are not intended as scores to be followed and memorized, bar by bar, as in a Beethoven sonata, but as a documenting of and guideposts to his two-row techniques, to help learners in their potential adoption of Kimber's intuitive approach to fashioning tune accompaniments on the Anglo concertina. These transcriptions include not only Morris and step dance tunes, but Kimber's English country dance tunes and the music for the popular quadrille and couples dances of the late nineteenth century—Lancers, Caledonian and Alberts quadrilles, as well as polkas, schottisches, waltzes, barn dances, galups, and the like. These so-called "ballroom" dances—many of them very modern and popular at the time—were not favored by Sharp and others of the folk revival, nor were they considered as traditional folk music—much as we might similarly dismiss rock or jazz music in our own time. As a result, the "ballroom" tunes have tended to be overlooked as significant parts of Kimber's overall repertoire.

Embedded QR codes throughout the book either make his playing instantly accessible or—because of copyright limitations—provide at least a digitally produced rendering of the music score. We hope that Kimber's unique way of playing the Anglo resonates as fully with you as it does with my co-author Jarrett Branch and myself.

Dan Worrall
Fulshear, Texas
July 2, 2023

---

[1] See transcriptions and biography of Droney in Dan M. Worrall and James J. Branch, 2023, *Chris Droney of Bell Harbour and the Tradition of the Concertina in North Clare*: Rollston Press, Honolulu, 247pp.

[2] Mary Neal, undated, Typescript for autobiography 'As a Tale That is Told: The Autobiography of a Victorian Woman', p. 153-155. Vaughan Williams Memorial Library, London.

[3] Kenneth Loveless, 1962, "In memoriam: William Kimber," *English Dance and Song*, English Folk Dance and Song Society, London, March 1962, pp. 20-21.

[4] Theo W Chaundy, "William Kimber. A Portrait." *The Journal of the EFDSS*, Vol.VIII, No.4 (1959), pp.203-211.

[5] Dave Townsend and Andy Turner, 1999, Stylistic characteristics of William Kimber's Anglo-concertina playing: in the booklet of the CD *Absolutely Classic, The Music of William Kimber*. EFDSS CD03, London, p. 56.

[6] John Watcham, as quoted in Gary Coover, 2020, *The Anglo Concertina Music of John Watcham*: Rollston Press, Honolulu, p. 95.

[7] Kathryn Wheeler, Worcestershire Morris musician and dancer, personal communication, January 7, 2024.

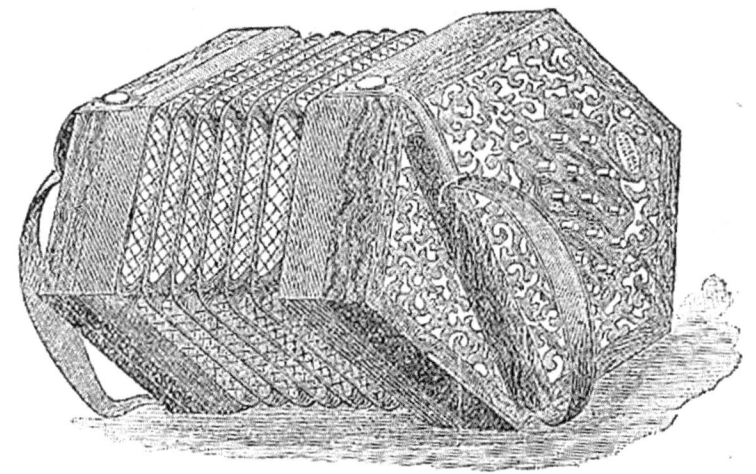

Acknowledgments

Our immense gratitude goes out to the many people who have contributed knowledge, insights, and materials to this work, both in its original form of 2005 and in this revised second edition of 2024. The original volume grew out of a long series of email exchanges with Essex musician Roger Digby, whom Dan met through www.concertina.net and has counted as a friend ever since. Roger provided encouragement and guidance at all steps of the early project, from initially suggesting publication through the editing of the final manuscript. On a first and subsequent trips to England, he introduced Dan to people and places of the fascinating world of English traditional music. The second edition was suggested by Gary Coover, another long-time friend and publisher of many concertina books through his Rollston Press in Honolulu.

The Vaughan Williams Memorial Library of the English Folk Dance and Song Society (EFDSS) is at the very center of most archival material relating to Cecil Sharp, William Kimber, Mary Neal, and others of the English folk revival, and the people of that archive have been very helpful in providing assistance and photographic materials. Macolm Taylor, two decades ago, and his present-day successor, Tiffany Hore, both directors of the library and archive, and the present librarian, Alexandra Burton, have produced many photographs and documents from the bottomless well that is their collection. In a similar manner, the chief officers of the EFDSS, Hazel Miller in 2005 and her successor today, Katy Spicer, have been generous in granting permission to publish information in both the early and second editions. Nigel Lynn, publishing consultant to the EFDSS, designed the original book, a task that has fallen to us for the present edition.

Other archives have granted access to materials that are also central to any study of William Kimber and his environment. Folk Arts Oxford, through its "Back to the Quarry" project, makes available on its website (www.merryville.uk) critical recordings made of Kimber by Theo Chaundy in the 1950s. There are also recordings of Rev. Kenneth Loveless as well as a very useful map of Kimber-related sites in the Quarry village. The Oxfordshire History Centre has kindly made available a number of period photographs with the able assistance of its manager, Mark Lawrence, and its photographic and oral history officer Helen Drury. Their archive assistant Anna Clark provided information on Kimber family burial sites, as did Helen Day, Parish administrator for Holy Trinity Church. Stephanie Jenkins, archivist of a wonderful local "Headington History" site—a part of the online site of Oxford History (www.headington.org.uk)—made available a number of period photographs of Headington Quarry. Any discussion of Headington Quarry history owes a debt to the late Oxford historian Raphael Samuel, whose seminal 1975 essay *Quarry Roughs: Life and Labour in Headington Quarry 1860–1920* is an essential historical reference for all things Quarry. A modern take on Quarry history is given by local historian Maurice East, who conducts walking tours through the old village area today, and who provided a wonderful photograph of his grandparents and other Quarry people in front of the Masons Arms pub at the turn of the last century.

Additional information on Kimber's life and his musical environment came from a variety of sources in the English traditional music and dance community. Any study of William Kimber will travel down paths that were blazed by Theo Chaundy, Kenneth Loveless, and Derek Schofield, each of whom has prepared an earlier biography of Kimber. David Atkinson, editor of the *Folk Music Journal* of the English Folk Dance and Song Society, kindly gave access to some of Chaundy's past work. Wes Williams supplied Kimber family information from the recently released UK 1921 census. We're grateful to Derek Schofield, Chloe Middleton-Metcalfe, and Dave Townsend for very useful advice on dance and tune history and sources, and to Andy Turner and John Watcham for patiently answering queries about Morris dance music and concertinas. Andy and Dave are currently the Musician and Squire, respectively, of the Headington Quarry Morris Dancers. In 2005 Dan had the great privilege of seeing the Headington Quarry Morris side dance on Whit Monday, and of meeting Kimber's grand-daughter, Julie Kimber-Nickelson. Stephen Rowling provided insight into the pipe and tabor and its comparison with the concertina in Morris use.

Besides the Vaughan Williams Memorial Library and Oxfordshire History Centre, we were kindly provided illustrations by Duncan Broomhead, keeper of the Morris Ring Photographic Archive; Christopher Sheffield, Duncan Drummond, and John Corlett of the Oxford University Morris Men and Oxford City Morris; and by Katie Howson. Randall Merris and Robin Harrison ably assisted with editing the first edition. Sally Antrobus skillfully copy-edited the second version, Andy Turner gave the manuscript a helpful critical read, and Drew Patterson kindly helped with cover design.

Those of us who enjoy listening to recordings of old-time traditional music owe a great debt to several collectors who were instrumental in recording and preserving William Kimber's music. Douglas Kennedy of the EFDSS helped Kimber make his studio recordings of 1935, 1946, and 1948. Field recordings in Headington Quarry were made by Theo W. Chaundy as well as by Peter Kennedy and Maud Karpeles, mostly in the 1950s. Those later recordings finally captured Kimber playing many tunes from his quadrille and couples dance repertoire, something that had been largely ignored by Sharp and others but had been an important part of the Quarry village's use of music and dance. In several visits over the years, Dan has been able to experience rural English traditional music sessions with Roger Digby, Katie Howson, Liz Giddings, John and Sue Cubbins, Deborah Matthews, Mark Davies and others; these sessions are surely descendants of the village dances and taproom amusements of Kimber's era. We both (Dan and Jarrett) hope to sample much more of this music at sites in southern and southeastern England after this book project is completed.

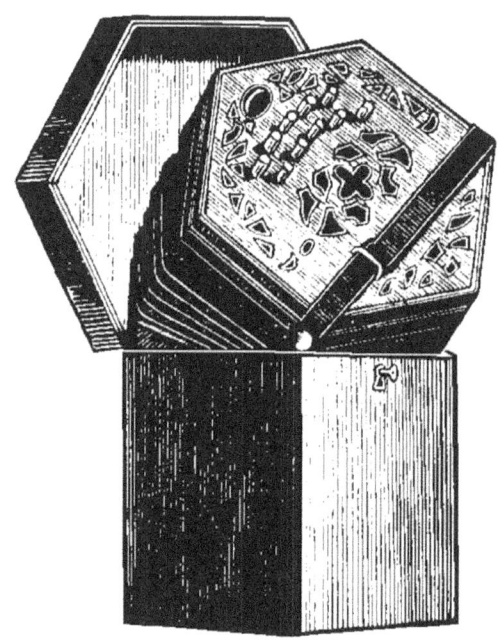

A Note on QR Codes and Audio Files Used in This Book

William Kimber recorded a number of tunes for the "His Master's Voice" label in the 1930s and 1940s. These recordings are now in the public domain, and QR codes linking to them have been added throughout this work. Kimber's later recorded music is still under copyright, so inserted QR codes for that music link to digitally generated audio files made directly from our transcriptions of Kimber's playing, as produced by the music writing software employed. These digitally generated audio files were made in order to check the accuracy of our transcriptions, and listening to them is of course a very far cry from listening to Kimber himself. However, for those who do not read music, or those who wish to quickly get the "gist" of a melody under discussion, these recordings may be helpful and are thus are included. A discography included in chapter 10 shows where the original recordings may be accessed. Finally, in the tutorial section of chapter 3, a few musical examples employ recordings of one of the authors (Worrall) in order to illustrate certain points on technique. These also are presented using QR codes.

All of these audio files can be accessed by pointing a smart phone at the QR code and opening up the website shown on the phone's screen. Things change rapidly in the digital world, and there is no guarantee that any of these QR codes and their internet links will still work five or ten years from now. To that potential eventuality, the discography included in Chapter 10 lists the archival or published sources of all of Kimber's known recordings.

William Kimber playing *Haste to the Wedding* via His Master's Voice, 1946

Haste to the Wedding, digital audio of the transcription

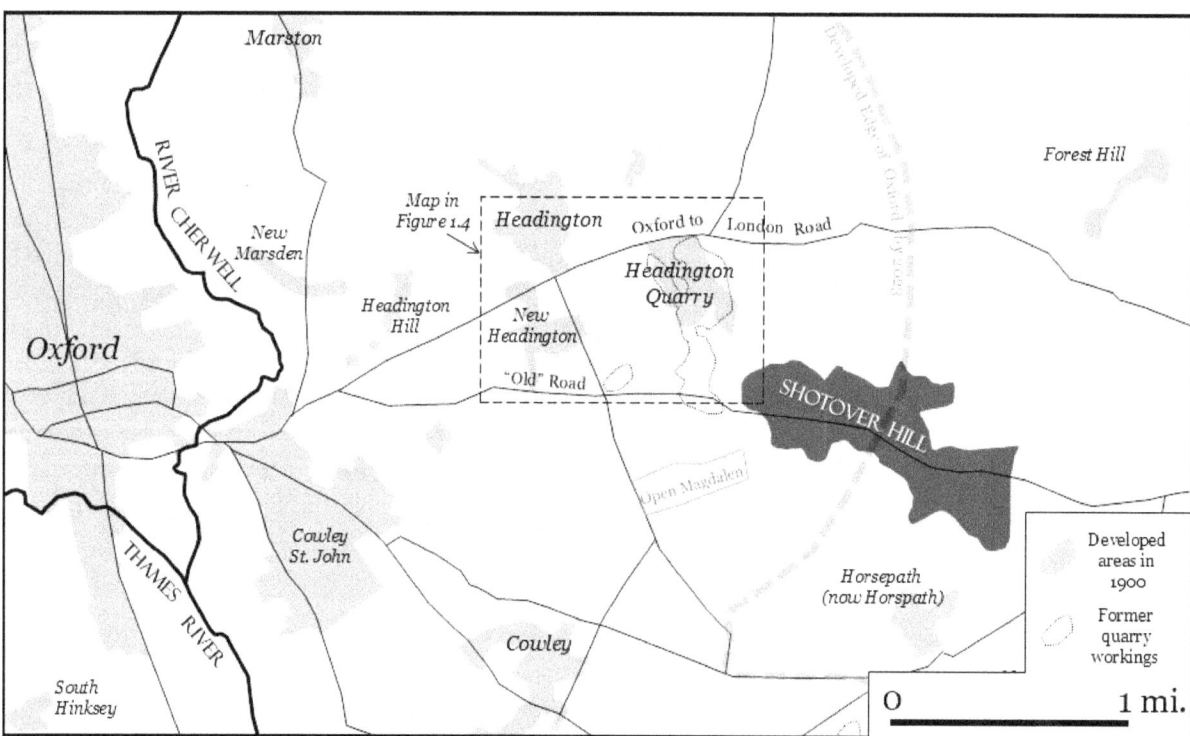

Figure 1.1. Headington and vicinity in the year 1900. Developed areas of towns and villages are shaded grey to represent their approximate extent in 1900, from the Ordnance Survey of that year. Main roads and areas of former quarry workings are also from the 1900 survey. The wide grey dashed line shows the approximate eastern limit of the developed area of the modern city of Oxford (2023) for reference. Dashed box shows the area of a more detailed map, Figure 1.4.

"All 'oles and alleys and 'ills, that's what Quarry is, all up and down."

A longtime Quarry resident interviewed by
Raphael Samuel, 1974

Chapter 1. Headington Quarry and Kimber's Early Years

William Kimber (1872–1961)—husband, father, bricklayer, gardener, Morris dancer, and musician—was very much a product of Headington Quarry. Its cultural environment, and his family's multigenerational history there, comprised a significant foundation upon which grew the man and his music. This foundation was laid long before he met Cecil Sharp while playing concertina for the Headington Quarry Morris side on Boxing Day in 1899, setting the stage for the English Morris dance revival. In this chapter we examine the cultural environment in Quarry village during Kimber's formative years in the late nineteenth century.

During William Kimber's youth, Headington Quarry and the neighboring villages of Headington and New Headington had not yet been pulled into the suburban orbit of nearby Oxford (Figure 1.1). Headington was old and established; it had Bronze Age, Roman and Saxon roots, as well as a royal tithe and manor dating to AD 1004. Its parish church of St. Andrew's dates from at least the twelfth century. This contrasts greatly with two upstart villages to the south. New Headington was laid out only in 1852 as a kind of residential suburb of Headington.[1] Headington Quarry village had rougher origins as a series of waste stone pits and dying stone quarries that began to be settled in earnest in the 1820s by young people from Headington and outlying areas who, lacking financial resources, needed cheap land on which to build their residences and lives.

To the west lay Oxford, a rapidly growing university city that was to swallow all three Headington villages in the early twentieth century. To the east of the Quarry village lay Shotover Hill, rising above the otherwise gently undulating Oxfordshire plain. Just south of Shotover Hill lay the village of Horsepath (now Horspath), which, like Headington Quarry, was a place with stone quarries. The earliest known ancestors of William Kimber came from there.

Family beginnings

William Kimber's second great-grandfather, Anthony Kimber senior, was born in Horspath in 1769 (Figure 1.2). He married Catherine Juggins from nearby Garsington in 1791, and they had three children together in Horspath between 1791 and 1819. Anthony and Catherine lived in Horspath until they died, in 1841 and 1856, respectively.

Horspath was an ancient place dating back to Romano-British times, when there was a pottery kiln there. It has a manor house dating from 1513 as well as the Church of St. Giles dating back to the twelfth century. The town changed its name from Horse Path to the perhaps less prosaic form Horspath in 1912. From census records, Anthony Kimber was a "labourer," but it is not clear if he was in the local stone trade. In similar fashion to Headington Quarry, many of Horspath women ran laundries for Oxford colleges.

Anthony and Catherine's firstborn, Anthony Kimber junior (1791–1870) also worked as a "labourer" at a time when census records did not distinguish between stoneworkers and agricultural workers. He married a woman named Susannah (1787–1833), also of Horspath, at an Oxford church in 1811, and she bore him eight children between 1811 and 1824, all while living in Horspath. William Kimber's grandfather, Job Kimber (1823–1898) was one of these children. Anthony junior and Susanna moved to the Headington Quarry area sometime after the birth and death in infancy of their last child, Robert Kimber, in 1824, but certainly by 1833, the year that Susanna died there, when Anthony junior reached the age of 41.

By 1841, census records show that Anthony junior, at age 50, lived near "Headington Mill" (probably the old Headington Windmill, site 11 of the map of Figure 1.3) where he worked as an agricultural laborer. The windmill was active until about 1876, after which it was demolished. This site is adjacent to an old quarry, part of the Headington Quarry group of quarries, and is not far from the "Old Road" to London. Anthony junior and his family were part of the early nineteenth-century migration of rural poor to derelict stone pits in the Quarry area, where land could be had either by purchase at low cost or by simply squatting; more on this later. By 1851, when he was 60, census records show that he was living in "Headington Quarry," and by 1861 the census reports that he lived in a house along the Old Road. This could still have been his original house in this area; location records are absent. He apparently never remarried after Susannah died, and he died in Headington Quarry in 1870.

Job Kimber (1823–1898), one of the children of Anthony junior and Catherine, came as a child with his parents to Headington Quarry. He married Francis Haynes (1814–1892) from Marston in 1845, at St. Andrew's church in nearby Headington; there was no church in the young settlement of Headington Quarry at that time. They had five children together at Headington Quarry between 1845 and 1856. The second of these was William Kimber senior (1849–1931), who was William Kimber junior's father. Job is the oldest member of the Kimber family known to have been a member of the Headington Quarry Morris side. William Kimber senior recalled being taken by his father Job to the final Lamb Ale at Kirtlington in about 1860; Job may still have been an active dancer then.[2] It is possible, although unlikely and undocumented, that Job's father Anthony junior may have joined the Quarry side as an adult, but certainly not in his youth and young adulthood, as he was living in Horspath. Job was buried at Holy Trinity churchyard in Headington Quarry next to his wife Francis, who had died six years earlier.

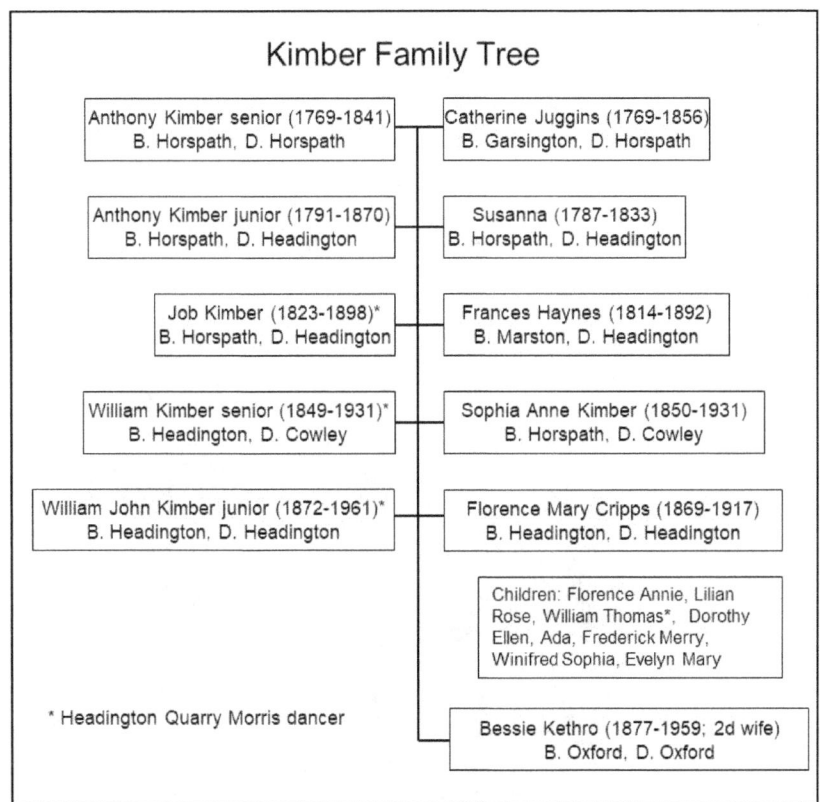

Figure 1.2. A Kimber genealogical chart, sourced from census data. The compilation was greatly aided by the Kimber-Marshall family tree on www.ancestry.com.

William senior (1849–1931), second son of Job and Frances, was born in Headington Quarry and baptized at the new Trinity Church there just as it opened, although he also was included in the baptism papers of Headington St. Andrews, the parent parish. He was a brickmaker in his early life. He married his cousin Sophia Anne Kimber, a frock maker from Horspath, at St. Giles Church in Horspath in 1872 (Figure 1.3). She and her husband shared a grandfather, Anthony Kimber senior. Sophie, according to Theo Chaundy, "was an expert smocker: she could make two smocks a week, ready to wear, for two shillings and twopence a smock."[3] They settled in Headington Quarry and from at least 1861 lived in what is now known as Huggins Cottage along the Old Road in the Titup neighborhood (site 9, Figure 1.4), technically a part of the Shotover district (Figures 1.6 and 1.7). William senior and Sophia had eight children while living in Headington Quarry: William junior (1872–1961), Thomas (1874–1939), Richard (1876, died in infancy), Arthur Thomas (1877–1922), Ada (1878–1880), Arthur (1880–1950), Ada (1886–1965) and Alice (b. 1887). During the 1870s and 1880s, including the birth year of his first son William (1872), the family lived at the previously mentioned Huggins Cottage on the Old Road, not far from the old mill environs where his grandfather Anthony Kimber junior had first settled in the area.

Like his father Job, William Kimber senior was a member of the Headington Quarry Morris side, and he claimed to have begun dancing for it at the age of eighteen (in about 1868), and to have led the side from about 1872, when he was twenty-two years of age.[4] He ceased dancing for the Morris after the 1887 Jubilee celebrations at the Oxpens in Oxford City.[5] A builder and brick man by trade, he eventually left the Quarry. By 1901 he became a foreman for the Oxford Corporation works, a steady job that he retained for several decades. He and his wife moved to 88 Divinity Road, in Cowley, and were living there at the time of the 1921 census, when he was listed as still working for the Oxford Corporation. At that time, they were living at that residence with two grown children, Arthur and Ada Martha.[6] Both William senior and Sophia died in 1931 and are buried at Holy Trinity Church in Headington Quarry.

William Kimber junior (1872–1961) was born at Huggins Cottage and spent his boyhood there. He later told Cecil Sharp that he recalled his father "playing the Morris airs to his son when he was in the cradle, to lull him to sleep, and that he taught him to dance as a schoolboy."[7] His father played fiddle, concertina, and tin whistle, and as William junior recalled, "I learned all my lot from the cradle."[8] William junior and his siblings were all taught Morris dances by their father, and during the daytime his mother would allow young William to play his father's concertina.[9] He attended the Headington Quarry National School until the age of eight, when he began to work as a bird-scarer, and by the age of fourteen he was apprenticed to the building trade to become a bricklayer. By the age of fifteen, William junior danced briefly with the Quarry Morris side during the Jubilee year of 1887,[10] the last time his father danced publicly. He married Florence Mary Cripps (1869–1917) in 1894 at St. Andrews Church in Headington, and by the time of his famous Boxing Day meeting with Cecil Sharp, the couple already had three of what eventually became six children, the last born in 1906. By 1896 they were living at a new brick row house on Lime Walk on the Highfield Estate in New Headington (site 4, Figure 1.3). Florence died in 1917, and he remarried three years later, to a widow, Bessie Kethro (1877–1959); they had no children together. William Kimber and his first wife Florence are buried together at Holy Trinity churchyard in Headington Quarry.

The number of concrete facts and stories tied directly to the Kimber family in Headington Quarry before and during William junior's youth—before his "discovery" by Cecil Sharp in 1899 at Sandfield Cottage—are few, and form only the bare patchwork sketched above. To get a better understanding of the Kimber family's background, we must first turn to broader historical and social accounts of Quarry village, its inhabitants, and its surrounding landscape.

Figure 1.3. William Kimber senior (1849–1931) with his wife, Sophia Anne Kimber (1850–1931). Photo courtesy of the Oxfordshire History Centre.

Headington Stone

Shotover Hill, which lies between the village of Horspath and the former village of Headington Quarry, rises some 80m above the undulating plain that surrounds the City of Oxford (Figure 1.1). The low outline of the hill can be seen in the distance in the frontispiece (pp. v-vi). It is made prominent by a cap of Whitchurch Sandstone of Lower Cretaceous age, a local variant of which is called the Shotover Ironsands, rich in reddish hematite. The strata underlying the hill resemble a layer cake, with the age of successive lower and thus older flat-lying layers beneath the Whitchurch

Figure 1.4 (next page). Headington and Headington Quarry in 1900, from the Ordnance Survey of that year. Numbered circles have been added to highlight places of interest:

1. Sandfield Cottage, where Kimber and the Headington Morris men were dancing on Boxing Day, December 26, 1899, and were seen by Cecil Sharp. The house was subsequently destroyed in the late twentieth century, but its former location is marked by a Blue Plaque.
2. The Chequers inn and tavern, where the recently re-formed Headington Morris Men were photographed in 1899. Behind and north of the pub can be seen the outline of a quarry known in later years as Saccy Horwood's pit. Here traveling people were known to camp in the winter on the broken ground of the pit floor. Quarry Morris dances and also social dances were held there during special occasions. Today the quarry pit has been filled in.
3. Holy Trinity Church, where William Kimber was baptized on 25 January 1873, and where he was laid to rest in the adjacent graveyard in 1961. William's father, William Kimber senior, was also baptized at this church and buried here.
4. Approximate location of the former Kimber home on Lime Walk on the Highfield Estate. William Kimber lived here in one of a number of newly built workmen's houses with his wife, Florence Cripps Kimber, from 1896 until 1908. The houses no longer exist.
5. The Britannia public house, a site of Morris dancing and the annual Odd Fellows feast at Whitsuntide.
6. Crown and Thistle public house, built on the site of the former Titup Hall. Kimber's birthplace is slightly east of this inn, in the former Titup neighborhood (see 9). At the time of writing, this pub is no longer in business.
7. Magdalen quarry (also known as the Workhouse Quarry, for the old workhouse that lay to its east) was one of a number of stone quarries in Headington Quarry. It is presently the site of William Kimber Crescent, named for Kimber in 1958.
8. Six Bells public house. It is adjacent to a quarry area where the Headington Quarry Morris men danced on Whit Tuesdays, and where the annual Sheep Roast was held.
9. Huggins Cottage, the birthplace of William Kimber. He was born here in 1872 to William Kimber senior and his wife Sophie Anne Kimber.
10. William Kimber built his last home, Merryville, at 34 St. Anne's Road (now 42 St. Anne's Road). It was built in 1908, after this map was drawn, although the NW-SE –trending dashed line shows that the future St. Anne's Road was already a dirt path. The house now carries a Blue Plaque, added in 2011.
11. Former site of Headington Mill, a windmill that had ceased operation by 1876. William Kimber's great grandparents, Anthony Kimber Sr. and Catherine Juggins, moved near here ca. 1833 or earlier, where Anthony was employed as an agricultural laborer.

Sandstone reaching down, at ground level in the surrounding plain, into the Jurassic era. At the lower reaches of the hill's slope, these Jurassic strata consist in part of outcrops of Wheatley Limestone, a rock composed largely of tiny shell fragments and corals. It is locally called "Headington Stone," with variants including a harder "Headington hardstone" and a softer "Headington freestone," and has been quarried there for a millennium. Saxon King Ethelred mentioned a "fulen pitte" as a landmark in 1004, within the area called "Hedena's dun" (Hedena's hill).

Stone from Headington quarries was used in the construction of many buildings in Oxford, starting at the bell tower for New College (1396) and continuing with Magdalen College (1468), Brasenose College (1509), and Christ Church Cardinal College (1525). By the seventeenth century several colleges owned and operated their own quarries at Headington, including All Souls, Balliol, Brasenose, Christ Church, Corpus Christi, Lincoln, Oriel, Magdalen, and Queens. The popularity and high use of Headington stone in Oxford construction was primarily because of distance (these are the closest quarries to Oxford), its cream color, and the relative ease of working it.[11] The Old Road to London was improved from a dirt path in 1574 to carry Headington stone to Oxford.[12] Nearby Horspath also has abandoned quarries where this stone was formerly worked.

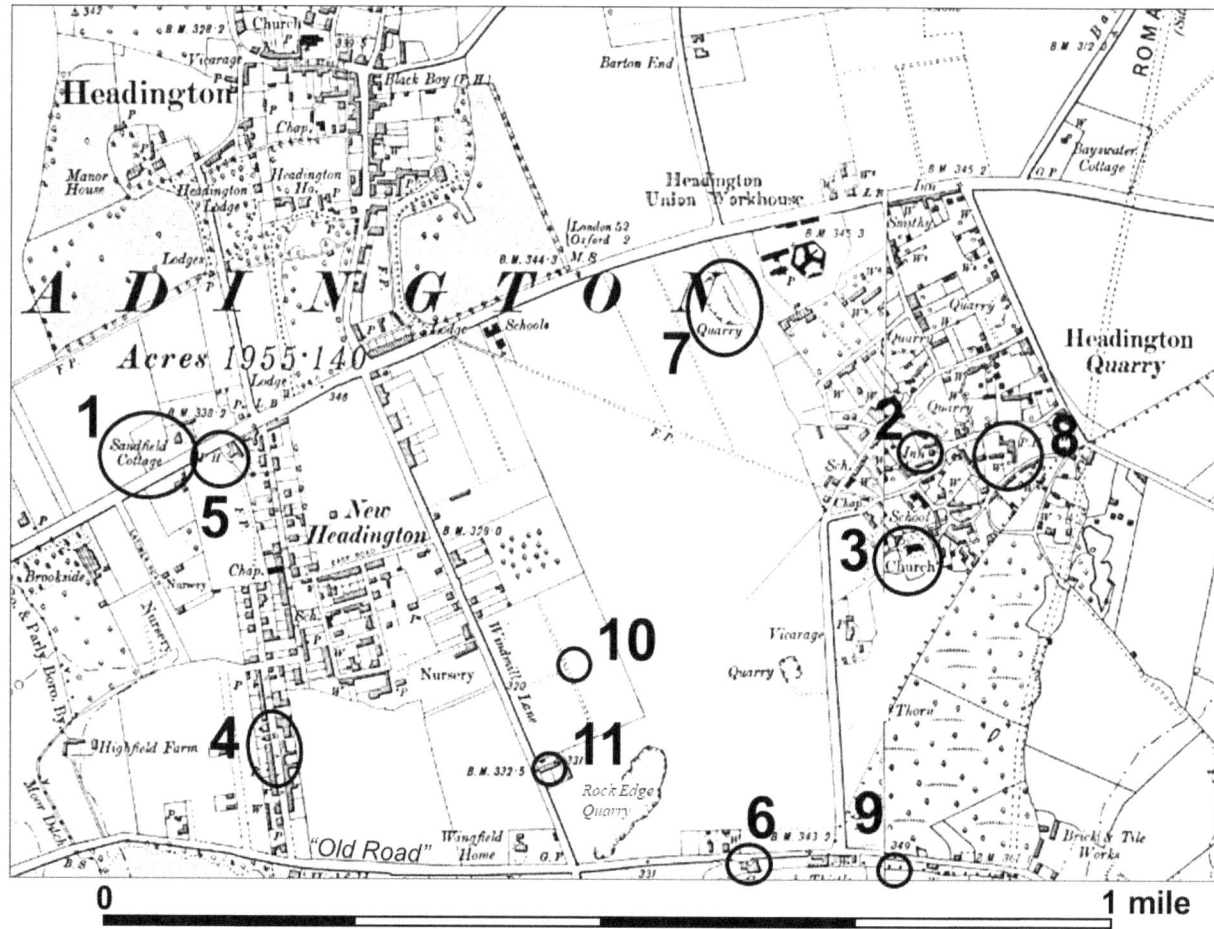

It is not known whether outside stonecutters were brought in to help with this rapid rise in construction use for Oxford buildings, but one may guess that this might have been the case, according to Chaundy.[13] Traditional stonecutting areas in medieval times include Cornwall, Wales, and the Isle of Portland. In the latter place, strangers on the Isle are known as "kimberlins." Stonecutters began to settle in the Quarry area, close to their place of work, at least by 1630, when there were complaints of cottages built without license by "lewd and disorderly persons."[14] The quarry area began as a series of pockmarked quarries on the level plain at the foot of Shotover Hill. As workings progressed, quarried areas from which commercially viable rock had been removed were left behind as waste, and squatters could move in, apparently with comparative ease. By 1797, when population figures are first available for the Quarry, it was at most a tiny hamlet, with about 68 persons. A map of that year shows ten buildings in and around the central quarries, and two more buildings along the Old Road to the south of the main quarries.[15]

By about 1750 it became known that Headington stone in Oxford buildings eroded rather quickly with time, a major flaw. From that time, Headington stone was primarily used in places where it was not as exposed to the elements, whereas Headington hardstone continued to be used more liberally. The use of Headington stone declined steadily in the nineteenth century. Only a very few quarry pits were still in use by 1900, and the last pit ceased operation in 1947. Most of the now-dormant Headington quarries have long since been built over by Oxford suburbia, but two are

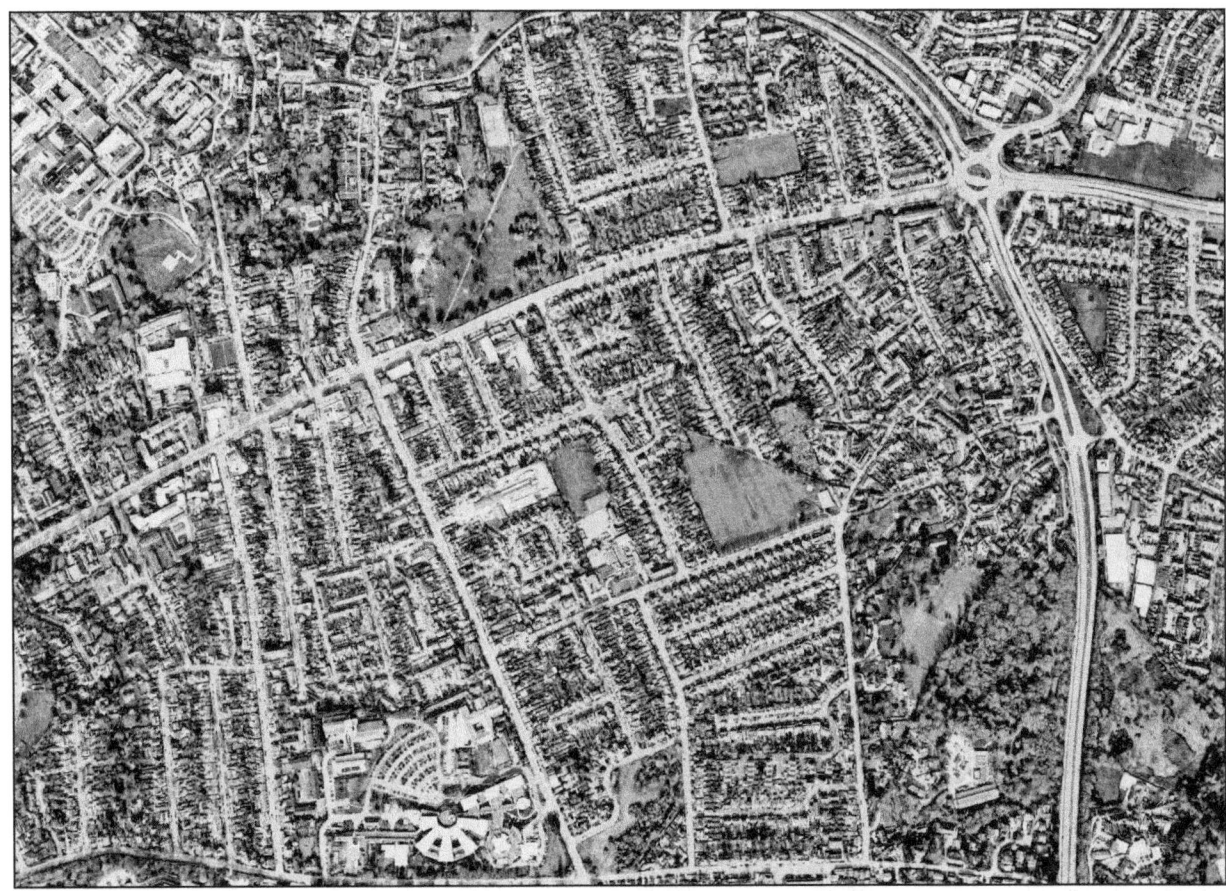

Figure 1.5. Modern aerial photograph of the same area as the map in Figure 1.4. The dense pattern of urban housing contrasts greatly with the formerly rural setting of the Quarry in 1900. From Google Earth, 2023.

preserved as Sites of Special Interest and may be visited today in Headington Quarry. Magdalen Quarry, formerly known as the Workhouse Pit, is at the end of William Kimber Crescent (site 7, Figure 1.4), and Rock Edge (formerly the Crossroads Pit) is at the southeast corner of Windmill Road (just south of site 11). Local Headington Quarry buildings that used Headington hardstone include Holy Trinity Church (1849) and the Headington Quarry National School (1864), both well known to William Kimber in his youth. In the churchyard of Holy Trinity Church is the intricate headstone of William Kimber, an ornamental monument that includes a lovingly carved concertina and some Morris bells (see chapter 2, Figure 2.19). Set soon after his death in 1961, it already shows the effects of erosion of this relatively soft stone.

A tale of two villages

The rapid decline of quarrying in the late eighteenth century, and especially in the early nineteenth, had a profound impact on Quarry village population. Counter-intuitively, the population increased dramatically. As already mentioned, stonemasons' homes were always present around the quarries, but as quarry pits were abandoned, impoverished people came in and "squatted" on unused bits of quarried land as well as on surrounding unused pieces of "common" moor land. Such was the origin of the Quarry community, and it led to a very higgledy-piggledy (or perhaps one should call it "organic") original arrangement of homes and gardens (Figure 1.8).

Figure 1.6. Huggins Cottage, where William Kimber was born in 1872 and lived with his parents Sophia Ann and William Kimber senior as well as five siblings. The house is on the southeast end of the Old Road, in the former Shotover census (see map of Figure 1.4, site 9). The family lived at this house until they moved by 1891 to a location at the current address of 2 Woodbine Cottages.

Figure 1.7. The Titup neighborhood along the "Old Road" to London, with Shotover Hill in the distance, ca. 1900. On the right is the Crown and Thistle public house, built in the 19th century to replace an old inn called Titup Hall (site 6 on the map of Figure 1.4). The name 'Titup' reportedly refers to the first flat land east of Oxford on the Old Road where it would be possible for horses to canter; the phrase "titup" would bring the horses to that canter. Image and history courtesy of Stephanie Jenkins at the Headington History online website, www.headington.org.uk.

Figure 1.8. Headington Quarry's irregular layout of houses and cottage gardens, in a pre-1918 photograph. The house sites and garden plots were carved out of abandoned waste land in and around old rock quarries by villagers exercising squatters' rights, and hence were larger than normal for the time. In these gardens, the residents variously raised vegetables, orchard fruits, poultry and a few pigs. Many Quarry women also used their garden space to dry clothes for their laundering work. Photographer unknown; from W. J. Arkell's *Oxford Stone*, 1947, and from Rafael Samuel, *Headington Roughs*, 1974.

For example, Headington parish churchwardens in 1869 noted of the squatting on a piece of their land that began in about the 1820s:

> ... *two small huts were erected upon this land, and they were inhabited by some poor people, and from time to time the buildings have increased into two cottages and the occupants have enclosed a piece of the ground as gardens, but for none of this do they pay taxes.*[16]

Much of the population growth in Headington Quarry came from nearby Headington village, and the abandoned quarries became an inexpensive place for the young of that "enclosed" village to start their new lives (Figure 1.9). The growth became pronounced in the 1820s, when the hamlet of Headington Quarry more than doubled from 118 (in 1821) to 270 (in 1831). This was the time when Anthony Kimber junior and his wife Susanna (William Kimber junior's great-grandparents) moved from Horspath to the Quarry vicinity with their eight children, as mentioned. They set up their habitation near a former windmill and the adjacent Rock Edge quarry (site 11, Figure 1.4) and seem to have been part of the early nineteenth-century settling of the area in and around the old quarries.

By 1851 the relatively young Quarry village, including the small collection of houses lying along the Old Road that was called the "Titup neighborhood," had 403 inhabitants. Nearly all the inhabitants of the rapidly growing village had been born either in nearby Headington village or in the surrounding area (in the Kimbers' case, Horspath). The incoming people were very young; in 1841 fully 60% of the population were 35 years of age or younger.[17]

The result was a young village of relatively impoverished rural young people, in homes that were scattered about a highly irregular, hummocky landscape of abandoned (and a few still active) rock quarries. As a villager of 1920 remembered it, it was "all 'oles and alleys and 'ills, that is what Quarry is, all up and down"[18] (Figure 1.10). Oxford historian Raphael Samuel's excellent social history of the people and culture of the former Quarry village ("Quarry Roughs: Life and Labour in Headington Quarry, 1860–1920: An Essay in Oral History,") in his 1974 book *Village Life and Labour*,[19] is a key source for the descriptions of old village life that follow.

As mentioned earlier, Headington Quarry was once part of a trio of formerly independent villages carrying the name Headington (Figure 1.1). The older village of Headington (also called Old Headington) lay to the north of London Road, about a half mile northwest of the quarries. It was a "proper" English village containing a Manor of Headington that dated from at least the tenth century, replete with a grand house, estate, and formerly a Lord of the Manor. The village also includes a Church of England parish, St. Andrews, where Job Kimber married his wife, Francis Haynes,

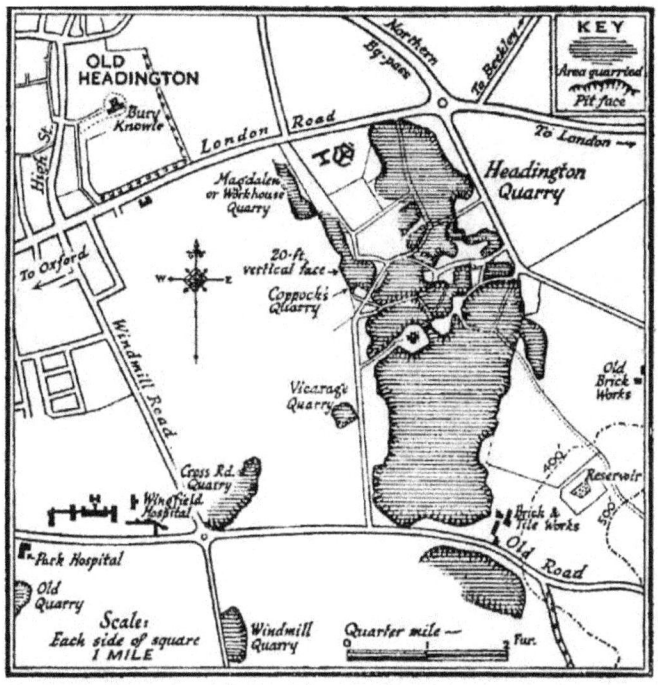

Figure 1.9. The extent of rock quarries of Headington Quarry in the nineteenth century, from an old map. Individual dwelling places are not shown. From Oxford City Council, 2010, Headington Quarry Conservation Area Proposal.

Figure 1.10. Looking towards Saccy Horwood's pit and adjacent houses, 1906. Courtesy of Oxfordshire History Centre.

in 1845. The village of New Headington was the youngest of the trio, begun in 1848, with lots sold from 1853 and cottages built thereafter.[20]

Those of us not native to England might be forgiven for having a mental image of "typical" English villages that are something like the slightly twee and squeaky-clean villages in parts of the Cotswolds. Just such an image is portrayed by Ronald Blythe in his 1969 study of a small Suffolk village, Akenfield:

> *Evidence of the good life ... is there for all to see. . . . . a tall church on the hillside, a pub selling the local brew, a pretty stream, a football pitch, a handsome square vicarage with a cedar of Lebanon shading it, a school with a jar of tadpoles in the window, three shops with doorbells, a Tudor mansion, half a dozen farms and a lot of quaint cottages. Akenfield, on the face of it, is the kind of place in which an Englishman has always felt it his right and duty to live. . . . . the real country, untouched and genuine.*[21]

Of the two villages, nineteenth-century "Old" Headington with its old Manor and its Church of England parish was much closer to that ideal than Headington Quarry could ever be.

Quarry was a young and highly unusual place of seized house sites in and around abandoned quarry pits, with less than well-to-do residents. At its cultural heart, it was a working class "open" village with a very independent-minded populace who wanted to keep it open and a bit isolated. "Open" villages like Quarry were surrounded by either common land or what the villagers considered common land. In proper "enclosed" villages like Old Headington, the common land of previous centuries had typically been converted to private ownership. Samuel, writing of the period from 1860 to 1920, could tick off the characteristics of "open" Headington Quarry village that separated it from its slightly more posh and "enclosed" neighbor to the north:

> *The whole setting [of Quarry village] was make-shift and extemporary. The village had grown up higgedly-piggedly, with no ivied church or village green to serve it as a focus; no regular pattern of lanes. . . . but a maze-like multitude of alleyways and paths, whose obscurity contributed to the legendary difficulties faced by the County Police when they ventured into the village. Sand pits, working or abandoned, twisted and turned the physiognomy of the village into ups and downs and waste. . . . Development of the brick-making industry during the second half of the 19th century with its attendant trails of diggings, added a fresh perimeter of waste. No pretty stream coursed through the village, though abandoned clay pits filling up with water provided the village horse keepers and donkey owners with a liberal supply of ponds. The approach to the village was marked neither by meadow land or leafy lanes, but by the smoking brick kilns of Titup on the one side, sand pits and the Union Work Castle [workhouse] on the other. . . . On the other side were the clay hills, where the lime pits were said to be burning both day and night. There were no shops in the Quarry, with or without doorbells, down to a very late date. . . . As for the village school, . . . [in 1897, windows] had to be blocked up to protect the classroom from the epidemic of stone-throwing by the more unruly Quarry children.*[22]

Where enclosed villages created a class of agricultural workers who paid constant deference and servitude to the Lord of the Manor and other gentry who owned the land, the nineteenth century Quarry was surrounded by open land that in many ways defined the village economy. Beyond the collection of squatters' house sites in and around the abandoned quarry pits, the open land was used by villagers for agriculture and the grazing of livestock; for collecting firewood, for gathering Christmas trees and boughs for sale in Oxford; for poaching rabbits, an important part of the local diet; for hunting birds and other small game (William Kimber junior found his first employment at the age of nine as a bird-scarer[23]); and all manner of such pursuits. Because of the value of such foraging and agricultural activities, villagers actively resisted any effort to enclose these surrounding common lands. Opposition to attempts at enclosure brought about legendary struggles, which the villagers always won up until the time of suburbanization. Perhaps the best example is that of the fight for the "Open Magdalen," a strip of land south of the Quarry village that had long belonged to Magdalen College in Oxford (see map, Figure 1.1). A farmer named Richard Pether attempted to enclose (fence in and establish possession for) this strip of land in the 1850s, with the purchased acquiescence of Magdalen College, leading to years of Quarry villager activity in what Samuel called:

> *mass trespasses, large-scale raids for wood, and the illegal grazing of cows. . . . Quarry children were quite as assertive in defending common rights as their parents, and took a leading part in the fight for the Open Magdalens—particularly in the incendiary fires which marked its later stages. They treated the whole hinterland as their own, not only the commons, but the farmers' fields."*[24]

The dispute rumbled on for decades, stretching from the time of William Kimber senior's infancy to William Kimber junior's boyhood, until by 1881 Magdalen College no longer claimed any rights to the property.[25] The affair serves to mark a sign of distinction of "open" Headington Quarry—a rough and tumble, somewhat scrappy place with a citizenry prone to fiercely resisting efforts of outsiders to encroach upon it—in contrast to the more established, "enclosed" Headington village with its stately manor house and public buildings, yet less independent inhabitants. According to Samuel,

> *Quarry had no parish church until 1861, no mansion house. At the time of the 1841 census, there was not a single person who might have been recognized in polite society as a gentleman. There was no servant-keeping in the village.*

Villagers were proud, independent, and as we will see, self-sufficient people. The village also had more than its share of people with rough edges, who were known in neighboring villages (especially rival Old Headington) as "Headington Roughs." As an Old Headington man remembered, "They were real tough, you didn't want to mix in too much with them."[26] County police were said never to venture into the Quarry alone, but always in pairs. Children were known to throw stones at unpopular teachers and at the windows of schools, and telegram boys sent in from the Old Headington Post Office were similarly targeted.[27]

Theodore Chaundy, an Oxford professor and Morris dancer who befriended Kimber and wrote of him, noted that the Quarry was:

> *... a more or less closed community of families. There was always a great shortage of surnames in the Quarry, and nicknames were everywhere in vogue. Anyone from Quarry will reel off a whole string of them: Drummer Bread, Dot-eye, Ferret (four brothers), Splasher, Dead'un, Moggy, Duck'em, Smarty, Shrimp. . . . The women too had their nicknames, not always complimentary, and they are best omitted. A well-known Quarry story is of the boy at Sunday School who, asked to name the three creeds, replied "Harry, Tom, and Tough-un."*
>
> *William Kimber himself was always "Merry Kimber" and he lives at "Merryville."*[28]

Samuel found that Quarry old-timers had affectionate memories of "gypsies" (Romany), who usually wintered over in the very middle of the village in the pit behind the Mason's Arms public house.[29] There was intermarriage between the villagers and gypsies, and villagers reported, "They were good to us." Samuel noted that a gypsy fiddler, Sampson Smith, was an occasional musician and dancer for the Quarry Morris side in the 1870s,[30] and Smith was to come to the Kimbers' defense in a famous quarrel of 1910 between Cecil Sharp and Mary Neal, described in the following chapter.

Brickmaking and bricklaying

At the same time as the decline in quarrying stone, local industry was saved by a second commercially valuable geologic unit, the bluish Kimmeridge Clay that overlies the Wheatley Limestone and outcrops immediately to the east of the village. By the middle 1800s, Quarry villagers were digging out this clay to produce handmade bricks. Brickmaking soon became a major occupation and bricks a prime village export. Brickmaking clay was dug by hand. The process was described by Edna Mason (1989):

> *In early summer [the brick clay] was mixed, usually at Shotover with a spade, although there are stories of it being trodden with bare feet, a common practice in some places. Then it was shaped in molds brick by brick. A skilled worker could probably produce up to 700 bricks a day, and during the comparatively short period he might take his wife and older children to help mold. The bricks would then be dried and finally fired. It was all heavy work, which nevertheless called for a considerable degree of skill.*[31]

Developing concurrently with the trade of brickmaking was the related occupation of bricklaying, a relatively easy transition for many of those formerly involved in building with stone and masonry.

That transition to brickmaking can be illustrated in the family history of the Kimbers in the Quarry. The occupation of Job Kimber (1823–1898, born in Horspath but moved to Headington Quarry in the 1820s) is not fully known; he was called a "labourer" in census records, but stonework was a major occupation in Horspath at that time. However, his son William Kimber senior (1849–1931) was a brickmaker in his younger years, and later became a foreman of a (bricklaying) building crew. William Kimber junior was apprenticed in the building trade in 1886 and spent most of his working adult life as a bricklayer.

Village working life

The Quarry during William Kimber junior's youth may not have been a very genteel place, but it was a mostly self-sufficient place. There were no charities or soup kitchens (once a frequent occurrence in Old Headington), nor was there much abject poverty.[32] This was due largely to the multifaceted local economy with its independent work force, as well as a shared work ethic that the village "took care of its own." In the 1960s Samuel interviewed then-aged surviving members of the old village workforce, from which the following descriptions are summarized.[33]

A vicar in 1897 wrote of the village that "the inhabitants are all working men; half of them being employed in the brickyards, and most of the rest being bricklayers, masons, carpenters and labourers in the building trade." Typical of that vicar's time, he left out the working women, who ran a number of laundries out of their homes. They cleaned linens and cloths for the colleges of nearby Oxford, laying out the week's wash to dry in their back gardens. Nearly none of them were sent out to service as maids and nannies in the genteel homes of Oxford, nor did the men hire out as servants there; they preferred to work independently at home or in the building trade in the surrounding countryside. Some women also assisted their husbands in the brickyards, molding bricks.[34]

Work in the quarries, brickyards, and building trade was enormously fickle. Men were hired by the job, usually as individuals. When the project finished, the worker had to find new employment. This was not wage-earning, but jobbing. Moreover, in the wintertime, both brickmaking and bricklaying ceased for weeks at a time, as cold weather interfered with the curing of mortar and with making bricks. That meant expected and periodic lapses in income that had to be made up. The laundries helped, of course, especially in households where the men did not work, either because they were disabled or laid off (especially in winter), or because of a dependence upon beer, as one old villager recollected:

> *Nearly all of the women in the Quarry used to take in laundry work 'cos half of their husbands didn't take any money home . . . they used to sup that in beer while they was at work . . . women had to do laundry work to keep the family going.*[35]

But there were many other ways in which these resourceful people kept up. There were nearly always odd laboring jobs to be had in the off time, including trenching and draining for farmers, foundation work, laying drainpipes, and the like. There was also work clearing rabbits for farmers, using ferrets and nets. The rabbits, of course, could then be sold to other villagers as an inexpensive meat source. Rabbits were also caught illegally by poachers on large woodlands of outlying estates and sold. It was a largely open secondary trade. At harvest time there were farming jobs like cutting grain, making sheaves and bringing them in. This too was temporary work done by the job.

Others not in the stone, brick, and building trade included well diggers and horse and cart men. The carts would take laundry into Oxford on Monday and deliver it back on Friday. Heavy haulers brought large loads of lumber and bricks to job sites or brought coal to homes. The haulers typically did the loading and unloading. All of these jobs included hard, heavy work. Beer was often given out at the job site to induce the men to work harder.

Almost all villagers had a secondary source of income aside from their primary occupation, which consisted of cottage gardening. Because of the "higgledy-piggledy" way the village was laid out, with most original house sites obtained by squatting on land, the average home had a much larger than average cottage garden for that time (Figure 1.8), which was put to very good use. There were vegetables and orchard fruits to be cared for, chickens to be raised, eggs to be preserved, and pigs in sties at the bottom of the garden. Raphael Samuel interviewed the son of builder's labourer William Green, who remembered the family's back garden:

> *We had ... fruit trees all down the centre ... vegetables – potatoes and so on ... we had the well half way down the garden – where we got the water – pig sties half way down ... hen houses ... something of everything ... We never bought any vegetables.*[36]

Tommy Webb's garden, related Samuel, was behind the Mason's Arms public house, and "used to be an orchard ... used to be a laundry too ...currant trees, apple trees ... a monstrous walnut tree. Vegetables. And we used to have a lot of pigs up there."[37] There were also small allotments, many of them established by an Allotment Extension Act in 1882 where Quarry villagers applied for additional gardening land.

During the growing season men would return home from their day jobs and go immediately to their garden or allotment, and work until dark. When the weather grew colder, it was time to slaughter the pigs, which provided the family's meat during the winter months. One of those raising pigs was William Kimber junior, who owned a sow and eleven piglets in 1913 before disaster struck, as he wrote to his friend Cecil Sharp:

> *I have had the misfortune to lose my sow and eleven small pigs. I tried my best, so did the vetinary [sic] surgeons but it was no good, you see she had a slight cold and this caused her to farry a month before time. It's all gone and buried—as you know bacon is up in price so is pigs[;] these eleven & sow would have been worth 14 pounds sterling. Now I have lost my whole summers work throwed away, its fairly knocked me up.*[38]

Figure 1.11. "A good crop of pigs," from the *Biggle Swine Book* of 1899, Philadelphia.

Kimber was raising more stock than his immediate household needs called for and was counting on selling the extras. Although there were no shops in the Quarry village in the old days, there were traders among the villagers, providing another way of raising extra money with pigs. By 1914 there was a pork butcher in town, who would trade in such home-reared pork. Even as late as 1929 Kimber raised pigs and fowl for extra money. In a letter to Maud Karpeles that year he wrote:

> *You see, we chaps down here go in for pigs and fowls with our gardens and allotments. I had four pigs worth £5 each. Well, they caught a chill. I have lost one and I am afraid another is going; you never know where it will stop. May clear the lot out then my bank is broke. So, you see its very worrying, in fact it's made me feel a bit queer. Still, we must hope for the best.*[39]

Besides gardening, yet another secondary source of income for villagers came from foraging for supplies in the woodlands around Shotover Hill, to the east of the village. There were acorns to feed the pigs; ferns for pig litter; berries; mushrooms; blackthorn, whitethorn, and furze for firewood. Holly branches could be cut in winter and sold in Oxford as Christmas decorations. Nothing was overlooked, including blackbirds netted for pies, and the rabbits that were caught by the dogs and ferrets of the village poachers. The villagers counted the open lands surrounding the village as their own collective property, regardless of what old deeds may have specified.[40]

A photograph from about 1905 (Figure 1.12) shows a group of Quarry villagers in front of the Mason's Arms public house, which is still in business today. Local historian Maurice East has detailed the history of some of the villagers in the photo, including pub landlord William Goodall (standing in the center with the bowler hat; he was East's great-grandfather) and his wife Rose Goodall, seated in front of him with the first three of a later total of eight children. The man seated third from the left is "Gaffer" Carey with his dog, and another man seated to his left holds a young puppy. Dogs were highly regarded in the Quarry and were important not only in protecting the village from outside intrusion but also for poaching rabbits. As East recalls:

Figure 1.12. A group of Quarry villagers in front of the Mason's Arms public house, ca. 1905. Photograph courtesy of Quarry historian Maurice East, a great-grandson of the pub owners in the photo. See text for more information.

> *Gaffer Carey would have been one of the Quarry Roughs. . . . I asked my Gran before she died about this photograph. . . . I said "Why did they call him Gaffer?" She said, "He was in charge." . . . The Careys [were a] big poaching family. They were always up at Shotover, bringing rabbits and pheasants down to feed people. . . . People in Quarry grew up on rabbit; [it was] vital to their diet.*[41]

Seated next to Rose, with the neck scarf, was Charlie Gurl, whom Rose married after William Goodall died in his forties. Charlie Gurl was "a proper Rough" and a well digger.

> *These guys . . . had been living the life of Riley . . . they just did a little bit of this, a little bit of that, a bit of poaching, and then go on the booze for few weeks. . . . They lived by their own rules, and there was some rough justice. . . . Whether it was bloody-mindedness, there was this sense of individualism.*[42]

Life of Riley notwithstanding, it is difficult to imagine today, in our world of relatively secure wages and a safety net of government subsidies, how difficult and undependable work was at that time. Quarry resident Waggle Ward told Raphael Samuel the story of Dusty Web, who worked during the day on Oxford sewers, then worked all night on his garden allotment and on poaching rabbits:

Uncle Dusty . . . had an allotment on Quarry Field, when he lived in St. Thomas's, and he used to come up a digging (in his allotment), and if the wind was a-blowing at night, he'd leave the digging, and he'd go a-rabbiting all night—he'd walk from there, when he come from rabbiting—he'd have a cup of tea in Granny Webb's—he'd walk back down St. Thomas's, he would, and he'd go to work all day, and he'd be a digging on the allotment at night in Quarry. Tell me where another man 'ud do that today? They ain't born to do it. They was bred different—horses they was, I reckon. . . . My Mam's uncle that was. He was a man and a half, he was . . . a man and a half.[43]

The Church in Quarry life

The Quarry village in the early nineteenth century had no church of its own and was connected only by a mud track across an open field to St. Andrew's Anglican church in adjacent Headington. That old footpath is indicated by the letters "FP" at the center of the map in Figure 1.4. An attempt in 1805 to enclose that field, thereby closing the footpath and preventing access by Quarry residents to St. Andrews churchyard, caused an uproar among Quarry residents, who fiercely protected their perceived common lands, and they protested by smashing the fence around the enclosure. A number of Quarry men went to jail. The Church of England in Headington at this time apparently did little to help the "roughs" in Headington Quarry, and its curate wrote: "The inhabitants of Quarry say that as they are to be deprived of their funeral path they will not come to Church at all but will intend to have a Methodist preacher come to them."[44]

Figure 1.13. The Church of the Holy Trinity, Headington Quarry, built in 1849, as it appears today. Both William Kimber junior and senior were baptized at this church, and both, along with Job Kimber, were buried in its churchyard.

The villagers were as good as their word, and money was raised for a Methodist church, which was built with local labor and opened in 1830. George Coppock and others (1933) reported that "not a penny" came from outside the village.[45] The villagers were then outside the reach of established state religion. By 1847 the bishop referred to Quarry as an "abandoned" district where "evil" found a "ready home." He sought to have a branch of the Church of England built within the village, which was done without local input in planning or labor participation, with funds raised from the outside. This was the Church of the Holy Trinity, completed in 1849 (Figure 1.13). Not surprisingly, the initial village response was tepid at best, and not helped by the bishop's comments at its opening, when he prayed that the Lord would cleanse the village of unclean spirits that "infested it and . . . made it notorious." By 1865 the outside diocesan society that had provided the funds reported that "of Headington Quarry it may be said, that the Church exists there . . . through this Society. Had it not been for the endowment provided by this Society, the Church would soon have closed."[46]

In spite of that rocky start, the Kimbers were at least participants in the parish from the beginning. William Kimber senior was baptized there in 1849 as the church opened, and William junior followed suit in 1872. Both are buried next to their wives in the Holy Trinity churchyard.

Village social customs

The Holy Trinity parish newsletter of June 1956 carried a piece about William Kimber junior's life in that parish—he was then 83 years of age—that summarizes the surprisingly large number of activities available to a young person in a small rural village:

> *Mr. Kimber is still living in the parish, where he was born and brought up. On leaving Quarry School at the age of nine his first job was "bird starving," [scaring] but it was [in] the building trade that he found his life's work. He was a chorister as long ago as the 1880s, during the incumbency of the Rev. C. P. Longland.*
>
> *In his younger days Mr. Kimber took part in most of the activities of the parish. Many still remember him as a drummer with the drum and fife band or presiding at the Sheep Roast for Quarry Village Feast. At Christmas he went out with the Mummers. He also played cricket and has been a member of the Foresters for more than 60 years. As a bell-ringer he went to the neighbouring parish of Old Headington. His chief delight, however, is Morris dancing, having first danced with the Quarry team in the local celebrations at the time of Queen Victoria's Golden Jubilee at the age of 15. Now 83 he is still playing for the present team, passing on his great love of the Morris to new generations of dancers.*[47]

The Quarry may have been a relatively isolated place, but Kimber clearly made the absolute most of it. This section explores some of these social activities in more detail.

May Day. Each May Day was celebrated with a May horn, or "peeling horn," blown from early morn by village boys, who made them using larch bark (Figure 1.14). As William Kimber remembered,

> *Before the tin horn come up, it was the peeling horn. You could go to a larch tree and pull off a piece of larch [bark], a couple of yards long. Well, then you used to wind him up. Start big at the bottom, sort of form a bell, till it come to nothing, and you'd pin it all together with thorns—hazel thorns—off the hedge. And on the top. Where you'd form the mouthpiece, you'd get a bit of inside willow, the inside of the willow bark, and tie that across. And when you blow that'd make a sort of shrieking noise . . . that was the peeling horn. You'll hear them when it begins to get in May again . . . now they have bugles. . . . Yes, that's the first of May."*[48]

Placing loud horns in the hands of rowdy village boys was bound to cause the occasional kerfuffle, and such was the case in May 1887. In the early evening hours of Sunday, May 7, just before chapel, a boy named Percy Kimber blew a May horn perhaps too close to the ear of another lad, John Basher, who promptly hit Percy twice, once on the ear and once in the face. The assault made it to the magistrate, where Percy's cousin William Kimber junior (then aged 15) testified on Percy's behalf

Figure 1.14. "Peeling horns" made from larch bark, collected by Percy Manning in Ducklington, Oxfordshire, in 1897. The items were later placed at Cecil Sharp House in London but were destroyed by German bombing during World War II. Image from Manning, 1897, in *Folklore, a Quarterly Review*, vol. 8.

that Percy's eye was "very much puffed up." The attorney hired by Basher's family for the defense said that Percy had thrust a May horn into his client's face and blown it, and that they "had no witnesses to call, as those who saw the disturbance were [all] relations of the complainant." The magistrate ruled for Percy Kimber and fined a young and aptly named John Basher two shillings and sixpence.[49]

Samuel notes that children went about the Quarry village on May Day, singing and begging. William Kimber remembered the verse that accompanied the Quarry children and their May garlands:

Good morning, missus and master, I wish you happy May
I've come to show me garland because it is my day
This branch of May I've brought you and at your door it stand
It is but a bud but it's well spread about
It's the gift of Our Lord's and so I wish you all Good Day.[50]

This practice is somewhat similar to that seen at that time in Bampton-in-the-Bush, west of Oxford, where historian and antiquarian Percy Manning reported that parties of children formerly roamed around dressed in white with red, white, and blue ribbons, one selected as "Lord" and another as "Lady" with her "maid." The Lord carried a stick adorned with flowers and ribbons (his sword), and a collecting box. The Lady carried a mace with sweet-smelling herbs and flowers. The Lady sang a song, the Lord then kissed her, and the money box was handed around.[51]

Annual Sheep Roast and other feasts. The village Sheep Roast, in November, was a big annual two-day affair with wide participation in the village. It was noted in the *Oxford Journal* of 1861 as occurring on Sunday, November 24, for the roasted sheep, with "other amusements" taking place the following Monday.[52] In 1899 it took place at the pit near the Six Bells (Figure 1.15). Several "ladies and gentlemen . . . as is customary, assisted in turning and basting the sheep" in what was called "an ancient custom." A collection was made for the widows and orphans of the war in South Africa.[53] In 1904 the *Journal* reported, "Practically all the villagers interested themselves in the preliminary ceremonies, and between 80 and 100 of them partake in the feast which follows," which was held inside the Six Bells.[54] In 1905,

A large number of people visited the Six Bells at Headington Quarry to witness the roasting of the carcasse for the annual sheep roast. This is an old custom, a consecration feast of the church, peculiar to the district. . . . The sheep was fastened to the spit and the "roasting" began about eleven o'clock on Monday morning, and during the course of the afternoon a record number of visitors were admitted to the field [pit] where it was proceeding. In the

Figure 1.15. The Quarry Sheep Roast of 1899. The sheep was roasted at the edge of a quarry pit near Six Bells public house, using a half ton of coal. A canvas tarp over the fire insured against rain. Image courtesy of the Oxfordshire History Centre.

evening a large number were present at the carving and distribution of the sheep, and a merry evening was spent."[55]

A Quarry villager recalled to Samuel that:

The roast was just for the adults, the children weren't allowed in for that object at all, [but] you were allowed to go and dip your bread in the fat. The baster usually took a long fork and flopped it about in the fat pan. . . . Nothing [else] happened till 7 o'clock at night, nothing except the sheep roasting. Then they [the adults] started eating and having a booze up."[56]

There were other attractions at the annual roast, sometimes on the second day. "One regular visitor at the feast was old Mother Humphries, who had a stall where she sold gingerbread and mint humbugs. She wore a red shawl, and the raw November weather tinted her nose to match the shawl. There were cheapjacks, halfpenny roundabouts, and once even a boxing booth to add to the attractions."[57] Among the other attractions were the village Morris dancers. According to Kimber, the annual sheep roast was:

[A] booze up and a good feed. You'd never make a Morris dancer but you have plenty of beer—you never stop for no food. Get a bit of bread and cheese and munch that, and you was always getting plenty of beer . . . down the hoppers, because beer was corn that time of day. They had some malt amongst it, no chemicals in them days. When I think back, I have to laugh."[58]

Clubs had their special feasts, too. For example, the Old Club and the Foresters celebrated on Whit Tuesday with a supper, preceded by all sorts of games and amusements, including:

> *. . . climbing the greasy pole for a leg of mutton; cock-chasing, when the men with their hands tied behind them tried to catch the bird with their teeth; and grinning through a horse's collar. Another form of amusement was for a man to lie flat on his back holding a huge stone over his chest. The quarrymen were then challenged to break the stone. The Morris dancers, too[,] were in great evidence, dancing the old dances to the fiddler's tunes. A supper finished the day, which had been eagerly looked forward to by all in the village.*[59]

Christmas and the Mummers. At Christmas time there were roaming carolers, but they seemed mostly to be children with begging tins; one of Samuel's sources said that "the more respectable would keep away [from caroling]."[60] But Kimber remembered that there were also mummers going out, and handbell ringers, and two village bands.[61] Of course, his first meeting with Cecil Sharp in 1899 was on Boxing Day with the Quarry Morris men, who like the other groups were out collecting funds.

The mummers were dressed in strange garments, and processed through the village performing their play, which was a version of the old story "St. George and the Turkish Knight." According to Coppock and others (1933), a Quarry version was as follows:

Enter Father Christmas:
> *In comes I, old Father Christmas,*
> *Welcome or welcome not,*
> *And I hope old Father Christmas*
> *Will never be forgot.*
> *[year] is a very great age for me.*
> *If you don't believe what I say*
> *Let King George come in and clear the way.*
> *In my hand I carry a can.*
> *Don't you think I'm a funny old man? Step in Jack Finney!*

Enter Jack Finney:
> *My name is not Jack Finney*
> *Nor John Finney, but Mr. Finney, and Mr. Finney I will be called.*
> *Step in, fiddler.*

Enter fiddler:
> *In comes I, as 'ant been hit*
> *With my big head and little wit:*
> *My head's so big and my wit's so small*
> *So I've brought my fiddle to please you all.*
> *Jack's gone to Ireland,*
> *Jim's gone to France,*
> *So we'll all rise up, and have a merry dance.*

The practice of the mummers' play lasted until World War I, and then disappeared.[62]

Social dances. On October 22, 1870, two years before William Kimber's birth, the *Oxford Journal* carried the following account of the festivities—including dancing—surrounding the close of Headington Quarry's annual cricket season:

> *Proceedings commenced with a match between the married and single, which ended in favor of the former. The weather was fine and warm, and caused a large attendance of spectators from Oxford and the neighbouring villages. At the close of the match the players, with a number of friends, sat down to an excellent dinner at the Six Bells. . . . After the removal of the cloth, toasts, speeches, and songs agreeably diversified the proceedings, and a very pleasant evening was spent. During the evening the lads and lasses of the village danced on the village green to the strains of the Headington string band.*[63]

Such social dancing also happened during other club and feast nights. Kimber played tunes for a variety of social dances that reflected the times during which he played (see Chapters 6 and 7), including a few old country dances but more often couples dances like waltzes, polkas and schottisches, as well as quadrilles. At a Whitsuntide dance, Kimber recalls:

> *[There was] all the old-fashioned dancing; they'd know no other. I shall never forget . . . well we'd [done] one set of quadrilles . . . it was the Caledonians . . . they hooted at us, all these old women, these old dancers did. They didn't want such damned stuff as that. They wanted some of their own. They said, "That wasn't dancing—bowing and scraping and stooping about." Quadrilles . . . there were three lots of quadrilles, you see. Not Lancers; that's a separate thing with itself. There was the Caledonian Quadrilles, the Polka Quadrilles, and the Alberts.*[64]

Other dances were sponsored by travelling people. Saccy Horwood's quarry pit, near the Chequers tavern, served as a campground for travelling people, and as a place where the gypsies would have a pony roundabout. The favorite gypsy haunt, however, seems to have been the pit at the back of the Mason's Arms public house.[65] As already mentioned, it was a favored place for these travellers to winter over (Figure 1.16). The Bucklands, a family of travellers, would put on shows at Whitsun and in November at the sheep roast, and operated a pony roundabout.[66]

In many parts of Oxfordshire it was common in the late nineteenth century to see wooden platforms during festival days, often covered with canvas, operated for profit by gypsies as "dancing booths," where villagers could partake in social dancing.[67] There is no mention of dancing booths in the Quarry by Samuel or by Kimber, but it seems likely that since gypsies regularly wintered over in the Quarry, such dancing platforms would have made their appearance there too. Music for social dancing was often to the tunes of a local gypsy fiddler. Sampson Smith was such a fiddler, and even though a gypsy, he both danced and occasionally played the fiddle for the Quarry side in the 1870s.[68] William Kimber junior accredited the gypsy folk for bringing many old dance tunes into the Quarry.[69] Peter Kennedy once asked him if the gypsies offered an entry into village culture for new tunes and dances. William replied, "I know they did. Not our Morris there, but other dances. [And] I know they're great carol singers."[70]

Figure 1.16. The steep edge of Saccy Horwood's pit, 1900, with parts of Quarry village in the background. Saccy Horwood lived in a cottage at one end of this pit. According to the Headington History website, "In his youth he had been a Morris dancer, but ill-health reduced him to totting [scrounging for useable plants] for a living, including bringing watercress from Ewelme....he also caught snakes on the brickfields to sell to university laboratories and acted as a rag-'n'-bone man. He also sold fish, grew potatoes for sale, and caught birds to send to London. He also put on a weekly open-air show in Quarry known as 'Saccy in the Tub.' He may have acquired his nickname from habitually carrying a totting sack on his back." Postcard courtesy of Stephanie Jenkins.

During Sharp's collecting of Quarry tunes and dances from Kimber, Morris and country dances were of prime interest. The tunes of couples dances and quadrilles elicited little or no interest either from Sharp or later from leaders of the English Folk Dance and Song Society (EFDSS); these tunes were considered tawdry and modern—and indeed, they were the popular dances of the late Victorian and early Edwardian eras and hence comprised some of the latest dance steps for Quarry villagers. Luckily, a small batch of tunes from Kimber's social dance repertoire was recorded in the 1950s by Theo Chaundy and Peter Kennedy in separate sessions, and transcriptions of them are presented in Chapter 7. Much of what is considered "English country music" (English traditional music) played in pubs today descends from the tunes for those rural dances.

Morris dancing

Amidst all the various sorts of income-generating activities available to Quarry men—brickmaking, pig raising, digging, freight hauling, foraging, poaching and such—there was yet another means of secondary income available to certain men of the Quarry: Morris dancing. We tend to think of such dancing today as a weekend hobby, perhaps, or as an important social tradition that needs volunteer participation to continue. In late nineteenth century Quarry it also provided a not negligible kind of extra income, and available sources indicate that this was how it was typically approached: with a sense of professionalism. As historian Edna Mason put it, writing about an earlier period in Headington Quarry, 1820–1860, when William Kimber's grandfather, Job Kimber, was an active Quarry dancer:

> *A seasonal occupation which never appears in the census returns was that of Morris dancing, although it seems to have been confined to a fairly small number of families, most of them stone and brick workers. Usually thought of as a pastime, it was also a valuable source of extra income. Traditionally the dancers performed locally at Whitsuntide, but they would dance their way to London between the hay and the corn harvests. On a good day, they could hope to make as much as 10 shillings a day each and they expected to make at least as much as they would in the harvest field—another indication of multiple occupations for the stone and brick workers.*[71]

The Quarry Morris men dancing in the snow and bitter cold in the famous morning encounter of Boxing Day 1899 at Sandfield Cottage (more on that later) were there at that unusual time for one reason, as William Kimber recounted, men from the team saying: "We're hard up, so let's have a go of some sort to see if we can't get a bob or two."[72] They apologized to the lady of the cottage for being out at Christmas—they knew that Whitsuntide was the proper time—but there was no work "and they thought there would be no harm in trying to earn an honest penny."[73] Joseph Trafford related that when dancing took place in the streets of Oxford, "undergraduates would throw hot pennies at the Morris men. The poor old fiddler Frank Cummings carried to his grave a scar which he received through a burn so caused."[74]

References to the occurrence of Morris dancing in southern England extend to the fifteenth century, but the records regarding the inception of Morris dancing in Headington Quarry village are vague at best. Historian Keith Chandler has studied the beginnings of Morris dancing in the Quarry and notes that regular ongoing activity can only be firmly documented there for the years from 1840 to 1888.[75] As discussed earlier, the Quarry consisted of only a few stonemasons' dwellings before 1820, when the population was documented as only 106 persons, and the village began to grow in the 1830s. Frank Cummins (b. 1798), the side's fiddler for over forty years, appears to have joined the side ca. 1841, playing until his death in 1885.[76] Joseph Trafford (b. 1838), a dancer who participated in a revival of the Headington Quarry side in 1897, was reportedly active in the side from the 1840s, and Chandler surmises that Job Kimber probably danced by that time as well, possibly even as early as 1838.[77] Job Kimber, William junior's grandfather, was thus likely to have been the first Kimber to dance in the Quarry side. He reportedly took his young son William Kimber senior (1849–1931) to a final "Lamb Ale" [annual Morris festive gathering of sides] in nearby Kirtlington in 1860, where Job danced with the Quarry side. A set of bell pads and sticks collected by Percy Manning at Headington Quarry reportedly dated back to the middle of the nineteenth century (Figure 1.17).[78]

A photograph from about 1876 shows the side at a time when Cummins, Trafford, and Job Kimber's son William Kimber senior were active (Figure 1.18). William Kimber senior, who as previously mentioned was taken as a child by his father Job to the Kirtlington Ale in 1860, claimed to Cecil Sharp that he began to dance at the age of eighteen (ca. 1868), led the side by age twenty-two (1872), and danced during the year of the Golden Jubilee of Queen Victoria in 1887. He retired from the side in 1888, after a last private "shake-up" with the side.[79] William Kimber junior

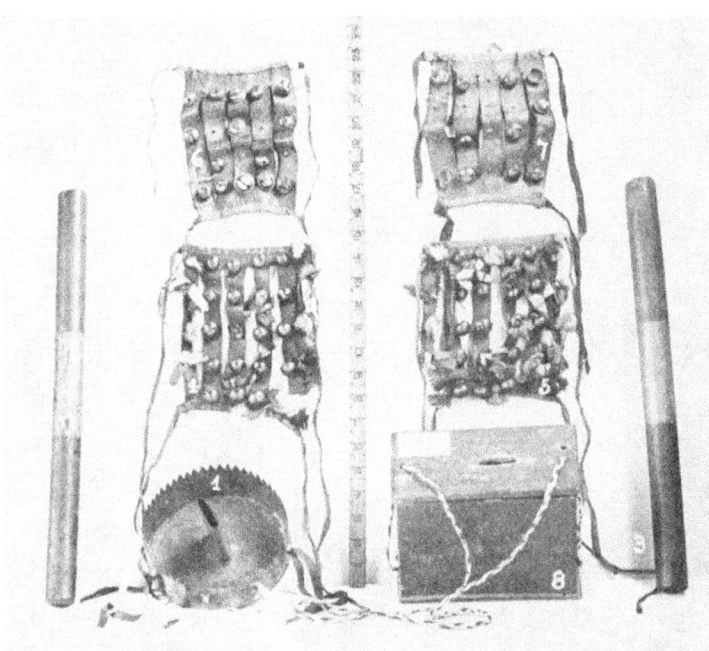

Figure 1.17. Oxfordshire Morris dance materials collected by Percy Manning, 1897. The two bell pads at top are from Headington Quarry. The sticks are also from Headington. The other two bell pads are from Taston, ca. 1840. The treasury box (ca. 1830) and cake tin are from Bampton. Manning, 1897, in *Folklore, a Quarterly Review*, vol. 8. The items were later placed at Cecil Sharp House in London, but were destroyed by German bombing during World War II.

reportedly often tagged along with the Quarry team and started to dance himself at the Jubilee celebrations, at the Oxpens in Oxford.[80]

The biggest event of the annual Morris dancing calendar was Whitsuntide week. It followed the holy day of Whitsun (Pentecost Sunday), which occurs annually on the seventh week after Easter. Dancing was formerly a weeklong event. William Kimber junior remembered Whitsuntide in his father's time:

[It] was a big thing about here then. . . . Everywhere that father went, of course, me being his oldest son, I went with him. . . . Every Whitsuntide, after they'd brushed up and got ready, it was a big week. They danced the whole week, the old dancers did, but their last time of dancing was in 1887.[81]

Kimber also recalled that there was "a club feast every day. In the morning [on Monday], we always done Oxford, [then] back to Oddfellows and the Britán"—Britannia pub in Oxford, where the Havelock Lodge of Oddfellows had their club feast. "Whit Tuesday was Quarry, two clubs there." According to Chaundy, they also attended mass and danced through the village, including at the big quarry pit by the Six Bells public house. They danced "Whit Wednesday, Melton. Whit Thursday, Great Haseley and Marlowe. Saturday, Long Crendon and perhaps some other places coming back . . . they'd get home Sunday."[82] The dancing was nearly continual during those feast days. Joseph Trafford remembered that in his younger days he would wear out a pair of shoes after just three days of dancing.[83]

The dancers were village working men. In the side of 1899, for example, William Kimber was a bricklayer, as was George Coppock. Sip Washington (the side's Fool) was a well digger, as was "Old" Mac Massey. "Young" Mac Massey was a builder's laborer.[84] They danced for money and for beer during the week of Whitsuntide. Collections were taken by the "fool" with his tin box. At these events, free beer was an additional privilege of dancers.[85]

The fiddler in those times, as noted, was Frank Cummings, who played for the side for some forty years. Toward the end he developed an infirmity, and "was taken round in a donkey-cart when he became too weak to stand to play. Before the donkey-cart came into use he was carried round on the men's shoulders."[86] Sharp reported that William Kimber senior played concertina and fiddle, and that he often played for the Quarry side when Cummings was unavailable or unable. Cummings was reportedly the source of many of Kimber senior's tunes. By the time William Kimber senior was twenty-two, he was the leader of the Headington Quarry Morris side, and danced continuously up to the Jubilee Year of 1887. After the side's appearance during the royal Jubilee Year it went dormant.[87]

The side practiced their steps at the club room of The Chequers, a pub at the center of the village. Dancer Joseph Trafford recalled that he "once won a wager by dancing every step of the jig 'Jockie to the Fair' on an upturned beer-barrel." Such

Figure 1.18. Headington Quarry Morris dancers, ca. 1876. William Kimber senior is seated to the right of the fiddle player. Seated, from left to right: Frank Cummings (fiddle player), William Kimber senior, James Hedges, John Horwood, Robert Cooper, probably John Haynes (the Fool). On ground in front, Joseph Trafford, Robert Trafford, and an unknown money collector. Used with permission of the Oxfordshire History Centre.

taproom events were typically all-male affairs. The taproom of Quarry pubs often saw the men also step dancing hornpipes, or dancing reels with each other (Figure 1.19). An example of such a reel in the transcriptions (Chapter 8) is the *Headington Morris Reel* recorded by Kimber; it is a version of the tune *Solder's Joy*. Of dancing such reels in the taproom, Kimber recalled:

> *Jack Hall from Horton . . . he used to come over and play a wooden whistle and his little dub. He'd sit with his old smock on and a high hat and dub away then. It was in the taproom, as you might say, it was six or seven of 'em a-reeling, dance a reel, mainly reels. That's what they mainly danced.*[88]

The "whistle and dub," more commonly called the pipe and tabor, was a standard instrument for Morris in older times, but was eventually replaced by the fiddle and, later still, the concertina. Regarding the numbers of dancers for reels danced in the taprooms, Kimber recalled:

> *[There were] sometimes four, sometimes six. It's all the same method how you split up. . . . Say you was going to dance the Headington Reel. Put one three over there, one three over here. They can dance a three-handed reel that way. See, there's no crossing over. Well then, the dance for four . . . the two centers facing the two outsides, you see, for the B music, then they changes places, them two . . . that's all there is in that dance. That's the four-handed reel. So, not enough to make up six, they make up four. Not enough to make up four, they make up three, you see?* [89]

Morris dancing had been commonplace during the eighteenth and early nineteenth century English countryside, but was decidedly less common by the end of the nineteenth century. The Quarry Morris side, after largely disbanding in 1887, was revived briefly in 1898–1899 when Oxford antiquarian Percy Manning (1870-1917) obtained the old photograph of the Headington Quarry Morris men shown in Figure 1.18. At that time, he thought the photo might date to 1864. Manning engaged two former Headington Quarry dancers who were in the photograph to recruit new dancers for the purpose of reviving the old custom during a presentation on old customs that he had planned. He later recalled the event:

> *I had picked up a photograph taken in 1864, of the dancers, and I discovered that two of the men, James Hedges & Jack Horwood, who were represented in that photo, were still living in Headington. With Carter's aid, I persuaded them to get a side together in the Autumn of 1898, which practised under the tuition of Hedges & Horwood during the winter. By the spring they were ready to dance and were provided with the necessary dress and equipment, on the exact lines of my old photo. The whole training was carried on by themselves, without any interference from me or from any outside source, so that there was no possibility of contaminating the pure tradition.*[90]

The practices were at the club room of The Chequers Inn in the Quarry (Figures 1.20 and 1.21). The recruited men, as later recalled by William Kimber senior (who, although a member of the side until 1887, did not take part) were William "Mac" Massey, his son Charles Massey, William "Sip" Washington (as the Fool), "Curly" and "Spuggle" Coppock, Richard "Dobbin" Kimber (William Kimber junior's cousin), Edward "Durgin" Morris, and John "Waggle" Ward.[91] Joseph "Jolly Joe" Trafford, the oldest dancer remaining at that time, was also consulted. To provide music, dancer James "Gran" Hedges approached Quarry resident Mark Cox, an "outsider" who had married a Headington woman and who played the violin to play for the side. Cox learned some of the side's dance tunes on the fiddle by listening to the whistling of dancers Hedges and Horwood.[92]

Figure 1.19. Step dancing in the tap room of a Norfolk pub. From *The Graphic*, October 22, 1887, and from Reg Hall's *I Never Played to Many Posh Dances* (Musical Traditions, 1990).

Manning arranged for the reformed side to dance at a lecture he gave on "Old Customs" at the Corn Exchange in Oxford on March 13, 1899. The side danced *The Blue-Eyed Stranger, Constant Billy, Country Gardens, Rigs o' Marlow, How D'ye Do Sir, Bean Setting, Haste to the Wedding, Rodney, Trunkles,* and *Drawback (Hunting the Squirrel).*[93] The transcriptions for all of these tunes are in Chapter 4. The dances were interspersed with folk songs sung by the Magdalen Choir and the Cathedral Choir, both of Oxford. The Morris side's appearance as "Ye Olde Headyngton Morris Dancers" was well attended and well received (Figure 1.22).

The side danced later that year (1899) at Whitsuntide (the week following May 21 that year), both in the streets of Oxford (Figure 1.23) and at Headington Quarry.

As part of that tour, the side danced at Sandfield Cottage on the London Road, at the invitation of Mrs. Dora Birch (Cecil Sharp's mother-in-law). She had previously engaged the company of Knowles and Son for some building work on the house, which she had just purchased. William Kimber junior was the foreman, and during an exchange of pleasantries one day in April, she had asked him to describe the hobbies and activities of the village. Among other things, he told her of the Quarry Morris side, and she invited them to stop by during their upcoming Whitsuntide activities. As Kimber recalled,

Figure 1.20. The Chequers Inn, Headington Quarry, as it appeared in 2023.

Well, when Whitsun come and we was round, we went in [at Sandfield] and we danced, and I can see it now. We danced and an old lady came to the window [to] see us dance. That's right. She said it was very pretty, and would we—whenever we were out—would we always call and let her see us dance? [I said,] "Yes we will." Well, we did . . . that same year, coming on to Christmas.[94]

In June of that year the Quarry men were photographed by Henry Taunt (Figures 1.24, 1.25).[95] They were dressed in new finery, including white shirts and trousers, white caps with badges, and with most sporting ties and baldricks. William Kimber was not among them.

By December 13, the side appeared again, at a fundraiser for the Boer War in South Africa, as mentioned by *Jackson's Oxford Journal* of December 16, 1899:

Figure 1.21. Headington Quarry Morris men at practice, ca.1898–1899. John Horwood and James Hedges were engaged by folklorist Percy Manning to form a new Morris side for one of Manning's lectures on local history. The dancers wear baldricks (ornamented shoulder belts) and white trousers but did not yet have the white team caps of later photographs. Photograph courtesy of Vaughan Williams Memorial Library and the Morris Ring.

A MORRIS DANCE.

Figure 1.22. The Headington Quarry Morris Dancers at the Corn Exchange, March 13, 1899. From the *Oxford Review*, May 16, 1899. Image courtesy of the Vaughan Williams Memorial Library.

In the hope of further increasing the total of the local Transvaal War Fund, the members of the St. Clement's Gymnastic Class gave a concert and gymnastic display on Wednesday evening at the Constitutional Hall, Cowley-road. ... A further attraction was the appearance of 'Ye Olde Headyngton Morrys Dancers', whose quaint antics greatly amused the company.[96]

William Kimber junior was not present at the Corn Exchange lecture of March 1899 nor at the scenes photographed by Taunt in June, but he was at the first Sandfield Cottage visit in May. The reasons for his absence are not fully known, but there is a back story that may partially explain it. His father, William Kimber senior, had played fiddle for the previous Quarry side after the death of Frank Cummins in 1885, but after the side's last public appearances in 1887 he removed himself completely from the Morris group. Like many of his era, William Kimber senior had an alcohol problem in his youth and early adulthood. In November 1873, when he was twenty-four and already a father, he and his older brother Richard Kimber (1845–1925) were arrested at night on a Headington street by a police officer who "saw the defendants fighting and causing a great disturbance in the village. They were both very drunk and offering to fight anyone in the place."[97] Beer flowed freely at many if not most Morris dance engagements in the Quarry. William junior in 1914 told Daisy Daking, a member of the early EFDSS, of these early days and the drinking in his father's day. In her words:

The old Headington Side used to be frightfully debauched and go off at Whitsuntide for weeks and weeks and never come home to their wives. They would be drunk the whole time and turn up at the end of the trip with no money at all. Then Old Kimber [William Kimber senior] got converted and turned Methodist, so set his face against the Morris. But he had taught all his sons and daughters, and they loved it, though he did all he could to discourage it.[98]

Recognizing what must have been an ongoing problem, William Kimber senior ceased dancing with the side at some time after their Jubilee appearances in 1887, and according to Daking joined the local Methodist Church. That conversion seems to have happened before 1901, when Kimber senior began working a steady job as a building foreman at the Oxford Corporation. Such a conversion to Methodism and abstention from drink was not limited to Kimber senior. Historian Michael Heaney notes that "Daniel Lock of the Morris side at Minster Lovell, Oxfordshire also embraced religion towards the end of the century. Lock said he stopped Morris dancing because of his wife's influence: 'She saw it lead to drinkin' and spendin' money and 'twere true enough'."[99]

When Percy Manning helped reconstitute the Quarry Morris side in 1898–1899, Kimber tried to dissuade his son, William junior, from dancing with the renewed Morris, fearing that drink would cause him similar problems.[100] Perhaps for that reason, William Kimber junior—although he had danced briefly at the Jubilee event in 1887 as a fifteen-year-old, and was well tutored by his father in the dances and tunes—missed the side's revival at the Corn Exchange event in March 1899. With all the positive press that followed this successful event, Kimber junior may then have decided differently and rejoined. By Whitsuntide 1899 (late May), he was dancing with the group, as noted earlier. But then he is absent from the photographs of the side taken by Taunt on June 26, where Mark Cox is prominently on display as the side's musician. When Henry Taunt took those photographs, Kimber and his wife Frances had two toddlers at home, and Frances was expecting their third child, William Thomas Kimber, who was born a few days later on July 1. It is possible that Kimber was needed at home, just as Mark Cox was absent at the side's Boxing Day dancing later that year. Kimber was the Headington Quarry side's musician on Boxing Day, December 26, 1899, playing his concertina.

Figure 1.23. Headington Quarry Morris dancing in Cowley Road, Oxford, Whit Monday, most likely in 1899. The fiddle player at left is Mark Cox. Photographer unknown. From *The Pearl* magazine of 1947, and Raphael Samuel's "Headington Roughs" (1974).

The concertina comes to Headington Quarry

Before relating the often-told tale of that most impactful Boxing Day, it is worth reflecting on the coming of the concertina to the Kimbers and their village. As mentioned earlier, William Kimber senior played fiddle for the Quarry side in the 1880s, and played both fiddle and concertina to his son William junior from a young age. By Boxing Day 1899, when Kimber junior first played the instrument for Cecil Sharp, William junior was the skilled musician for the side using the concertina, and his melodies were transcribed by Sharp. This generational transition in the Quarry's Morris music from fiddle to concertina was mirrored in other English communities of the time and reflects the increasing availability and popularity of the new and unusual free reed instrument—not unlike the rise of the electric guitar a century later.

Morris dance music in the Midlands of England during William Kimber senior's lifetime had been in transition from being played primarily on the pipe and tabor to being played on the fiddle. By the 1870s, however, there were concertinas used by several Morris sides. The earliest known occurrence of a concertina in a Morris group (1874) was in south Derbyshire, where a writer documented the Boxing Day visit of:

Figure 1.24. The Headington Quarry Morris dancers, June 26, 1899, standing in front of The Chequers. Left to right: William Washington, Charlie Massey, George Coppock, John Horwood, Mark Cox (with fiddle), "Old" Mac Massey, George Coppock, Richard Kimber, James Hedges. Photograph by Henry Taunt, courtesy of the Oxfordshire Historical Centre.

A troop of seven morris dancers, but dressed more after the fashion of [Negro] minstrels than the traditional mummers, an effect which was increased by five of them having blackened their faces. The tallest and most ungainly of the party was caparisoned as a woman. To the sound of a concertina they danced burlesque waltzes and quadrilles. . . . This incongruous medley of a performance was concluded by a "walk round" of the whole company singing, with more vigour than accuracy, the very unseasonable and inappropriate glee, "in a little boat we row."[101]

Other early appearances of the concertina in Morris dancing include Shrewsbury, Shropshire, in 1878; Wheatley, Oxfordshire, 1870s, a concertina with pipe and tabor; and Winchcombe, Gloucestershire, a concertina and a melodeon by the 1880s.[102] Of the Shrewsbury occurrence, the concertina was coming in as the Morris dance was on the way out. An observer later wrote:

The last specimen of morrice dancing seen by me in Shrewsbury was during the bad winter of 1878–1879, when about a dozen unemployed men performed a morrice dance through the streets of Shrewsbury to excite the sympathy of the benevolent. The music was supplied by a concertina, and the dance was to the tune of "There is nae luck about the house." The men had short sticks in their hands, and when they "set to partners" the sticks were struck sharply against each other. The dance was certainly a novel if not a pleasing one. The faces of the men were not blacked.[103]

By 1888 concertina use was common and often it replaced the fiddle, as in Ely, Cambridgeshire:

> *The streets were [formerly] tolerably filled by village ploughmen, fantastically dressed, dancing to the strains of a violin, ploughs being dragged on the roads; but this year, these implements of agriculture were conspicuous by their absence, and fiddles were supplanted by concertinas. Some of the morris-dancers, it would appear, had no connection with agricultural pursuits.*[104]

Imported inexpensive German-made concertinas were available in London by the 1840s, and that trickle became a flood in the 1850s and 1860s, when these instruments surged into the rural countryside. It is difficult to overstate how popular the concertina was in the late nineteenth century for working-class people in both urban and rural areas. Rural English youth were drawn to the concertina not just for the amusement it provided but for the chance to make extra money playing for events and social dances. A London writer in 1885 described the musical scene in the then-impoverished southern English countryside as follows:

> *A show of hands as to the most satisfactory [rural] instrument would probably result in favour of the German concertina. This foreigner . . . has helped drive out the fiddle and to spoil the ears of a rustic people. It is now the concertina that is the rule at rural*

Figure 1.25. The Headington Quarry side, June 26, 1899. The side was resurrected with the encouragement of Oxford lecturer Percy Manning. Mark Cox is the fiddle player. William Kimber was not part of the group on this occasion. Photograph by Henry Taunt, courtesy of the Oxfordshire Historical Centre.

merrymakings, and the fiddle that is the exception. The concertina has an alluring charm in the way in which it lends itself to processional purposes. You may see a performer strolling along the moonlit roads, while a bevy of appreciative friends go with him, and listen to his playing. This peculiarity makes the concertina in demand at certain weddings in which, after church, the marriage party makes a ceremonial progress through the village, a concertina player heading the procession. There is something of an antique simplicity in these processions, in the high priest of the solemnity flourishing his instrument in curves like those of the skater, as he wafts melodious incense, and in the noisy jollity of the people who follow him. . . . This may be thought an unfavourable picture of village music, but it is true for a great part of the villages in the South of England, at least. On the one side there is a deep and sincere love for music, and on the other the most meager of opportunities for learning or for guidance in it.[105]

Cecil Sharp reported that Kimber senior played fiddle to his son (born in 1872) "when he was in cradle & bed to lull him to sleep."[106] As mentioned, during the daytime William junior's mother would allow young William to play his father's concertina,[107] suggesting that at least by the late 1870s the family had one. William Kimber junior's granddaughter, Julie Kimber Nickelson, has stated that

Figure 1.26. William Kimber with Morris regalia and his two-row Anglo concertina, ca. 1906. The image is from Cecil Sharp's *The Morris Book* (1911). The photo first appeared in the London *Daily Chronicle* of January 4, 1907.

Willliam Kimber junior "was very passionate about the music; he had to be right. And then a concertina club opened in the Quarry, and he and his brothers joined it. He used to play regularly."[108] Derek Schofield added that the concertina club met in a local taproom and that William's brother Tom (1874–1939) also played.[109]

An early printed tutor for the twenty-button German concertinas by Charles Minasi, published in London of 1846, indicates that these instruments were being played by at least some musicians in a harmonic manner (chords on the left hand, melody on the right) from the very beginning of the instrument's appearance in England in the 1840s and 1850s.[110] The Kimber style requires a snap and quickness tailored to the needs of Morris dancers, played with volume at a rapid dancing speed that would not be easy on a typical, rather wheezy inexpensive German concertina of that era. That more complex harmonic playing would be best accomplished on a better crafted, English-made Anglo concertina, which began to be made in London in the 1850s. The earliest published photograph of William Kimber junior with a concertina appeared in the London *Daily Chronicle* in January 1907 (see next chapter). The instrument shown in the photograph was a hexagonal Anglo concertina with two rows of keys (Figure 1.26).

The earliest advertisements for Anglo concertinas in the Oxford press were in the *Oxford Times* from 1878 through the early 1880s (Figure 1.27). C. F. Mallett's Musical Repository in Oxford listed Anglo concertinas as early as 1878. In 1879 R. Taylor's Music Repository also carried Anglo concertinas and included an image of one of them, upside down. By the next year, 1880, the image had been corrected and the Anglo was shown right side up. Taylor's apparently also carried less expensive German concertinas, as their stated prices for "concertinas" started at 2s at a time when Anglo concertinas started at about £1.[111] The images show a simple two-row

Anglo. Its grid pattern, arranged in a semicircle, somewhat resembles that of an early Lachenal two-row Anglo owned by Stephen Chambers, noted collector.[112] The Lachenal company was known for its mass production of concertinas and was growing rapidly from the 1870s, when about 3,500 Anglos per year were manufactured, to the 1880s, when production of Anglos peaked at about 6,000 per year. No other maker of English concertinas in that era came close to Lachenal's production volume.[113] With this in mind, it would seem most likely that Kimber senior acquired one of these Lachenals that were sold in Oxford, probably during the period 1878–1883.

It is worth recapping the state of music in the relatively isolated Quarry village at the time of William Kimber junior's youth. There were several fiddle players and at least one pipe and tabor player. Both Kimbers, senior and junior, could play the tin whistle. Both, at different times, were members of the village fife and drum band. Kimber senior became a member of the Methodist church, which was a rather severe place, probably not given to high-church organ and choral music. Young Kimber thus came from a musical background that was primarily melodic, with not much exposure to highly chorded music with particular chord progressions, as one might experience in large churches, orchestras, brass bands, and university music schools. When the concertina came to the village, this new-fangled instrument had lots of potential for making chords, but that potential took time to develop.

Most new Anglo concertina players will play it along-the-row and purely melodically, essentially mimicking the sound and compass of a fiddle. The fact that there was a concertina club in the village suggested that there was some experimenting going on. At nearly this same time in Sussex, young Scan Tester (1887–1972) learned how to play in octaves from his older brother Trayton,[114] but he never made the jump to a chorded, harmonic style as did Kimber. Kimber and perhaps his father used a more complex style of playing utilizing the right hand for melodies and the left hand for rhythm and partial chords; that style was ideally suited to the Morris. It is not known how much of

Figure 1.27. Early advertisements for the Anglo concertina in Oxford. Upper: *Oxford Times,* July 13, 1878. Lower: *Oxford Times,* June 21, 1879.

that particular manner of playing the instrument was learned from others, but there are some clues. As mentioned above, several early printed tutors from as early as 1846 showed the basics of playing in a harmonic manner, but of course the Kimbers and indeed many other village musicians of his day did not read music. A good indication that the harmonic style was used by street musicians of that era is given by Henry Mayhew's 1856 interview of a young busker who played on the steamboats on the Thames: "I like the concertina, because it's like a full band. It's like having the fiddle and the harp together....The fiddle is pretty good, but nothing, to my fancy, like the concertina."[115] Kimber's take on this accompaniment style, with his unusual and very rhythmic chording, is discussed in detail in Chapter 3. Suffice it for now to say that as often as not, his chord choices—especially the "unusual" ones—were dictated by a combination of the constraints of the two-row concertina and the techniques he applied in playing it.

Family life

As William Kimber reached the age of nineteen, in 1891, his family moved to what are now called the Woodbine Cottages on Headington Hill, just off the Oxford to London road and west of the mapped area shown in Figure 1.4. Here he and his two younger brothers, Percy and Thomas, were employed as bricklayer's labourers. In 1894, at the age of twenty-two, he married Florence Mary Cripps at St. Andrew's Church in Headington. Florence (1869–1917) was originally from Cold Harbour (also called Cold Arbour), a neighborhood on the south side of the village of South Hinksey, to the south of Oxford, perhaps three miles from Headington Quarry. Her father was an Oxford stonemason named Thomas Cripps. By 1891, at the age of twenty-two when she met William, she was living near St. Ebbe's Church in central Oxford. At first the newly wedded couple took up residence in a row house on New High Street in New Headington, three quarters of a mile west of the central part of Quarry village. Their first child, Florence Annie, was born there the following year, and by 1896 they moved into a brick row house on Lime Walk in New Headington that has since been destroyed (site 4, Figure 1.4).[116] There their daughter Lilian Rose was born in 1896, and their first son, William Thomas, was born in July 1899.

It was as a family man that Kimber began playing concertina for the Quarry Morris side, perhaps in the beginning when their relatively new fiddle player Mark Cox was absent. Doubtless the experience of dancing for a public lecture by Percy Manning at the Corn Exchange in Oxford gave new spring to the steps of the Quarry side and lent an air of respectability to the enterprise, which may have made the move easier for Kimber, whose father, a recovering alcoholic, was against encouraging participation in the Morris. By late 1899, in the last few days of the nineteenth century, the Quarry Morris side was ready to emerge again, this time in winter snow. This meeting would eventually result in changing Kimber from an anonymous rural villager to a nationally known and respected figure in the English folk revival.

The Boxing Day meeting, 1899

December 1899 in Oxford was colder than normal, and a string of freezing days in the middle of the month had shut down most building and brickmaking activities (among other things, it is difficult for mortar to set when the temperature is so cold).[117] As a result, many in the Quarry Morris side were temporarily out of work.

As mentioned earlier, they decided to try dancing to generate some income. Unlike the dancers of the revived side, their fiddler, Mark Cox, may not have been relieved of work that day, and in any event William Kimber took over duties as the side's musician. One of the places they visited that day was Sandfield Cottage, which they had visited in May and to which they had been asked to return. Unbeknownst to them, Mrs. Birch was joined by her daughter, Constance, and her son-in-law, Cecil Sharp. Kimber related the meeting as follows:

> *About three weeks before Christmas that set in and froze. It froze us all out. Main part of us were in the building trade—pretty well all of us were in the building trade. It froze us out; well honestly we was all hard up. Well of course at that time, Christmas time, the carol singers were out, the Mummers was going out, the handbell ringers was going out, and the two village bands was going out. Christmas Boxing [Day] our chaps got together and they said, "Well, what about us?" I said, "Look at the weather." "Oh well, we be hard up," they said. "Let's have a bit of a go of some sorts [and see] if we can't get a bob or two?" Well, it was settled that we should.*
>
> *Well, we went round and we got to Sandfield Cottage and went in; we started. The first dance was* Bean Setting, *in this snow—still, we got through it. A gentleman come to the window, and this gentleman had got a shade over his eye, and they stood and watched us dance.*

This man was forty-year-old folk music collector Cecil Sharp (Inset Box), and the eye patch was there to help ameliorate a painful and acute sensitivity to light in one eye. The dancers included William Kimber at the concertina, J. Hedges, Bill Massey, J. Horwood, R. Kimber, George Coppock, Charles Massey and W. Washington as the Fool.[118]

> *Well, as we were a-coming away, this gentleman comes to the door—the front door—and he asked me if I could find time the next day to go up and play them two tunes over to him as he'd seen danced—that he should like to take 'em down. I said yes, I'd come up, and [then] I went.*
>
> *I played those tunes over to him and he took 'em down and he went across to the piano and played 'em and I was never so much surprised. In all my life I'd never seen nothing done like that before, in my life, never. Of course, in those days it was strange. That was* Bean Setting *and* Constant Billy. *Well, we had a glass of wine and a biscuit and a long chat and as I was coming to the front door this gentleman give me half a sovereign and said, "We may meet again some day." That gentleman was Cecil Sharp. That was the first meeting with him and the first two tunes that he took down. Boxing Day, 1899.*[119]

The tunes that Sharp recorded from Kimber that day as well as later included just the melody line (e.g., Figure 1.28). As Kimber later said, "I just played the treble [for

Cecil Sharp

Cecil J. Sharp (1859-1924) was born in South London, son of a slate merchant. He earned a B.A. at the University of Cambridge in 1882, and then emigrated to Australia for a few years, lecturing in music. He returned to England in 1893 and married Constance Dorothea Birch. He taught music in London. While visiting his sister-in-law at Sandfield Cottage in 1899 he saw Morris dancing and met William Kimber for the first time.

In 1904 he resigned his teaching post and began to collect, compose, lecture, and write about folk songs full time. Sharp eventually collected some 1600 songs from hundreds of sources in England. In 1905, working at first with Mary Neal, organizer of the Esperance Girl's Club in London, he began collecting and notating Morris dances and later rapper and sword dances, from across England. He also collected and published a number of English country dances. In 1911 he co-founded the English Folk Dance Society, which later merged with the English Folk Song Society in 1932 to become the EFDSS. During World War I, he collected songs of largely English origin in the Appalachian mountain region of the US.

Sharp and Kimber, though of vastly different social backgrounds, became lifelong friends, and often worked together in collecting and performing hundreds of Morris dances. It is Sharp's undeniable legacy that thousands of English and Anglo-American folk songs and dances were saved from oblivion by his tireless work.

Image courtesy of the Vaughan Williams Memorial Library, EFDSS, London.

him],"[120] meaning that he played only the right hand for Sharp, leaving out his left hand rhythmic harmony, so that Sharp could easily transcribe the melody. His characteristic style of playing the concertina (melody on the right hand, accompaniment on the left) was clearly already in use, and he was a seasoned player. Cecil Sharp called him "a first-rate performer on the concertina."[121]

The half-sovereign (50p) that Sharp gave Kimber was, according to Kimber, "a Godsend. The day before we got eight bob apiece (40p) out of our dancing, and I hadn't had no money for three weeks. That was a Godsend to the wife when I got home, I tell you."[122]

It would be three years, and a new century, before Kimber was to meet Cecil Sharp again, but a stage had been set that would change Kimber's life forever. It wasn't the only stark change that he would meet in the early years of the new century, however. An automobile company that was to set up a factory in nearby Cowley in 1913 would thoroughly change forever the character of the small village that had nurtured Kimber and his music.

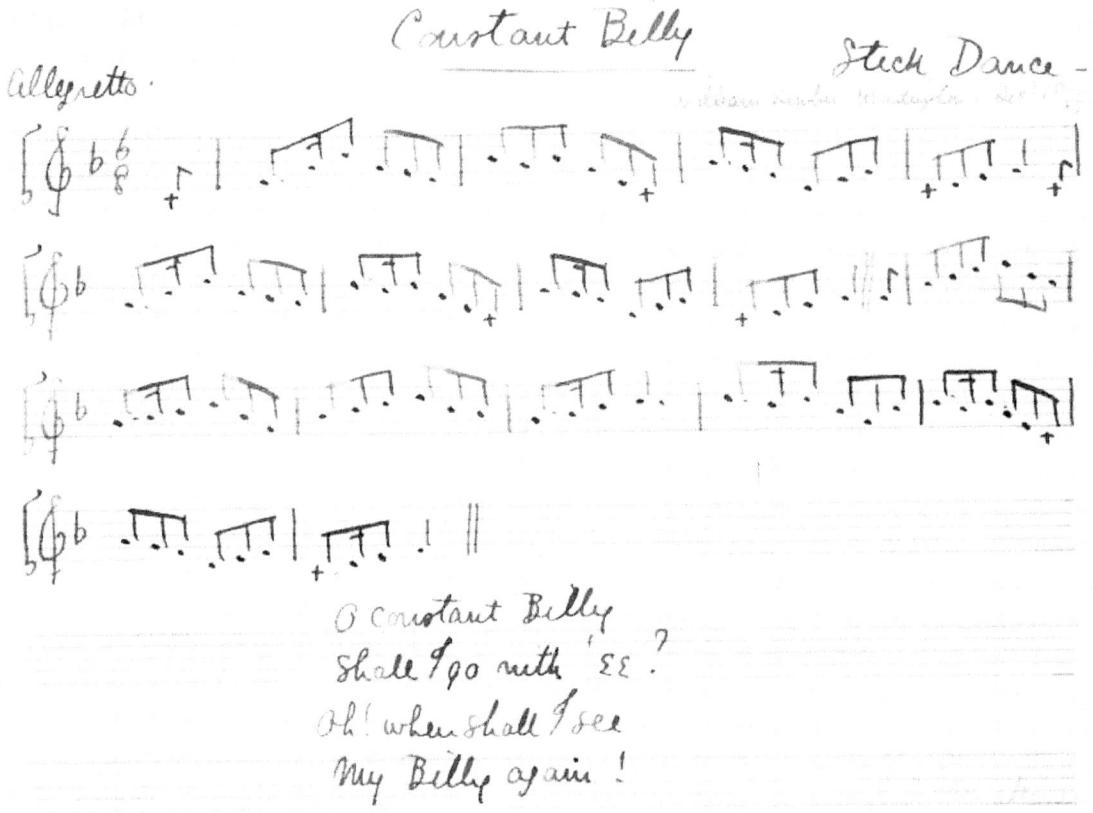

Figure 1.28. The Morris tune *Constant Billy*, as noted by Cecil Sharp from the playing of William Kimber in late December 1899. Image courtesy of the Vaughan Williams Memorial Library, EFDSS, London.

---

[1] Headington History, an online resource of Oxford History, entry by Stephanie Jenkins, https://www.headington.org.uk/history/timeline_briefhistory/index.html.
[2] Keith Chandler, 1993, *Ribbons, Bells and Squeaking Fiddles: The Social History of Morris Dancing in the English Midlands, 1660–1900*, Middlesex, UK: Hisarlik Press, p. 149.
[3] Theo W. Chaundy, 1959, "William Kimber: A Portrait." *Journal of the EFDSS*, vol. 8, no. 4, p. 204.
[4] Cecil Sharp, "Folk Dance Notes," manuscripts housed at Vaughan Williams Memorial Library of the EFDSS, London, volume 1, p. 251ff., as quoted in Chandler, 1993, p. 149.
[5] Chandler, 1993, p. 149.
[6] United Kingdom census of 1921.
[7] Cecil J. Sharp and Herbert C. Macilwaine, 1911, *The Morris Book part 1*, Novello, second edition.
[8] William Kimber, 1956, as interviewed by Theo Chaundy, tape 1, Chaundy collection, www.merryville.uk.
[9] Chaundy, 1959.
[10] Chaundy, 1959, p. 115.
[11] Phil Kerry, 2020, "The Stones that Built Oxford," www.goldholme.com/history-stone/the-stone-that-built-oxford.
[12] Facts in the preceding two paragraphs are partly taken from "Headington History: The Quarries," website of Oxford History, entry by Stephanie Jenkins, www.headington.org.uk/history/quarries, accessed May 2023.
[13] Chaundy, 1959.

[14] Edna Mason, 1989, "Headington Quarry c. 1820–1860: A Study of a 19th-Century Open Village, *Oxoniensia*, vol. 54, p. 364.
[15] Mason, 1989, p. 364.
[16] Headington Charity Commission archives, 1869, as quoted by Samuel, 1974, p. 142.
[17] Mason, 1989, p. 367.
[18] As quoted by Raphael Samuel in his Headington Quarry Transcripts, Morris and Coppock, fol. 5.
[19] Samuel, 1974, pp. 139–263.
[20] Headington History, an online resource of Oxford History, entry by Stephanie Jenkins, https://www.headington.org.uk/history/timeline_briefhistory/index.html.
[21] Ronald Blythe, 1969, *Akenfeld: Portrait of an English Village,* New York: New York Review Books, republished 2015. The quote is from the Introduction.
[22] Raphael Samuel, 1972, "Headington Quarry: Recording a Labouring Community: Oral History," vol. 1, no. 4, *The Interview in Social History: Part 1*, pp. 107–22.
[23] Chaundy, 1959.
[24] Samuel, 1974, p. 154.
[25] "Open Magdalen, Open Brasenose, and Brasenose Wood," in Headington History, an online history site, www.headington.org.uk/history/misc/magdalen_brasenose_woods.html. Accessed July 2023.
[26] Samuel, 1974, p. 149.
[27] Samuel, 1974, p. 149.
[28] Chaundy, 1959.
[29] Samuel, 1974, p. 147.
[30] Samuel, 1974, p. 162.
[31] Mason, 1989, p. 372.
[32] Samuel, 1974, p. 157.
[33] Samuel, 1974.
[34] Samuel, 1974, pp. 157, 170.
[35] J. A. Coppock, as quoted by Raphael Samuel in his Headington Quarry Transcripts, Oxford County Museum, fol. A.8.
[36] Samuel, 1974, p. 191.
[37] Samuel, 1974, p. 191.
[38] Correspondence, William Kimber to Cecil Sharp, October 15, 1913. Vaughan Williams Memorial Library.
[39] William Kimber, letter to Maud Karpeles, June 14, 1929. Vaughan Williams Memorial Library.
[40] Samuel, 1974, pp. 208–13.
[41] Maurice East, 2021, "A Rough Guide to Quarry with Maurice East," Chippie Townie Tours, recorded by Trish Elphinstone and posted on YouTube. Used with permission of Maurice East.
[42] *Ibid.*
[43] As quoted by Raphael Samuel in his Headington Quarry Transcripts, Oxford County Museum, Ward, fol. A, 4–5.
[44] Mason, 1989, p. 374.
[45] G. A. Coppock, B. M. Hill, and Edmund Arnold Greening Lamborn, 1933, *Headington Quarry and Shotover: A History Compiled on Behalf of Quarry Women's Institute,* University Press by John Johnson, p. 30. That church was on Trinity Road and was replaced by a larger chapel in 1860 on Quarry High Street, which ceased operation as a Methodist church in 2004. The building is now used by the Cornerstone Church.
[46] See Samuel, 1974, p. 158.
[47] Anonymous, *Headington Quarry Parish Magazine*, June 1956. Copy at Vaughan Williams Memorial Library.
[48] William Kimber, as recorded by Peter Kennedy, 1951, *William Kimber Talking*, an interview of William Kimber with Maud Karpeles at Kimber's home, December 4, 1951. Folktrax recording CD 383, track 23.
[49] "The May Horn Nuisance," *Oxford Chronicle and Reading Gazette*, May 14, 1887, p. 2.
[50] *William Kimber Talking*, as recorded by Peter Kennedy, 1951, Folktrax CD 383, track 23.

[51] Percy Manning, 1897, "Some Oxfordshire Seasonal Festivals, with Notes on Morris dancing in Oxfordshire," *Folk-lore, Transactions of the Folk-Lore Society*, vol. 8, pp. 307–24.
[52] *Oxford Journal*, November 23, 1861, p. 8.
[53] *Oxford Chronicle and Reading Gazette*, December 2, 1899, p. 3.
[54] *Oxford Chronicle and Reading Gazette*, December 2, 1904, p. 9.
[55] *Oxford Chronicle and Reading Gazette*, December 1, 1905, p. 11.
[56] Research notes from interviews, Raphael Samuel, Oxfordshire History Centre, Oxford.
[57] *Ibid.*
[58] *William Kimber Talking*, as recorded by Peter Kennedy, 1951, Folktrax CD 383, track 28.
[59] G. A. Coppock et al., 1933, p. 66.
[60] Samuel, 1974, p. 206.
[61] *William Kimber Talking*, as recorded by Peter Kennedy, 1951, Folktrax CD 383, track 6.
[62] G.A. Coppock et al., 1933, pp. 57–58.
[63] "Headington Quarry," *Oxford Journal*, October 22, 1870, p. 7.
[64] *William Kimber Talking*, as recorded by Peter Kennedy, 1951, Folktrax CD 383, track 31.
[65] Samuel, 1974, pp. 146, 147, 185.
[66] Samuel, 1974, p. 162.
[67] Keith Chandler, Musicians in 19th Century Southern England: Keith Chandler's Short Essays, online at Musical Traditions, www.mustrad.org.uk/articles/d_booth1.
[68] Samuel, 1974, p. 162. Also, Cecil Sharp, manuscript notes, Vaughan Williams Memorial Library, p. 253.
[69] Chaundy, 1959, p. 204.
[70] *William Kimber Talking*, as recorded by Peter Kennedy, 1951, Folktrax CD 383, track 32.
[71] Mason, 1989, p. 372.
[72] Chaundy, 1959, p. 205.
[73] Maud Karpeles, 1967, *Cecil Sharp*, London, p. 25, as quoted by Samuel, 1974, p. 187.
[74] *Ibid.*, p. 56.
[75] Chandler, 1993, pp. 147–57.
[76] Chandler, 1993, pp. 148–50.
[77] Chandler, 1993, p. 148.
[78] Manning, 1897, vol. 8, plate IV.
[79] Cecil Sharp, from his manuscripts at Vaughan Williams Memorial Library, as quoted in Chandler, 1993, p. 148.
[80] Derek Schofield, 1999, "Absolutely Classic: The Music of William Kimber," biographical notes in booklet to accompany a CD of the same name, EFDSS CD 03, p. 6.
[81] *William Kimber Talking*, as recorded by Peter Kennedy, 1951, Folktrax CD 383, track 2.
[82] William Kimber, as recorded by Theo Chaundy and others, 1956. www.Merryville.uk/collections.
[83] Coppock et al., 1933, p. 56.
[84] Samuel, 1974, pp. 241, 254.
[85] Samuel, 1974, p. 185.
[86] Coppock et al., 1933, pp. 53–56.
[87] Cecil Sharp, MSS "Folk Dances, Further notes on Headington Quarry Morris Dancers," p. 251. Cecil Sharp Manuscript Collection, Clare College, Cambridge (CJS2/11/1/251).
[88] William Kimber, 1956, as interviewed by Theo Chaundy and others, online at *Merryville: The online home of William Kimber* (www.Merryville.uk/collections), Tape 3, Whittle and Dub.
[89] *William Kimber Talking*, as recorded by Peter Kennedy, 1951, Folktrax CD 383, track 42.
[90] Percy Manning, "Notes on the Revival of Morris Dancing." MS Top. Oxon d.200, ff. 62–65. Bodleian Libraries, as quoted by Michael Heaney, 2023, *The Ancient English Morris Dance*, Oxford: Archaeopress, pp. 349–50.
[91] Bob Grant, 1999, "When Punch Met Merry," *Folk Music Journal*, vol. 7, p. 646.
[92] Coppock et al., 1933, pp. 5.
[93] Grant, 1999, p. 646.
[94] *William Kimber Talking*, as recorded by Peter Kennedy, 1951, Folktrax CD 383, track 4.
[95] Grant, 1999, p. 646.
[96] Heaney, 2023, p. 350.
[97] *Oxford Times*, December 6, 1873, p. 6, Bullingdon Petty Sessions.

[98] Daisy Daking, 1914, "The Log of a Fine Companion," manuscript diary, Vaughan Williams Memorial Library.

[99] Heaney, 2023, p. 233. Also see Chandler, 1993, p. 215.

[100] Sharp, "MSS Folk Dances," p. 252.

[101] An Old Fogy, "Christmas Visitors [Letter]." *Derbyshire Times and Chesterfield Herald*, January 6, 1875, as quoted by Michael Heaney, 2023, *The Ancient English Morris Dance*, Oxford: Archaeopress, p. 266.

[102] Dan Worrall, 2008, *The Anglo-German Concertina: A Social History, Vol. 1*, pp. 114–15. Also see Chandler, 1993, p. 180.

[103] *Shropshire Notes and Queries*, I and II, Shrewsbury, June 19, 1885, p. 61.

[104] Ely correspondent, *Cambridge Independent Press*, January 13, 1888, as quoted by Michael Heaney, 2023, *The Ancient English Morris Dance*, Oxford: Archaeopress, p. 268.

[105] "The Music of a Village," in *The Musical World* (London), April 4, 1885, pp. 221–22.

[106] Cecil Sharp, manuscript notes, Vaughan Williams Memorial Library, p. 252.

[107] Chaundy, 1959.

[108] Julie Kimber Nicholson, ca. 2014, "Music in the Family," an interview by Michael Heaney, "Back in the Quarry," Folk Arts Oxford, online at Back to the Quarry (folk-arts-oxford.co.uk).

[109] Schofield, 1999, p. 4.

[110] Charles Minasi's tutor for the two row German concertina, published in London in 1846, discussed both octave and harmonic (chords on the left hand, melody on the right) style playing, with musical examples; see discussion by Randall Merris and Dan Worrall, 2005, "Earliest known English-language concertina tutor: Minasi's 'Instruction Book,' 1846" at the Concertina Library, http://www.concertina.com/merris/minasi-german-tutor-1846/index.htm. In addition, George Jones published his *Chromatic Anglo-German Concertina Tutor* in London in 1876 that included examples of both octave and harmonic style playing; www.concertina.com/jones/Jones-Anglo-tutor-1946.pdf.

[111] Chris Algar, ca. 2007, "Lachenal Concertina Pricelists," www.concertinalibrary.com.

[112] Stephen Chambers, 2004, "Some Notes on Lachenal Concertina Production and Serial Numbers," *Papers of the International Concertina Association*, vol. 1, pp. 3–23, fig. 7.

[113] Worrall, 2008, fig. 43, p. 27.

[114] Reg Hall, 1990, *I Never Played to Many Posh Dances,* Rochford, Essex: Musical Traditions, Musical Supplement No. 2, p. 96.

[115] Henry Mayhew, 1856, "Concertina player on the steamboats," in *London Labour and the London Poor*, volume 3: London, Charles Griffin and Company.

[116] *Ibid*.

[117] Grant, 1999, pp. 647–48.

[118] Chaundy, 1959.

[119] William Kimber, as interviewed by Peter Kennedy, November 14th, 1956. Included as part of EFDSS LP 1001, London, 1963.

[120] William Kimber as interviewed by Theo W. Chaundy, 1956, Tape 3. Online at www.merryville.uk, a project of Folk Arts Oxford.

[121] Cecil Sharp and Herbert C. Macilwaine, 1907, *The Morris Book* vol. 1; revised in 1911, p. 35. Published for the Morris Ring, 1991, Letchworth Garden City, Herefordshire: The Hive Printers.

[122] William Kimber as interviewed by Theo W. Chaundy, 1956.

Figure 2.1. William Kimber playing for Morris dancers at an annual festival of the English Folk Song and Dance Society at Stratford-upon-Avon, 1946. Image courtesy of the Vaughan Williams Memorial Library.

[Kimber is] a bricklayer by trade and a dancer by profession.

—Cecil Sharp

Chapter 2. The English Folk Revival and Kimber's Later Years

The new century began quietly. The memories of the Boxing Day dances receded, and for William Kimber's part, he forgot about the man in the eyepatch who has expressed such interest in the Morris tunes. The Quarry Morris side continued to dance every now and then, for example at the Water Carnival celebrating the coronation of Edward VII in August 1902, and at a fundraising festival for the Radcliffe Infirmary in August 1905.[1] After that event, the old side's members began to fade away through age or other competing activities.[2]

Kimber and his family were still living on Lime Walk in New Headington in 1900. He and Florence welcomed another daughter, Dorothy Ellen, in 1902, and then another daughter, Ada, in 1903. By this time, at age thirty-one, he supported a wife and five young children. The back gardens in the row houses along Lime Walk were small, which must have been problematic, although there were village allotment grounds where extra gardening space could be arranged. Most Quarry families relied on home-grown produce and livestock to make it through the long dark winters, when many (especially those in the building trade) were apt to be out of work. There was never enough money, as Kimber wrote to his friend Cecil Sharp in December 1905: "I have only earned a few shillings this last month with so much rain and now frost and snow and the town is very bad off for trade. My Christmas doesn't seem as if it's going to be very bright."[3]

On March 7, 1906, his second son and sixth child, Frederick Merry, was born, and that addition was an impetus for the family to move to a larger place. In about 1908 Kimber obtained a garden lot along St. Anne's Road and built himself a two-story brick house, later to be known as "Merryville," for his nickname, Merry (Figure 2.2). The garden was much larger, which no doubt was a major draw. The backyard lot behind the rear edge of the house was only about 20 feet wide, but was about 110 feet long, into which the family crammed a vegetable garden, fruit trees, some chickens, and a pig stye.

It is difficult for us today to appreciate the work and commitment that went into that back lot. If you look via aerial photography at the lots today along that street—the houses are mostly all still standing – you will see lawns, patios, a few water features, ornamental trees, and even a trampoline or two in the backyards. Only a few have small vegetable gardens, at least from that aerial view. In Kimber's day, Quarry villagers would have been putting up preserves of berries, fruits and vegetables throughout the summer that were either grown in the backyard or in a small allotment (or in the case of berries, picked in the wild). When the weather turned cool, potatoes would be dug up and a family hog would be butchered in the backyard and salted down in a trough. Everything of this pig would be used but the squeal, as they say, providing the family with meat throughout the winter. In Kimber's case, as was the case with other villagers, he tried to raise more piglets than the family would need for food in order to sell or barter them for valued extra income. During that fall weather when today we might take our families on cool weather pleasure hikes in the forest, they too would venture out, but to gather acorns ("pig nuts") for feeding the swine and ferns for the pigs' bedding. Keeping them warm and dry was essential in preventing the pigs from catching the same colds and flu that their owners would catch. More than once, Kimber lost all his pigs to such maladies.

It was a busy life, and the income of a bricklayer was never enough, especially for a family with six children to feed. Raphael Samuel recorded a Quarry woman named Gaitha Kerry whose husband, like Kimber, was a bricklayer:

Figure 2.2. "Merryville," the tidy brick house that William Kimber built for himself and his family in 1908, at 42 St. Anne's Road, Headington (formerly number 34). A long garden in the back contained vegetable beds, chickens, and a pig sty. Kimber lived here until his death in 1961, and today the house displays a Blue Plaque honoring Kimber's time there.

Oh, you couldn't work in the winter [on bricklaying] because of the frost. I don't know what we did do. Nothing much, we had to save our money, we'd do the best. . . . We never did get much money. If we'd have half, a quarter, or been able to do like they do today it would have been a wonderful life. [How did you get by?] Well, you see, they had their own gardens, you never bought any vegetables, never such a thing, and you kept a chicken— chickens—or a pig, you made everything yourself, you see, you had your fruit, you made your jam, your pickles and everything, and I suppose really that's how we did get by. Because there was no "unemployment," nothing of that, no dole money or anything of that. Everybody had a garden, and everybody had an allotment. We never bought potatoes or anything of that,

> *you hadn't the money to buy them. Why, you couldn't buy those sorts of things, on the bit of money you had in those days, if you had a family.*[4]

In 1909 Winifred Sophia was born, and in 1912 the Kimbers' last child, Evelyn Mary, was born, bringing the number of children to eight, all living with their parents in that small row house. Tragedy struck in 1917, when William's wife Florence suddenly died. Life was not easy, and when we read of Kimber telling others of difficult finances, it can be understood that playing concertina for Morris dancing with the Quarry side, and later with Sharp, was seen as something more than a joy; it also provided a bit of needed extra income.

The Beginning of the Morris revival, 1905–1909

There was no immediate follow-up to meeting Cecil Sharp at Sandfield Cottage on Boxing Day 1899, and over the next six years Kimber had all but forgotten about Sharp. Kimber was recorded by Peter Kennedy in 1951 telling the story:

> *I didn't hear any more about it; I'd almost forgot it. But one day a lady came from London. She [had] tried to find me but couldn't. My wife couldn't tell 'em where I was working. But the next week I had a letter from her to say, would I come to London and learn some girls a few morris-dance tunes. They were giving a show at the Sir Edward Passmore Settlement at Tavistock Place at Christmas. She stated her terms, which didn't suit, and I wrote back and told her what it would be.*

With all those children at home, Kimber could ill afford to miss a day's wages (and pay the train fare), and he advised the lady of this. He also told her:

> *[I]t would be impossible for me to play the tunes and teach [dancing] at the same time. To do it all would take a long while, so I suggested bringing my cousin [Richard Kimber] with me, and it was arranged that we should go . . . and she'd meet us at Paddington Station. I was to keep my concertina in my hand so that I should be recognized.*[5]

The lady to whom Kimber referred was Mary Neal (1860–1944), who shares with Cecil Sharp the credit for beginning the revival of English Morris dancing. In her work helping poor working girls in London, she co-founded Espérance Girls Club in 1895, with an eye to providing a decent place of employment for impoverished young girls in London as well as a place to enrich their cultural lives and restore a sense of their English heritage. Part of those enrichment activities involved acquainting them with English folk songs and dances. Looking for suitable material, she approached Cecil Sharp in late summer or early autumn of 1905. By this time, Sharp was a well-respected expert on English folk song. He told her of the Headington Quarry Morris dancers that he had seen at Sandfield Cottage in 1899, and gave her William Kimber's name, which had set up the correspondence between Neal and Kimber.

Kimber continued his account, which has him at Paddington Station awaiting Mary Neal:

Mary Neal (1860–1944) was born to a prosperous Birmingham family; her father was a button manufacturer. As a young woman she began to help poor working girls in London, ultimately co-founding the Espérance Club. After she met Cecil Sharp in 1905, they began to collaborate on bringing folk songs to the girls, hoping to help them reclaim their cultural heritage. Neal expanded that effort to include Morris dance in 1905, by inviting Cecil Sharp's source, William Kimber, to London to instruct the girls in the Morris, the first time the dances were learned by village outsiders. Sharp, seeing the undeniable success of the girls in learning the dances and in popularizing the genre with the public, was inspired to collaborate further with Neal and to collect and publish more Morris material from the countryside.

Unfortunately, disagreements about performance and other issues drove Neal and Sharp—two strong-willed people—apart. With the founding by Sharp of the English Folk Dance Society in 1911, Neal ultimately drifted off to other pursuits, including the suffragist movement and penal reform. Until recently her pivotal role in beginning the Morris revival was underappreciated.

The image of Neal is from her autobiography, in the archives of the Vaughan Williams Memorial Library. The image of the Espérance dancers performing *Shepherd's Hey* is from Neal's *Espérance Morris Book* of 1910.

> *Well instead of her turning up, a gentleman turned up, which turned out to be...Mr. [Herbert] Macilwaine. So he took us to Cumberland Market, where this club was held, and we went inside and was just a-getting the girls into shape at the first dance which I always used—one of the easiest to start with—when Mr. Mack starts striking up two tunes, and I wondered where he got 'em from. And it didn't come to me all at once. . . . but I turned to him and I said, "Where did you get them tunes from?" He said, "You'll find out directly." Well, we went on for a time, and who should come in but another gentleman, and he said to me, "Don't you recognize me?" I said, "No, I don't[,]" and he put his hand up to his eye . . . and as soon as he did that, I said, "Ah! Sandfield Cottage!" He said, "That's right." It was Mr. Sharp; then I realized where Mac had got these tunes from as he'd played."*

By the time of their Christmas party on December 15, 1905, the Espérance girls had learned four dances from Kimber, including *Bean Setting, Laudanum Bunches, Blue-Eyed Stranger*, and *Constant Billy*, as well as a number of folk songs, some of them from Sharp's collecting activities.[6] The event was a big success (Figure 2.3). Of it, Mary Neal wrote in her autobiography:

And that night there awoke, after generations of sleep, a little stir of an older life, an older rhythm, an older force, in tune with a simpler life, a sweeter music. And that stir took place as we watched and listened to these workers of the city who sang and danced to the rhythm so long forgotten.[7]

Figure 2.3. A newspaper clipping from the London *Daily Chronicle* of January 4, 1907, recounting the recent reintroduction of Morris dancing and English song in London by the girls of the Espérance club. Image from www.maryneal.org.

Neal and Sharp then cooperated on the next series of lectures and performances, and a national movement began to take shape. On April 3, 1906, Sharp lectured on "The History of Folk Songs and Morris Dances," followed by the Espérance girls singing folk songs and performing six dances, at an event at the small Queen's Hall in Langham Place. The *Pall Mall Gazette* of April 4 called it "an unalloyed delight." Kimber was now a tradition-bearer of a dying art form, and his musical knowledge and dancing skills were much in demand from both Neal and Sharp. On May 25 Kimber visited the Espérance club again, teaching dances, and Sharp stopped in to get more Morris tunes from him.[8]

Espérance girls began fanning out across the country for the rest of the year, teaching their newly learned songs and dances to an appreciative public, and for his part Sharp had enough Morris dances from Headington Quarry to begin preparation of *The Morris Book*, volume 1. When he eventually published it in April 1907, he included a dedication to the Espérance girls and a tribute to his collaborator, Mary Neal. He also gave a nod to William Kimber and his cousin Richard Kimber, who had taught them:

> *The result of their coming far outran our fondest expectations. . . . Within half an hour of the coming of these Morris-men we saw the Bean-setting—its thumping and clashing of staves, its intricate figures and steps hitherto unknown—full swing upon a London floor. And upon the delighted but somewhat dazed confession of the instructor, we saw it perfect in execution to the least particular."*[9]

Sharp paid William £2 for the essential part that he had played in the endeavor.[10]

Kimber's tunes were attracting interest too, in ways that surprised him. On April 28, 1907, Kimber wrote to Sharp:

> *Last week I heard a piano playing opposite where we are working and I listened and to my astonishment it was playing* Country Gardens. *I could not work. I had to lay my trowel down and listen. My mates say, what's up, Merry? . . . They did not know the tune. I says I wonder where they got that from. One man said it was the* Vicar of Bray, *but as I told him there is a lot of difference in* Country Gardens *and* Vicar of Bray. . . . *Well the young woman kept playing for ten minutes so I just gave them* [his mates] *a turn on the planks, up close to the chimney stack. I danced in jig style, in the same time as you know, and I had a good mind to ask her where she got it from, but another thought struck me. I wondered if the* [Morris] *book was out, so I thought that by writing I should know for certain, and after I hear from you I shall certainly ask her. . . . It will soon be 12 months since I saw you all, it seems as if it were ages.*[11]

The young woman was indeed playing *Country Gardens* from the newly released *Morris Book*. A decade later Percy Grainger released a set of variations on *Country Gardens*, based on Sharp's release of the tune in the *Morris Book*, and that arrangement became an international hit.

By October 1907 Sharp again visited the Espérance girls and with the help of Herbert Macilwaine noted three more Morris dances from Kimber, who for his part also taught one of the girls (probably Florrie Warren) a solo Morris jig, *Bacca Pipes*.[12] By this time Sharp had begun collecting more Morris dances wherever he could find them, and by August 1908 he was busy with Macilwaine preparing the *Morris Book*, volume 2. This dance collecting shored up his reputation as an expert on the Morris, of which he had known nearly nothing at the Boxing Day event at Sandfield Cottage only a few years earlier.

At year's end 1907, two connected things happened that began to cause a very unfortunate rift between Neal and Sharp, who heretofore had been on very cordial and cooperative terms. On November 13 the satirical journal *Punch* ran a picture of a mixed Morris side of three women and three men dancing to the music of the magazine's namesake character Punch (Figure 2.4), with the caption:

> Merrie England Once More! *In consequence of the great success of the Espérance Girls' Club in promoting the revival of English Folksongs and Morris Dances in country villages, on November 14, at the Goupil Gallery for the purpose of furthering this admirable scheme.*

Neal, in her autobiography, reckoned that this cartoon marked a turning point in her relationship with Sharp, saying, "I took *Punch* to Sharp and as he looked at it I saw a sort of blind come down over his face." The idea of recreating a free-spirited "Merrie England" was close to Neal's heart, whereas a more sober-minded and academic Sharp saw his own efforts as documenting a dignified and dying art form to preserve it for a nation's cultural enrichment. As Neal put it, "Mr. Sharp wanted to make an exact canon for dancing and I wanted it to follow the traditional freedom of the old dancers."[13] This basic conceptual difference—and the competition that developed between the two for leadership of the new movement—portended trouble at a folk-dance conference that started the next day.

Figure 2.4. Illustration from *Punch*, November 13, 1907, showing a mixed side of Morris dancers led by the caricature Punch. From a Queen's Hall program from 1907.

Neal had organized a conference at the Goupil Gallery to discuss the formation of a national folk-dance society, which would elevate her club-level efforts that had, so far, been locally organized. There, Neal and Sharp had the first public disagreement, over the organization of the proposed society. Neal was in favor of a loosely run organization headed by herself, and Sharp preferred a more democratically run outfit governed with a constitution and bylaws. The effort to start a new organization failed, so Neal proceeded instead with a small private group instead of a public body.[14] It was the beginning of a serious run of disagreements between these two pioneers of the folk-dance movement. The pair and their nascent feud began to drag others into it, which unfortunately was ultimately to include the tradition-bearer, Kimber, and some others on the Quarry side.

By autumn 1908, after spending months in the field collecting Morris dance material, Sharp was in a much stronger position as an authority on collecting and disseminating Morris dance, and of course he was already well underway to becoming a recognized authority on English folk song. He began to have serious problems with the organization that Neal had started, including what he called "the impertinent assumption of the Espérance Society that they had originated the whole Folk-song movement."[15] On November 10 he disassociated himself from Neal's new organization, the Association for the Revival and Practice of Folk Music, preferring to go his own way. A Cambridge event in January 1909 was the last Espérance performance that Sharp attended.[16] The two leaders and their respective compatriots parted ways.

Meanwhile, back in Headington Quarry life went on as before. William Kimber, perhaps partly buoyed by earnings from his trips to London, purchased a lot on St. Anne's Road in New Headington, and around 1908 he built for his growing family the previously mentioned two-story home, "Merryville."

In early 1909 Cecil Sharp, now out from under the awkward association with Neal, held a number of enjoyable and popular events in which Kimber was a key participant. On February 25 Sharp began a set of three successive lectures at Steinway Hall in London that included childhood games, Morris dance, and folk song. Kimber danced solo jigs, as Sharp at that time had no team of dancers, and the Headington Quarry side of 1899 had apparently disbanded. On March 4 Sharp and Kimber gave the first of several lectures with dance examples at Steinway Hall. During the performance, Kimber's old concertina that had once been his father's came apart and was unplayable. The *Oxford Times* picks up the story:

> *At an exhibition at Steinway Hall on March 4th Mr. Kimber broke his concertina. An appeal for subscriptions was made to the audience in order to replace the instrument, the amount realized being about £7. Mr. Cecil Sharp has since presented Mr. Kimber with a valuable concertina inscribed "From the audience at Steinway Hall. March 4th, 1909."*[17]

Jeffries Brothers, of 23 Praed Street in London, was the top manufacturer of concertinas at the time, and Sharp was readily able to procure one (Figure 2.5). The instrument—today owned by Kimber descendants—has thirty buttons and three rows of keys; that is, ten more buttons and an extra row of keys as compared with his earlier two-row, twenty-button concertina. Analysis of his playing (see Chapter 3) shows that by this time his playing style was well set, and he essentially never subsequently utilized the added third row of buttons in any of his many recordings.

In February 1909 Sharp began teaching Morris dancing at the Physical Training Department of the South West Polytechnic in Chelsea. Sharp and Kimber began to train a women's team, and this was soon to pay off as a ready supplier of dancers for lectures and events. On June 10, 1909, Sharp gave a demonstration before King Edward VII, Queen Alexandra, and the rest of the royal family at Chelsea Hospital, with his new Morris team of Chelsea girls and well as Kimber. Kimber remembered:

> *It was a good affair, it turned out lovely. But after it was over, we went to tea in a marquee. I sat with Mr. Sharp and two more ladies, and on my right was the King and Queen Alexandra. After we'd had tea King Edward turned to me, he said that "I've seen your father dance in Oxford when I was at Christ Church." I said, "I know you have, your Majesty because I've heard my father talk about it."*[18]

Kimber later taught a men's side at Chelsea as well, which included promising young dancers George Butterworth and Douglas Kennedy. Kimber clearly enjoyed his time there, much preferring it to bricklaying.[19]

In April 1909 another special event occurred on "Shakespeare's Day" at Mansion House in London, for the Lord Mayor and Lady Mayoress. The *Oxford Times* reported:

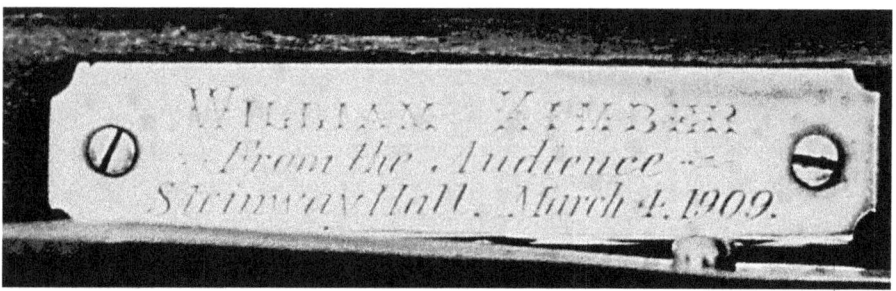

Figure 2.5. Kimber's thirty-button Jeffries Brothers CG concertina, photographed in 2005. The plaque is located on the upper edge of the wooden handrest.

The guests passed on into the Egyptian Hall to witness a performance of old English folk-songs, Morris dances, and singing-games. . . . Many of them would have been lost altogether if they had not been saved for posterity by the untiring zeal of Mr. Sharp. . . . The programme . . . opened with a selection of folk songs . . . after which Mr. W. Kimber and Mr. R. Dandridge, real Morris-dancers from Headington, in Oxfordshire, danced the quaint old jig, "Jockie to the Fair." Dressed in white coats and shirts, white shoes and crossover braces of red and blue, carrying handkerchiefs in each hand, and wearing below the knee short leather greaves, each carrying 12 bells, they alternately and finally together gave a very interesting exhibition of the jig steps and body movements of which the Morris dance consists. . . . Mr. Cecil Sharp, who accompanied all the songs and dances, is to be congratulated on the excellent work which he is doing in rescuing the tunes and steps of over 30 Morris dances, including the three which were given on Friday by Mr. Kimber and Mr. Dandridge.[20]

The three dances were *Jockie to the Fair*, *Shepherd's Hey*, and *Bacca Pipes*. The latter is a solo jig danced over crossed churchwarden-style clay tobacco pipes (Figure 2.6). After the dance, Kimber recalled,

There was two gentlemen there who very badly wanted these pipes for souvenirs. I said, "Well, the pipes don't belong to me . . . . [If Mr. Sharp] says you can have 'em, I've done with 'em; I've danced over 'em. . . . Anyway, they bid against each other for these two pipes till they got to a pound each. One had one and the other had the other, and they gave the two sovereigns to Mr. Sharp. But after it was over Mr. Sharp said to me, "Well, Kimber, I've never danced the pipes . . . you danced the pipes, this money must be yours.". . . I give my mate as had danced with me one, and I had the other meself.[21]

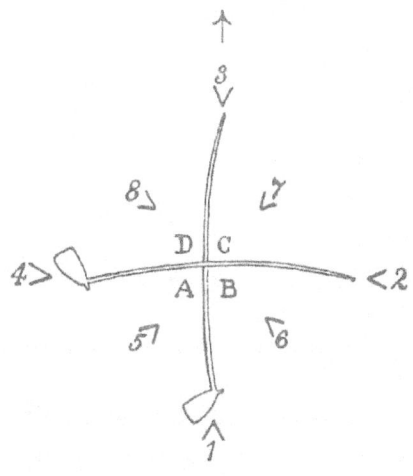

Figure 2.6. A drawing of crossed churchwarden pipes on the floor with dancing notation, which accompanies the description of the dance *Bacca Pipes* in Sharp's *The Morris Book*, 1911.

With the many lectures and demonstrations in 1909–1910, Sharp was gaining allies among the public and the powerful. Kimber was clocking a lot of trips to London and elsewhere to perform with Sharp, who relied on Kimber both to demonstrate the vitality of the dance and to play the old tunes on his concertina. Because bricklaying in the Quarry was by the job, not permanent employment, Kimber was able to juggle these two worlds and attend to both. Theo Chaundy summed up the situation from his interviews with Kimber:

Kimber found them a very nice lot at Chelsea and liked his work there much better than bricklaying. His two employments often clashed, but he never let his old friend down and, whenever Sharp wanted him in London, to London he went. "I want the day off to go to London." "We can't spare you, Bill, we want those cills on." He said nothing but went all the same. Then followed the usual sequel: "There's something for you at the office," the prelude to dismissal. "I've had the sack dozens of times," he tells you with a chuckle. But he was too good a workman ever to be out of a job. "I went down the road, and there was a man waiting for me: 'I knew you'd get the sack, Bill'." So he got another job within the hour. In any event, he found his dancer's pay better than what he earned as a bricklayer.[22]

51

Meanwhile, Kimber found time in 1910 to recruit a new and younger Morris team at Headington Quarry, which included his son William.[23]

In the midst of all the fun of these various engagements, the growing feud between Neal and Sharp continued to simmer on the back burner. Like Sharp's lectures, Neal's Espérance girls' performances and teaching were thriving, mostly in London. In January 1909 she gave an interview to the *Morning Post* in which she claimed to have discovered in Oxfordshire songs and dances that had, in fact, been based on Sharp's work, and this caused him anger. He immediately sent a rebuttal to the *Morning Post*, bringing their disagreements into the public press.[24] In June 1909 Kimber attended by invitation a last performance with the Espérance girls, in Oxford, but he did so only with Sharp's permission, which Kimber, sensing trouble, requested in advance. At this time Macilwaine withdrew from Neal's association, which caused Neal anger and a sense of betrayal.

Macilwaine continued to work with Sharp, however. In July 1909 Sharp and Macilwaine published their *Morris Book, part 2*, with more of Kimber's Headington dances and another dance, from Winster. In the second edition of that work (1911) Sharp and co-author Herbert Macilwaine had this to say of their friend from the Quarry:

> *Of Mr. William Kimber, Junior, they would add that besides the invaluable help he afforded them in recording the dances, his own vigorous and graceful dancing at various public displays has, by showing what traditional dancing can be and setting before the dancer of the revival a high standard of technical accomplishment, forwarded the movement in a practical and altogether admirable manner.*

The book included no references, however, to the earlier collaboration with Espérance, even though the girls there by that time had been dancing some of the new Headington dances in the book for some eighteen months. Also, Sharp inserted a few veiled barbs aimed at Neal, such as saying: "Here and there we have noticed in the would-be Morris-dancer a tendency to be over-strenuous, to adopt, upon occasion, even a hoydenish [tomboyish] manner of execution." Neal took this as a slight to her leading dancer and teacher, Florrie Warren, and was incensed, objecting bitterly in a letter to Sharp.[25] And so it went. Sharp wrote to Kimber, saying that there was "a big cloud coming up over the horizon."[26]

Conflict, 1910–1913

By 1910 the bitterness between Neal and Sharp came fully out into the open. It was a sad argument between the two pioneers, and as it dragged on, the tradition bearers in the Headington Quarry Morris side were unavoidably dragged in, causing very unfortunate personal rifts among these former dancers. The disagreements and insults might seem almost comic and petty today, but in the years leading up to the First World War there was a growing nationalist feeling among the British public and a nostalgic yearning for a storied past. The idea and practice of a dance that came from deep within England's history resonated with the general public, and a strong demand developed across the country for teaching and instruction, so that age-old traditions were preserved and protected. The Board of Education, in August 1909, published a new syllabus for physical education that gave encouragement to the teaching of Morris dancing in schools.[27]

In September 1909 Sharp became the director of Morris Dancing at the Chelsea Polytechnic School. In March 1910 Neal established a rival Espérance Guild of Morris Dancers and published the *Espérance Morris Book* to assert her own authority on the subject. There was no mention of Sharp's role in introducing Neal to Kimber, nor was William Kimber's name mentioned—she only mentions "two men in Oxfordshire." She emphasized the importance of learning from traditional dancers wherever possible, and that the movement "must be kept, in the true sense of the word, a "vulgar" movement, understood of the common people."[28] By this time Sharp had been collecting Morris dances around the country for several years and felt that he was the leading expert on the form as a whole. In April Sharp wrote to the *Morning Post* with a comment on Neal's new Espérance Guild: "It is to be hoped that the promoters will see that the guild is founded upon broad and comprehensive lines, and that they will allow their enthusiasm to be guided by those who possess the requisite experience and knowledge."[29] Neal had little use for experts and thought the knowledge of the traditional dancers themselves sufficed nicely. Neal's reply, in *Vanity Fair*, was stinging: "It behooves those of us to whom has been entrusted the guidance and helping of this movement for the renewal of beauty in life to tread reverently, and to see to it that the blighting touch of the pedant and the expert is not laid upon it."[30]

Neal, not content to make her position on teaching Morris dance known, next began to try to undercut Sharp's authority as an "expert." That meant also undercutting the veracity of Sharp's main source, Kimber, as a bona fide traditional dancer, even though Kimber had also been essential to the early Espérance movement. In October 1910 Neal and associates Clive Carey and Francis Toye travelled to Headington Quarry to interview other Quarry dancers about dance practice. They met with old dancers Joe Trafford and Jack Horwood, and fiddle player Mark Cox (she also met with a Mr. Cummings, who claimed to have danced sixty years earlier, but William Kimber senior later identified him as "Bass" Cummings, a resident of Marston, who, according to William Kimber senior, had never danced and was a member of the Marston village band. Kimber senior thought that Neal may have mistaken him for Frank Cummings, the side's long-deceased former fiddle player).[31] In Neal's notes, preserved at the Vaughan Williams Memorial Library, she heard criticisms from Trafford of Kimber junior's dance moves—in particular, a tendency to stamp and to keep his leg too straight on the back step for Trafford's taste. Cox claimed that *he* taught Kimber junior to dance, although Cox only became familiar with the side and the Morris when Manning reassembled the group in 1898; Kimber learned from his father, and first danced with the side as a teenager in 1887. Joe Trafford claimed that he taught Kimber's father, who only joined them infrequently as a "stop gap." William Kimber senior, on later seeing Neal's notes, vehemently disagreed with Cox and Trafford's statements as "untrue." Following Neal's meeting with the four men in Headington, she wrote to Archibald Flower—then in the process of deciding whether to task Sharp or Neal with the coveted leadership of the important Stratford-upon-Avon Summer School of the English Folk Dance Society—that: "We have indubitably proved that the whole basis of Mr. Sharp's contentions as an expert are entirely unfounded."[32]

Trafford and Cox came to the Espérance Club a week later to teach, and Clive Carey transcribed their tunes. Of Trafford, Neal wrote in the *Espérance Book, Part 2*, published in 1910, that "Mr. Trafford is a real expert in morris dancing, and . . . his opinion on the execution of the dances accounts for much."[33] Trafford, however, hadn't himself danced in thirty years, and of his teaching appearance at the Espérance Club, Neal's colleague Clive Carey wrote that "Old Trafford said it was very difficult to remember without a side of dancers. He changed something every time we went through the different dances. He could give no distinct names for the different figures."[34] Trafford and Cox were never invited back, and Neal's experiment in branching out from Kimber in Headington Quarry was ultimately a failure.

Sharp, hearing of Neal's maneuvers to undercut Kimber's authority as a traditional dancer, immediately wrote to Kimber in November 1910: "Miss N. is on the warpath . . . this is a very serious business, and it may do you and me a very great deal of harm. Will you put me in possession of all the facts as quickly as you can?"[35] Kimber replied immediately with calm reassurance:

Figure 2.7. Joe Trafford, Mark Cox, Jack Horwood, and "Bass" Cummings, who met with Mary Neal at Headington Quarry in 1910. From Neal's *The Espérance Book, Part 2 (1910)*.

> *Please don't get worried. I hope you can, and will think me still trustworthy and truthful in all I have told you. I have not altered as you know a bit from when you first took down these tunes from me. . . . But Quarry men will sell any time their birth right for ale and I know what Miss Neal's doing if money will do any good. . . . I am going home (old) tonight on my way home to see my father. . . . I am going to clear the air for once and for all. When my Dad speaks it's the truth.*[36]

Kimber later (in 1956) recalled more: "She come down to Quarry and tried to bribe all my side as I was dancing with them to say what I told Sharp was all wrong."[37] The next day (November 10, 1910), he wrote to Sharp again:

> *I have been round home last night and saw my father and also read your letter to him. It fairly surprised him. I am to assure you from him that the tunes all of them taken down by you from me are right, and the way I have taught you also is right.*[38]

Sharp, realizing that he must perfectly understand everything of the background of the Headington Morris side in order to counter Neal's claims, went to Headington Quarry to speak directly with Kimber senior. The father was of course still opposed to his son's involvement in the Morris, but this was now a matter of family honor. William junior tells what happened:

> *Well for my father to meet Mr. Sharp, I had a good deal of trouble over that—to get him to meet him—but eventually with the help of my mother, he sanctioned that he would meet him. . . . My proposition was that him and two of the oldest dancers should meet Mr. Sharp, which they did* [Sampson Smith and Jim Hedges]. *They was there on the Saturday afternoon as arranged, and I was the prisoner, I could say nothing. I was on trial. There was only one person who was allowed to barge in, and that was my old mother, well she would do! And this is what she said: 'I'd like to get hold of that beautiful lady; I'd just give her a piece of my mind, and tell her that . . . my son* [has] *always been brought*

> *up honest and to speak the truth. That was the only one as was allowed to speak during that interview. After it was over, I walked down with Mr. Sharp . . . and I said to him when a'coming down, "Are you satisfied now, Mr. Sharp?" He said "Perfectly, William, and I hope you never thought I mistrusted you."*[39]

In the final analysis Neal's attack on Sharp and Kimber failed. Neal had claimed Kimber wasn't a traditional dancer by Sharp's definition. David Sutcliffe, in his recent biography of Sharp, summarized what was shown to be reality:

> *In fact, William Kimber had learned the tunes and dances as a boy from his father and he danced briefly, aged fifteen, in the first Jubilee side in 1887, before the lapse of eleven years. Aged twenty-seven, he then joined the revival side in 1899. When Mark Cox was unable to play on Boxing Day, Kimber stepped in as a musician, playing the concertina. It is obvious that a complete novice cannot just set up as musician and lead a team of dancers.*[40]

After Trafford and Cox were discredited by Kimber senior and by Trafford's flawed dancing instruction with the Espérance girls, the attacks by Neal soon ceased, and Neal sailed off to the United States for a few months. From this moment Sharp began to emerge from the fracas as the clear national expert on Morris dancing. Neal, meanwhile, had managed to drive a very unfortunate wedge between members of the old Headington Quarry dancers over minor style issues (straight leg or bent on the backstep?) in her search for any issue to tear down Sharp and his teacher. The unfortunate effects in Quarry village were to last a long time. Two decades later, in a book of 1933 about the history of Headington and Shotover, authors George Coppock and others describe the folk custom of Morris dancing in the village this way:

> *In the autumn and winter of 1910, the [Headington] dances were noted, the tunes being played by Mr. Mark Cox and taken down. These tunes were published in the Espérance Morris Book, edited by Mrs. Mary Neale. . . . Mr. William Kimber . . . was responsible, under Mr. Cecil Sharp, for recording many of the dances at a later date, [and] was only an occasional dancer at the time when Mr. Cox fiddled. Later he [Kimber] acquired the tunes and accompanied the dances with a concertina. The music and dances obtained from this source differ slightly from those recorded in Miss Mary Neale's book.*[41]

This appears to have been an intentional dig at Kimber, either by the authors or their source, as the statement was completely false. Sharp had recorded Headington tunes from Kimber beginning in 1899, and Kimber taught tunes and dances to the Espérance girls beginning in 1905. By 1933 Kimber had long since become something of a nationally known figure in the folk music and dance world, and any local Quarry source of that information for that history book would have known this. The statement is a testament to the lasting damage made to the members of the old Quarry side by Neal's maneuvering in 1910, a painful result of the inability of Sharp and Neal to get along.

At a display of Morris dances at Stationer's Hall in London in January 1911, Kimber danced three jigs (Figure 2.8). The Master of Worshipful Company of Musicians, Alfred Littleton, proclaimed that he was like "a Greek statue . . . his grace and movements are absolutely classic."[42] Also in 1911 Kimber began teaching Morris dance on his own account, teaching a Morris side at Steeple Aston, a small village about twelve miles north of Oxford.[43] For Kimber, Morris dance continued to be not just a passion but the valuable source of extra income that it had always been.

Sharp moved on to collecting sword dances and then country dances, books on both of which he published in 1912. In Headington, Kimber recruited a new Morris side, which was to be active until its members were placed in service as soldiers in the First World War. He was aware that he had given Sharp most if not all of his Headington dances, and was always on the lookout for more. He tried to collect more Morris dances and tunes from his disapproving father, but to no avail. As Daisy Daking heard it (in 1914):

> *Young Kimber has taught the side all he knows, but means to get more out of his father if he can. The old man refuses to speak. Not long ago Old Kimber and Henry Franklin arranged to meet in a pub in Oxford and dance jigs. Young Kimber heard of this, and came down, meaning quietly to watch from behind something and see what his father did do—but the old man saw him, and never said a word, but went straight back to Headington without dancing a step.*[44]

William Kimber senior had by then sorted out the alcohol problems of his early life, and his eschewing of Morris dance, with all its social trappings, was part of his recovery. A bricklayer and builder by trade, he became a building foreman for the Oxford Corporation works, which provided steady income in his last decades. He and his wife moved to nearby Cowley in 1901, where they lived a quiet life until both passed away in 1931.

In July 1911 Sharp gained the directorship of the folk program at the Stratford-upon-Avon Summer School, which both he and Neal had coveted. He also received a very welcome pension for his work. At Stratford that year, he showed off five new teachers, two Chelsea Polytechnic Morris teams, and William Kimber. It was a huge success for Sharp in what had become a national celebration of things folk.[45] Later that year he helped guide the formation of the English Folk Dance Society, an organization that aimed to spread Morris dance through qualified instruction, nationwide. Sharp became the honorary director. In summer 1912 he published an amazing array of books: *Sword Dance, Country Dance I and II, Morris Book, volume IV,* and *English Folk Carols*. He also released a revised edition of *The Morris Book,*

Figure 2.8. William Kimber in full Morris dance regalia, ca. 1912, probably at the Stratford Summer Vacation School of the English Folk Dance Society. Vaughan Williams Memorial Library.

volume I. There could no longer be much argument as to who was the national expert on English folk dance. By 1913 Neal's rival efforts began to lessen, and her dance operations ceased entirely during World War I, never to return.

In 1912 William and Florence Kimber welcomed their eighth and final child, Evelyn Mary. Kimber continued working as a bricklayer, and that year built more houses in New Headington, at numbers 2, 4, 6, and 8 Gathorne Road, within a block of his house, Merryville, on St. Anne's Road.[46]

The war years, and change comes to the Quarry

The First World War brought the Morris revival to a halt. The Headington Morris dancers performed at Abingdon and the summer school at Stratford went forward in 1914, but then all organized folk dance activities were shuttered. Young people who would be dancing were drawn into the service. With nothing to do on the folk scene, and at the age of fifty-four too old to fight, Cecil Sharp went to America with his personal assistant, Maud Karpeles, there to begin a landmark multiyear study of folk songs in the Appalachian Mountains.

Image courtesy of Wikipedia Creative Commons

Maud Karpeles (1885-1976) and her sister Helen Karpeles first met Cecil Sharp in 1909, and soon Maud was teaching at Sharp's Morris, sword and country dance events, an activity she continued until Sharp's death in 1924. She was an early member and honorary secretary of the English Folk Dance Society (later the English Folk Dance and Song Society) and assisted Sharp in two song-collecting tours to the US Appalachians between 1916 and 1918. She acted as an amanuensis (writing assistant) when an elbow ailment prevented Sharp from writing for himself, and edited Sharp's manuscripts after his death. She published a biography of Sharp in 1967. Of William Kimber, she wrote:

It is fortunate that the dances of the Headington tradition were the first that Cecil Sharp saw and noted, for in William Kimber he was able to see the style and technique of the Morris Dance at its best. One has a vivid memory of his perfect carriage, the dignity of his bearing, his loose-limbed yet controlled movements and, above all, the sparkle of his step, which is one of the glories of the Morris Dance.

William Kimber has been described as 'a bricklayer by trade and a dancer by profession', but above all he was an artist, and that no doubt made the bond of friendship between him and Cecil Sharp – a friendship which continued unsullied for twenty years.

Kimber, by then well into his forties, was stationed at a military depot in Southampton during his war service. By chance Percy Manning was in the same company as Kimber; Manning died there of pneumonia in 1917.[47] Of Kimber's recently revived Headington Quarry Morris side (Figure 2.9), four of the dancers were to die or be wounded during the war, including his own son William, who was injured by a gas attack in August 1918 and two months later was severely wounded in the leg, leading to an extended hospital stay. The war years were a devastating time personally for Kimber, who wrote to his old friend Sharp in late 1918:

> *I should have wrote to you before, but I have been down in the dumps lately and it's not much to write about, if you have to write about trouble, that doesn't clash with what you and I have been used to, does it, but I have been hit hard again. Last year it was my wife* [Florence passed away on September 11, 1917], *this year October, my second daughter 22 years old, with "Flue," the one that used to dance so nicely* [Lilian Rose died during the 1918–1919 Spanish flu pandemic], *and my boy got wounded in October, his leg shattered almost blown away. He's still in hospital at Davidson Road War Hospital, South Norwood. I thought of you when I went to see him, as I passed through South Kensington, the old route to Chelsea.*[48]

Figure 2.9. William Kimber (right) and the Headington Quarry Morris Dancers outside the Six Bells public house, Headington Quarry, Whitsun 1914. Four of the dancers were soon to die or be seriously wounded during the coming war, including his own son William. Image from the Vaughan Williams Memorial Library.

The war years were only part of a momentous change that came to Headington Quarry in the early years of the twentieth century. It would be easy for a casual traveler today to miss the former villages of Headington and Headington Quarry while driving across the City of Oxford, as all of them have long since been completely over-run by rampant Oxford suburbanization. That wave of change began in 1913, when Morris Motors Limited built an automobile manufacturing plant at Cowley (Figure 2.10), east of Oxford, causing rapid urban expansion eastward as housing for workers was added. By 1929 government of these villages was taken over by the Oxford City Council and they began to lose their original identities. Local historian Maurice East, referring to the 1905 photograph of Quarry villagers that was taken in front of the Mason's Arms public house and discussed in the previous chapter (see Figure 1.12), described the ensuing social change that came to the relatively isolated and independent rural village of Headington:

Figure 2.10. The 1913 Morris Oxford, the first product of the new automotive plant in Cowley. Image courtesy of Wikipedia Commons.

> *This [picture] is really the end of the Quarry in a lot of ways, because a big change was going to come for all of these people. . . . These guys . . . had been living the life of Riley . . . they just did a little bit of this, a little bit of that, a bit of poaching, and then go on the booze for few weeks. . . . They lived by their own rules, and there was some rough justice. . . .Whether it was bloody-mindedness, there was this sense of individualism.*
>
> *For these people, it was all about to change. In 1905 just down the road at Longwell Garage, there was a guy called William Morris playing about with cars. In 1913 he set up a factory in an obscure little place called Cowley. By the 1920s he needed lots and lots of workers. Suddenly, all these boys [in the photograph], who had been poaching, doing occasional jobs . . . they had the option of very good blue-collar jobs at the factory, and that's where they went. And if they had building skills, they could be utilized in the new estates that were being built to house the workers [who were] to go in William Morris's factory. Suddenly in very short order, Quarry became part of Oxford, because Oxford grew up around it. [And these guys,] . . . when they did have the option of really good, settled work and employment, that's [what] they did. And that's why, when I was growing up in the Quarry, this was an area full of car workers. And there would be hundreds of bikes that would go along the bypass to the factory along the cycle path.*
>
> *So, that Quarry [in the photograph] ended, and by the 1930s, Quarry was now officially part of Oxford. It wasn't [anymore] this unique little place on the edge of town.*[49]

Even car builders, it seems, wanted Morris dance in their recreational activities. In 1926 William Kimber and Harry Woodcock (a member of the pre-World War I Headington team) founded the Morris Motors Social Club Morris Dancers, at Cowley.[50]

The effect of the new Morris Motors factory on the three formerly rural Headington villages was dramatic. Suburban infilling first took place in Headington proper. Sir John Betjeman, writing in a history of Oxford of 1938, brutally observed that Headington "is a mass of untidy speculative buildings, blaring arcades of shops and finally a neat council house scheme."[51] John Piper, in his *Shell Guide* to Oxfordshire of 1938, could add little that was positive: "Headington: How not to develop Oxford. Headington old village is just north of the by-pass fork—a place of slopes and corners. Looking uncomfortable under these folds of 'Oxford's bricky skirt'."[52] Reginald Turner, writing a travelogue for his 1949 book on Oxfordshire, had this to say:

> *Except geologically, Headington suggests nothing more than a deplorable Oxford suburbia on which it would be a pity to waste words. There is, it is true, the old village of Headington Quarry whose terrain is broken up into serried levels by its ancient purpose, but all around it the face of the land has been ravaged by the acne of speculative development.*[53]

That urban growth has continued to the present day, as can be seen by comparing the map of the Quarry area in 1900, Figure 1.4, with an aerial photo of the same area today, Figure 1.5. Nearly all the open space that formerly surrounded the village, allowing village subsistence use of outlying areas in farming, totting, and poaching, was rapidly taken by row houses, which meant that villagers by necessity became wage earners in industrial and other jobs. Even in the old village center, population density has increased by one to two orders of magnitude from the time of Kimber's youth to today.

After the First World War

The war and the suburbanization of the Quarry comprised a watershed in Kimber's life that separated his life experiences into two very different phases. Before 1905 Kimber was a bricklayer, a subsistence farmer, and an occasional musician/dancer in an obscure and somewhat peculiar Oxfordshire village. After he was exposed to the folk music and dance collecting activities of Mary Neal and Cecil Sharp in 1905–1906, he rapidly entered a national stage during the heady early days with Sharp in the English folk revival and became known to people who lived far beyond the confines of his rural village. Most of his musical repertoire and dances were formed and shaped by the culture and traditions of his former world and were merely drawn upon during the next half century of his life. After the war he was awarded much recognition, and still had much to contribute to the Morris dance movement, but at a more sporadic pace, with long quiet interludes at home and at bricklaying.

Figure 2.11. William Kimber at a performance at Chelsea Polytechnic, ca. 1920. From *The Dancing Times*, 1920, courtesy of the Vaughan Williams Memorial Library.

By 1920 Kimber was emerging from the dark days of war years, which saw the death of his wife and daughter and the maiming of his son. In May 1920 he danced the *Shepherd's Hey* at the Headington Orthopaedic Hospital and worked to rebuild the Quarry Morris team, which had been decimated during the war. The side soon included his youngest son Fred as well as his cousin's sons Harry and Arthur Kimber, plus Jim Phillips and Charlie Jones.[54] This side had staying power, and these men danced together for nearly five decades.[55] Kimber performed again at Chelsea in 1920 (Figure 2.11) as part of an afternoon of Morris dances, sword dances, and country dances. Of his performance there a writer for *The Dancing Times* exclaimed that "to see William Kimber, one of the traditional dancers of Headington, perform a jig, is to be carried back three centuries while enjoying the present."[56]

Another high point of 1920 was his marriage in June to the widow Bessie Kethro Clark (b. ca. 1882), whose first husband had died two years earlier in Headington; by that marriage Kimber also gained a stepdaughter. Bessie's father was William Joseph Kethro, an Oxford stonemason. Kimber seems to have written very little about either of his two wives, but it appears that he had been in desperate need of a woman's (and partner's) touch in a busy household. Bessie got a mention in a letter from Kimber to Sharp in November:

> *I hope if you come to Oxford again you will come up [to my] home, and have a look round. I have about got it straight again, and it seems very nice to have the home, home again. I was married on June 5 but as I say, I must tell you about it when we meet. I think you will say that I have made a very good deal. She is very clean and domesticated, and looks after the children well. So I am pleased to say I am in the pink. I feel as young and nimble as ever.*[57]

Hard times were always near, however. In a letter to Sharp in January 1921, Kimber thanked Sharp for sending him a used suit, and asked about a pair of used boots that Sharp had earlier mentioned. By later that year, however, Kimber joined the tide of Quarry men who had traded their former lives as intermittent jobbers to become wage earners in steady jobs. The census of 1921 shows that he had become a boilerman at the Headington Orthopaedic Hospital in Headington.[58] He never seems to have mentioned that job in his interviews, so it is not known how long he held the post, but it was no doubt a welcome hedge against hard times. At that time, he and Bessie still had four children at home (Frederick, Sophia, Mary, and Ada).

Kimber expressed a lingering nostalgia for the busier times and companionship with his friend Sharp before the war. After wishing Sharp a Happy New Year in a letter sent two days after Boxing Day near the end of 1921, he remarked:

> *It was very quiet here* [during Christmas and Boxing Day]. *I don't think I ever remember one so quiet. Not a single step of any sort. I was only thinking the other morning as I passed Sandfield Cottage. I looked at that room where you and I had our first tune, it doesn't seem all that time ago yet it's too true. A great many things have happened since then. And the old saying of bricklayers crossed my mind: "And you, old boy, have at last wound up your line," which makes a fellow just a bit down, as I always said, when I could not have a dance. I hope it would soon be all over for if ever one loved a certain thing in this world, the one thing I loved was the Morris.*[59]

In 1923, however, Kimber was teaching again, this time with the Oxford City police, who were raising money for an orphanage at nearby Redhill (Figure 2.12). Theo Chaundy related:

> *The City police detailed to keep the ring* [manage the crowds, at a May Morning celebration in Oxford, where Kimber played the concertina for the Morris dancers] *soon grew interested in the Morris and formed their own side (but on condition that they should avoid the indignity of a woman teacher!). Kimber was very ready to teach them, and they had much success until at a performance a 14-stone officer went through the platform. This discouraged them.*[60]

Figure 2.12. William Kimber with the Oxford City Police Athletic Club Morris Team, 1925. From the Vaughan Williams Memorial Library.

Sharp, for his part, never abandoned his old friend. On June 2, 1923 Kimber was presented the gold badge of the English Folk Dance Society (a predecessor, along with the Folk Song Society, of the modern English Folk Dance and Song Society), which he would proudly wear at events for the rest of his life (Figure 2.13). At a Festival of Music in Oxford, the president of the EFDS branch there, Sir Hugh Allen, made the presentation, in honor of Kimber's long and exemplary service to the folk dance movement. A few days later, Kimber wrote to thank Sharp and the organization:

> *Will you kindly thank the Committee for me for the medal, and say that I shall treasure it very much, and be proud to wear it. It will remind me of the very many happy hours I have spent with you dancing and also of the many friends that dance the dances I love so well. . . . Saturday was the best and happiest day I have had for many a day.*[61]

The evening after the presentation Sharp walked with Kimber and with Maud Karpeles to the train station. It was the last time Sharp and Kimber were together. Sharp, never a healthy man, who had worked many times through illness and pain, died of cancer in 1924. Kimber later recalled:

> *It was the worst blow I'd ever had. I'd lost all. His death ended a friendship of 24 years and six months to the day. Whenever he sent for me, I never failed him once. No, I never failed him once, even if it meant losing my job.*[62]

Figure 2.13. William Kimber at Stratford-upon-Avon, 1947. He is wearing his EFDS Gold Medal, presented to him in 1923. Photograph by W. Fisher Cassie, Morris Ring Archive

To Maud Karpeles, Sharp's former personal assistant and an EFDS contact for Sharp in coming years, he wrote:

> *Oh, I would have given all I possess if I could have only said good-bye. My only dearest friend gone, one I stood by through thick and thin; you will understand what I mean, won't you. But I am so glad he lived to see his work come out "top hole." He will never, never be forgotten.*[63]

In the years after Sharp's death, there was a movement to raise money for a headquarters for the English Folk Dance Society, as a memorial for Sharp and a place to keep his substantial library. A Mrs. Shaw of the EFDS wrote to Kimber, asking him to lay the cornerstone of the new building, in a ceremony planned for June 24, 1929. He wrote to Maud Karpeles, saying:

I shall be pleased to come. I have worked with a good many masons in my time. It's about 47 years ago that I first went on a building with my dad. But you will be the first lady that I have fixed a stone with, and you know I have fixed a few. I have been fixing stone for weeks now.[64]

The building was opened on June 7, 1930, but a part of its collection and a good bit of the building were destroyed by a German bomb during World War II.

William Kimber and Douglas Kennedy, August 1947, Stratford-on-Avon. Photo by W. Fisher Cassie, in the Vaughan Williams Memorial Library.

Douglas Kennedy (1893-1988) was a student at South-Western Polytechnic in London in 1911 when he was introduced to Cecil Sharp's Morris dance group there, and he joined the demonstration team of what was then the English Folk Dance Society; William Kimber was their Morris dance instructor. Kennedy married Helen Karpeles, sister of Maud Karpeles, in 1914; the Karpeles sisters were leaders in the nascent folk-dance movement. Kennedy served with distinction in the 14th battalion London Scottish regiment, and later the Royal Defence Corps, during the First World War, but four other members of the EFDS demonstration team were killed during the conflict.

After the war, Kennedy became a committee member of the EFDS, and after Cecil Sharp died in 1924, he became the director of the organization. In 1932 the EFDS merged with the Folk-Song Society to become the English Folk Dance and Song Society, under Kennedy's stewardhip. Kennedy encouraged and enabled William Kimber to make recordings with The Gramophone Company (His Master's Voice lable) in 1935, 1946, and 1948. In the late 1940s, Kennedy presented folk dance music on the BBC and encouraged public participation in dance events. After retiring from his directorship with the EFDSS in 1961, he continued to be active in folk music and dance circles until his death.

In his late fifties Kimber was still laying brick as his chief occupation, as well as keeping pigs and a garden and looking out after Morris dance requests, which came less often these days. In 1933 he wrote to Maud Karpeles to express sadness and perhaps frustration that he had not been in contact with the newly formed EFDSS and its new chief, Douglas Kennedy, for a long time:

It is almost 12 months since I heard or saw any of you. Honestly I thought after my last visit on the 6th December 1932 I had finished my career as a Morris Dancer with the E.F.D.S. I have often wondered after doing three things in one day that I did not hear from Mr. Kennedy. . . . I have never heard a word or seen anybody, and I quite thought that I had finished so long as London was concerned.[65]

As if to dispel any doubts about his standing, Kimber was invited to play at a BBC broadcast of a twenty-first anniversary celebration of the EFDS on December 6, 1932, only a few months after his letter to Karpeles. The broadcast linked celebrations of various local EFDS branches, in the year that the EFDS merged with the Folk Song Society to become the English Folk Dance and Song Society (EFDSS). He played at a concert of Oxfordshire folk music in 1934; at the EFDSS All-England Festival at the Royal Albert Hall in London in 1935; at the EFDSS First International Folk Dance Festival in London that same year; and at a concert of Traditional Musicians at Cecil Sharp House in 1936. In 1937, the EFDSS made an appeal for subscriptions to a special fund for William Kimber as well as for fiddle player William "Jinky" Wells from Bampton-in-the-Bush, as a retirement nest egg that established annuity payments for the aging musicians who had contributed so much to English music and especially to Morris dance.[66]

Cecil Sharp wrote down many tunes and dances from Kimber and felt free to share them with friends in the London music world, like composer Percy Grainger, who took Kimber's *Country Gardens* and arranged variations on it for the piano in 1918, and later arranged it for an orchestra. Grainger attributed the tune to Sharp, but not to Kimber, who was the tradition-bearer. Kimber heard the piece on BBC in 1932 and checked its identity in their play list. Then he wrote to Maud Karpeles:

> *This is how it appears in the Radio Times:* "Country Gardens (Handkerchief Dance) Arr. Grainger." *Now who is this Grainger,* [and] *what right has he to do this? There is a long story attached to Country Gardens. There is no other side that's got the dance but us. . . . The second time Country Gardens came on, I played my concertina with the band* [on the recording] *because I know my own fingering to a note, and the three parts too. But the many Folk Song and Folk Dance persons nowadays beats me, without mind. They have been in touch with the Dead, that's the only way that I can see it.*[67]

When once asked what he thought of Grainger's arrangement, Kimber said, "He didn't add anything. He murdered it. You couldn't dance to it."[68] Apparently unknown to Kimber, when Grainger's 1918 arrangement of *Country Gardens* became immensely successful (it reportedly sold 40,000 copies a week in the USA alone during its peak), Grainger offered half the considerable royalties to Sharp, who refused to accept the gift. As Derek Schofield pointed out in his 1999 biography of Kimber, it didn't seem to occur to either Grainger or Sharp that they might offer part of the royalties to the tune's source, Kimber, who could have certainly used the money more than either of them.[69]

In the late 1930s a new friendship brightened Kimber's days. Rev. Kenneth Loveless (1911–1995), an Anglican priest then living in east London (Figure 2.14), became interested in Morris dance and its music, and sought out Kimber in 1937. He later recalled:

> [Kimber] *had many callers at the cottage "Merryville" . . . seeking information, very often for their own advantage, and without proper consideration for William. But he was more than a match for such people. Very shrewdly and pointedly he would send them packing. I first met him way back in 1937 when at the Whitsun Morris dancing at Bampton-in-the-Bush. I had recently bought a concertina and after being introduced, timidly showed it to him. "That thing's no good," he said, "and you can't play it" (he was quite right, I couldn't!). "You come and see me at Quarry—I'll teach you to play." He was as good as his word, and he often used to say that I was the only person he had ever really taught to play, as he understood it.*[70]

Figure 2.14. Rev. Kenneth Loveless, MBE, playing William Kimber's Jeffries concertina, 1979. Kimber bequeathed the concertina to Loveless, and after Loveless's death in 1995 it reverted to the Kimber family. Photo courtesy of Gary Coover.

The two remained friends for decades. After Kimber's death many years later, Kimber's concertina was to go to Loveless. After the death of Loveless in 1995, it eventually returned to the Kimber family.

After the founding of the Morris Ring at Cecil Sharp House in 1934, Kimber was involved in their annual meetings for the rest of the decade and longer. As Schofield tells it, "he was a guest of honor. His toast was drunk, and he was invited to play for the dancing, teach the Headington dances, or comment on the dancing."[71] He was well on his way to become the recognized "Father of the English Morris." In fact, in a piece in the 1944 issue of *English Dance and Song*, the Boxing Day encounter in 1899 was called "the birthday of Morris Dancing."[72]

In 1939 Kimber played for a team from the Headington Quarry Senior School at a local folk dance festival and played for them at Bampton on Whit Monday.[73] Many of this team were called up for World War II service in 1940. There were Morris activities for younger dancers during the Second World War, notably May Morning at Oxford in 1941 and a summer school in Reading in 1943, both attended by Kimber.

In 1942, at the age of seventy, Kimber finally laid down his bricklayer's trowel in retirement,[74] but his music and dance activities continued apace. In 1947 the pre-war Headington Morris side regrouped at Kimber's urging, with an addition of younger members from St. Christopher's Guild.[75] By the late 1940s the EFDSS began a series of annual outdoor summer festivals at Stratford-upon-Avon, where the society displayed their activities to the general public, inviting participation. Kimber and Bampton fiddler Jinky Wells were perennial honored guests (Figure 2.15).

The Headington Quarry Morris dancers were admitted to the Morris Ring in 1949, and Kimber often played for their outings (Figure 2.16). This side has been active continuously to the present time. Chaundy noted in 1959 that "the modern Headington side is no longer a village side in the old sense, dancing only 'Headington,' unlike Bampton which goes on dancing 'Bampton,' but is a normal member of the Morris Ring making itself free of the riches of every tradition."[76] This, along with his playing at the summer schools, would explain the numerous non-Headington Morris tunes that found places in Kimber's repertoire (see Chapter 5).

Final years and legacy

In 1959, at the age of eighty-seven, Kimber was still teaching Morris dancing, including three classes at the Quarry secondary school (Figure 2.17). Even at this advanced age, the income from teaching was very important to him; he had had to

Figure 2.15. William Kimber waving goodbye to the crowd at Stratford-upon-Avon Summer School, 1946. From the Vaughan Williams Memorial Library.

Figure 2.16. William Kimber and the Headington Quarry Morris dancers, May Day 1949, Oxford. From the *Oxford Mail*, courtesy of the Vaughan Williams Memorial Library.

pursue a basic living income throughout his long life. As he told Theo Chaundy in an interview that year, "It's all educational. It doesn't matter to me, as long as there's money. I've got to live."[77]

Kimber's last years were laced with celebrations and tributes for a life well lived. In 1958 the City of Oxford honored him by naming William Kimber Crescent for him (Figure 2.18). Naming this new crescent was perhaps a bittersweet occasion for Kimber and others of the old village, as this bit of new suburbia was built over part of the old Magdalen Quarry, used for quarrying the stone for Magdalen College at Oxford in 1474 and one of many features of the old rural village that had disappeared. Very near to and south of William Kimber Crescent, a rock wall of that quarry has been preserved.[78] On

Figure 2.17. William Kimber and dancers from the Headington Quarry Secondary School, 1950s. Image courtesy of the Headington Quarry Morris Dancers.

Figure 2.18. William Kimber and members of the Headington Quarry Morris Dancers, October 19, 1958, at the inauguration of William Kimber Crescent, Headington Quarry. Photo by the *Oxford Mail*, in the Vaughan Williams Memorial Library.

Boxing Day, 1959 a plaque was unveiled at Sandfield Cottage commemorating the first meeting of Sharp and Kimber on Boxing Day, 1899. The cottage was later demolished, but the plaque is still there, placed on the new flats at Horwood Close.

The last big event that Kimber attended, in 1959, celebrated that same 1899 Sandfield Cottage event. Schofield described the Diamond Jubilee celebration of the Sandfield Cottage meeting:

Earlier in the year, 4–6 September, the Headington Quarry Morris Dancers organized a Morris Ring meeting for almost 400 dancers, representing 39 clubs: at that time, the largest meeting ever held. A marquee was erected at the Secondary Modern School for the Friday evening Ale and Saturday Feast. On Saturday there were twelve tours that travelled as far as Aylesbury and Banbury, followed in the afternoon by two main displays in Bury Knowle Park, Headington. At the Feast, William Kimber spoke "with marvelous assurance and with justifiable pride . . . and sat down to loud cheers and the singing of 'For He's a Jolly Good Fellow' (Morris Ring Logbook). Douglas Kennedy remarked that he had first met William in 1910, and paid tribute to the great debt Morris dancers owed to him. Dancing outside each of the public houses continued until closing time. The Church service on Sunday morning was exclusively for the Morris dancers—no one else could fit in the church—and was preceded by a procession headed by Arthur Kimber on a white horse!

This Ring Meeting also celebrated the Silver Jubilee for the founding of the Morris Ring, and was held a couple of days before William's 87th birthday. The event was extensively reported in the Oxford newspapers— "Ovation for Mr. W. Kimber" was the Oxford Times *headline—and even the* [London] Times.[79]

William Kimber died on Boxing Day, 1961 at age 89, collapsing of a heart attack when he went to his backyard for coal. He was laid to rest a few weeks later by the Headington Quarry Morris Men as pallbearers, all of them dressed in full regalia with the addition of black ties. The attendees included a full cross section of his family and friends and representatives from a wide variety of English folk organizations, including the EFDSS, the Morris Ring,

Oxford University Morris Men, Headington Quarry Morris Men, and a number of sides and other folk organization from around the country.⁸⁰ His obituary in the *Oxford Times* read in part:

> *"Merry" Bill Kimber, as he was known in Quarry, never belied his name and became a legend in his own lifetime—it being such a thrilling experience to dance with this dynamic figure, or, in later years, even to dance to the music of the old concertina which never seemed to be out of his hand. Ever young, he continued even in extreme old age to radiate far and wide his enthusiasm for the dance, and actively to teach the boys and young men of Headington Quarry to follow in his footsteps literally and metaphorically. . . .*
>
> *A striking figure, even in his latter days, William Kimber was the epitome of old English village life as it had been, and he carried over in the living tradition of the Morris much of the best of bygone times. It was no casual compliment which led the City authorities to name William Kimber Crescent, Headington, after him in 1958, though indeed, even without this reminder, he would ever be remembered with affection and gratitude as a source of inspiration and a fount of living tradition in the annals of English Folk Dance and Song.*⁸¹

Of Kimber, his friend Rev. Kenneth Loveless—a Morris dance enthusiast; and in later days vicar of the Anglo Catholic Shrine of the Holy Trinity in Hoxton; and, in the early 1980s, Squire of the Morris Ring—said:

> *His real memoriam is in the hundreds of Morris dancers he has taught and influenced, and in the brilliance of his playing, which to my knowledge was quite unequalled even to within a few weeks of his death. His sense of rhythm, his wonderful natural ability to use the right chord and the proper use of the bellows which so many Anglo players seem to know nothing whatsoever about—all these are things that I and many others will long remember.*
>
> *On a cold and bleak day, 30th December, we who loved him laid him to rest beside his wife and daughter, in the little churchyard at Headington Quarry. My mind was taken back through the centuries to our great tradition of English Dance and Song, and the simple music of the countryside which this noble old man had done so much not only to preserve, but to perpetuate. . . . We shall not look on his like again.*⁸²

Figure 2.19. William Kimber's headstone in the Holy Trinity churchyard, Headington Quarry. Photographed by Gary Coover in 1979, prior to noticeable erosion of the soft Headington stone in recent years.

[1] David Sutcliffe, 2023, *Cecil Sharp and the Quest for Folk Song and Dance, a New Biography*, London: The Ballad Partners, pp. 249–50. Venues are from the *Oxford Times* Oxford Times of August 16, 1902, and August 5, 1905.

[2] R. W. (Bob) Grant, 1990, "Headington Quarry and Its Morris Dancers, a Brief Chronology up to 1961," *The Morris Dancer*, vol. 2, no. 10, p. 156.

[3] William Kimber to Cecil Sharp, December 15, 1905; Sharp correspondence, Vaughan Williams Memorial Library.

[4] Rafael Samuel, 1974, "Quarry Roughs: Life and Labour in Headington Quarry, 1860–1920, An Essay in Oral History." In Rafael Samuel, ed., *Village Life and Labour*, London: Routledge and Kegan Paul, p. 189.

[5] William Kimber, as interviewed by Peter Kennedy, December 4, 1951. Included as part of Folktrax CD 383, William Kimber Talking.

[6] Sutcliffe, 2023, p. 153.

[7] Mary Neal, 1940, *As a Tale That Is Told: The Autobiography of a Victorian Woman*, unpublished autobiographical manuscript at the Vaughan Williams Memorial Library, p. 145.

[8] *Ibid.*, p. 153.

[9] Cecil J. Sharp and Herbert C. Macilwaine, 1907, *The Morris Book* (volume 1): London, Novello and Company.

[10] Letter from William Kimber to Cecil Sharp, December 15, 1906. Vaughan Williams Memorial Library.

[11] Letter from William Kimber to Cecil Sharp, April 28, 1907. Vaughan Williams Memorial Library.

[12] Derek Schofield, 1999, "Absolutely Classic: The Music of William Kimber," biographical notes in booklet to accompany a CD of the same name, EFDSS CD 03, p. 14. Also Sutcliffe, 2023, p. 267.

[13] Neal, 1940, p. 159.

[14] Sutcliffe, 2023, pp. 265–67.

[15] Letter from Cecil Sharp to Lucy Broadwood, November 10, 1908; Sharp Correspondence, Vaughan Williams Memorial Library.

[16] Roy Judge, 1989, "Mary Neal and the Espérance Morris," *Folk Music Journal*, vol. 5, no. 5, p. 556.

[17] *Oxford Times*, May 1, 1909.

[18] William Kimber as recorded by Peter Kennedy, November 14, 1956. In notes to accompany *William Kimber*, EFDSS LP 1001, 1963.

[19] Theo W. Chaundy, 1959, "William Kimber: A Portrait." *Journal of the EFDSS*, vol. VIII, no. 4 (1959), p. 207.

[20] "Headington Morris-dancers at the Mansion House," *Oxford Times*, May 1, 1909.

[21] William Kimber as recorded by Peter Kennedy, November 14, 1956. In notes to accompany *William Kimber*, EFDSS LP 1001, 1963.

[22] Chaundy, 1959, p. 207.

[23] Grant, 1990, p. 156.

[24] Sutcliffe, 2023, p. 286.

[25] Judge, 1989, p. 559. Also Sutcliffe, 2023, pp. 297–98.

[26] William Kimber, as interviewed by Peter Kennedy, December 4, 1951. Included as part of Folktrax CD 383, William Kimber Talking, track 11.

[27] Judge, 1989, pp. 559–60.

[28] Mary Neal, 1910, *The Espérance Book, Part 1* (3rd edition), London: J. Curwen & Sons, p. 5.

[29] *Morning Post*, April 1, 1910, p. 5. As quoted in Judge, 1989, p. 562.

[30] Mary Neal, "The Revival of English Folk-Music," *Vanity Fair*, April 14, 1910, p. 462. As quoted in Judge, 1989, p. 563.

[31] Maud Karpeles, 1910, shorthand notes of Mary Neal's interview notes with Trafford, Cox, Horwood and Cummings on October 24, 1910, with comments in margin by William Kimber senior.

[32] Neal to Archibald Flower, October 25, 1910, Sharp Correspondence, Vaughan Williams Memorial Library. As quoted in Judge, 1989, p. 565.
[33] Neal, 1910, *The Espérance Book, Part 2,* London: J. Curwen & Sons, p. xiii.
[34] Thyra McDonald to Clive Carey, November 30, 1910. Clive Carey manuscripts, Vaughan Williams Memorial Library. As quoted by David Sutcliffe, 2023, p. 338.
[35] Sharp to Kimber, November 7, 1910, Sharp Correspondence, Box 5, Vaughan Williams Memorial Library. As quoted by Judge, 1989, p. 566.
[36] Kimber to Sharp, November 9, 1910, Sharp Correspondence, Box 5, Vaughan Williams Memorial Library. As quoted by Derek Schofield, 1999, p. 20. Also see Sutcliffe, 2023, p. 342.
[37] Chaundy interview with Kimber, as quoted by Sutcliffe, 2023, p. 342.
[38] Kimber to Sharp, November 10, 1910, Sharp Correspondence, Box 5, Vaughan Williams Memorial Library. As quoted by Judge, 1989, p. 566.
[39] William Kimber, as interviewed by Peter Kennedy, December 4, 1951. Included as part of Folktrax CD 383, William Kimber Talking, track 22.
[40] Sutcliffe, 2023, p 342.
[41] G. A. Coppock, B. M. Hill, and Edmund Arnold Greening Lamborn, 1933, *Headington Quarry and Shotover, a History Compiled on Behalf of Quarry Women's Institute*, University Press by John Johnson, pp. 55–56.
[42] *Musical Times*, March 1911, copy at Vaughan Williams Memorial Library, cuttings book 6.
[43] Grant, 1990, pp. 156–57.
[44] Daisy Daking, 1914, "The Log of a Fine Companion," manuscript diary, Vaughan Williams Memorial Library.
[45] Sutcliffe, 2023, p. 364–65.
[46] Stephanie Jenkins, "William Kimber," Headington History website, www.headington.org.uk.
[47] Schofield, 1999, p. 26.
[48] Correspondence, William Kimber to Cecil Sharp, December 12, 1918. Vaughan Williams Memorial Library.
[49] Maurice East, 2021, "A Rough Guide to Quarry with Maurice East," Chippie Townie Tours, recorded by Trish Elphinstone and posted on YouTube. Used with permission of Maurice East.
[50] Grant, 1990, p. 158.
[51] Sir John Betjeman, 1938, *An Oxford University Chest*, London: John Miles. Quoted by Stephanie Jenkins in the online *History of Headington* (www.headington.org.uk).
[52] John Piper, 1938, *Oxon (Oxfordshire) Shell Guide*, London: Batsford. Quoted by Stephanie Jenkins in the online *History of Headington* (www.headington.org.uk).
[53] Reginald Turner, 1949, *Oxfordshire,* London: Paul Elek. Quoted by Stephanie Jenkins in the online *History of Headington* (www.headington.org.uk).
[54] Schofield, 1999, p. 26.
[55] Grant, 1990, p. 157.
[56] Mark E. Perugini, 1920, "Expression in Dance,"*The Dancing Times*, London, 1920. In papers of Maud Karpeles, Vaughan Williams Memorial Library.
[57] William Kimber, letter to Cecil Sharp, November 14, 1920. Vaughan Williams Memorial Library.
[58] United Kingdom census of 1921.
[59] William Kimber, letter to Cecil Sharp, December 28, 1921. Vaughan Williams Memorial Library.
[60] Chaundy, 1959, p. 209.
[61] William Kimber, letter to Cecil Sharp, June 18, 1923. Vaughan Williams Memorial Library.
[62] William Kimber as interviewed by Chaundy, 1956; also see Chaundy, 1959.
[63] William Kimber, letter to Maud Karpeles, June 27, 1924. Vaughan Williams Memorial Library.
[64] William Kimber, letter to Maud Karpeles, June 14, 1929. Vaughan Williams Memorial Library.
[65] William Kimber, letter to Maud Karpeles, October 30, 1933. Vaughan Williams Memorial Library.

66 Schofield, 1999, p. 28.
67 William Kimber, letter to Maud Karpeles, April 4, 1932. Vaughan Williams Memorial Library.
68 Chaundy, 1959, p. 209.
69 Schofield, 1999, p. 45.
70 Rev. Kenneth Loveless, "William Kimber," date not known but after 1961, 5 pp. I confess not to know the source of this copy, which originally came (decades ago) from the Vaughan Williams Memorial Library, EFDSS. It is roughly equivalent to a shorter biography by Loveless in the jacket notes to accompany the 1974 LP, *The Art of William Kimber*, Topic 12T249.
71 Schofield, 1999, p. 33.
72 *Ibid.*, p. 34.
73 Grant, 1990, p. 159.
74 William Kimber as interviewed by Chaundy, 1956, number 6.
75 Grant, 1990, p. 159.
76 Chaundy, 1959, p. 208.
77 William Kimber as interviewed by Theo Chaundy, June 16, 1959: www.merryville.uk, Chaundy collection, tape 6.
78 Stephanie Jenkins, "Magdalen (or Workhouse) Quarry," online at the Headington History website, www.headington.org.uk.
79 Schofield, 1999, pp. 43–4.
80 "Funeral of Mr Kimber," *Oxford Times*, January 1, 1962.
81 "'Merry' Bill Kimber," *Oxford Times*, December 12, 1961.
82 "In Memoriam, William Kimber,'" *English Dance and Song*, March 1962.

Figure 3.1. William Kimber at the Bedford Morris Ring meeting of 1950. From the Morris Ring Archives, W. Fisher Cassie, photographer.

I go for the easiness of the bellows, see? . . . It's quite a different method altogether.

I don't want so much of low notes. Treble, that's what the dancers want.

—William Kimber, as recorded by Theo Chaundy, 1956

Chapter 3. Playing Like Kimber: Style and Technique

The rural village of Headington Quarry offered a multitude of musical events during the typical year, most of them involving dancing, and William Kimber was an active musician. Long after his emergence onto the national folk dance scene as a tradition-bearer for Morris dance, some fifty-six of his tunes were recorded over the period 1935 to 1958. These recorded tunes include representatives of four major types of dance music: Morris dance, step dances, country dances, and quadrilles and couples dances (the latter two are often called ballroom dances). Kimber played for all of these dance types in his village during his youth in the late nineteenth century. It was there, in Headington Quarry, that he developed his unique playing style on what was then a relatively new instrument, the Anglo concertina. He crafted his playing style to suit the needs of these village dances.

The purposes of this chapter are both to demonstrate how Kimber created his unique sound and to give Anglo concertina players (especially beginners) a few tips on how to recreate it. His playing is not an exercise in muscle memory work or an application of harmonic theory, and the aims of this chapter and the transcriptions that follow in subsequent chapters are not to induce learners to memorize button numbers. Far from it. There are a few relatively simple techniques that Kimber uses to produce the basic framework for his sound, and these can be learned and then applied to most traditional tunes. It is a very accessible and relatively easily learned style.

Why is Kimber's sound so unique?

It is a bit difficult to express the exact ways in which Kimber's playing is unique. In reviewing the Kimber *Absolutely Classic* CD some years ago, Essex musician Roger Digby described it as "crisp, precise, controlled, dignified, unmistakable, and unerringly rhythmic."[1] Oxford musician and Headington Morris dancer Dave Townsend, who along with Andy Turner (currently the musician for the Headington Morris side) transcribed a few of Kimber's tunes on the 1999 *Absolutely Classic* CD's booklet, said of Kimber's playing:

> *It's lovely, light, brisk, neat playing . . . so unlike most playing that you hear these days. It's so full of vitality. They seemed to have danced quite fast, and he played quite fast for them to dance to . . . this is music that gets you off the ground. . . . His playing is, in so many ways, completely definitive.*[2]

"Light" and "crisp" are certainly parts of his uniqueness, but alone they are not enough to describe it. Andy Turner adds another word: "English," to describe Kimber's playing of the tune *Double Lead Through*, although as Turner notes, the tune itself is French in origin.[3] Getting perhaps closer to the essence are these additional comments by Townsend and Turner:

> [Kimber brings in] *unexpected harmonies at many points. . . . The charm and quaintness of the effect on our ears, accustomed to the usual sequences of western harmony, may not have been apparent to Kimber or to his immediate audience. . . . Kimber's harmonies are nothing like those that anyone trained in western art-music would have produced.*[4]

Putting it all together, we might characterize his playing as light, crisp, and eminently danceable, with unexpected harmonies that give it a quaint, charming, and vaguely English sound. Certainly, that is the impression I got when I first heard a recording of Kimber, in 1975.

A musical critic writing in London in 1885 described rural concertina playing of the time:

> *[The concertina] helped drive out the fiddle and to spoil the ears of a rustic people. . . . The concertina has an alluring charm in the way in which it lends itself to processional purposes. There is something of an antique simplicity in these processions. . . . On the one side there is a deep and sincere love for music, and on the other the most meager of opportunities for learning or for guidance in it.*[5]

Mary Neal had two words for that lack of "guidance" when describing Morris fiddlers: *musically unlettered*.[6] Although of course more than a bit condescending, that brief description helps explain the uniqueness of Kimber's sound to our ears. Most of us who follow folk and traditional music today have had some or much academic exposure to the structure of western harmony, through participation in a church choir, secondary school band or orchestra, by taking piano lessons or college courses in music theory, or simply by listening to the myriad styles of western music on recordings and broadcasts. Such music is all around us every day of our lives. When playing unaccompanied melodies, we are predisposed to "hearing" in our heads the proper chords that should be played with them. The harmonic progression of standard chords, or the weekend musician's shorthand "three chord trick," are embedded in our brains today in a way that likely was not the case for isolated rural people like Kimber in the late nineteenth century, when there was no broadcast or recorded music in village cottages, and when Headington Quarry existed as somewhat of a cultural island. As a general rule, notes Roger Digby, in rural English villages in the middle to late nineteenth century there was "probably very little harmony, unless the village schoolmaster wrote some arrangements for a village band."[7] The harmonies in Kimber's left-hand accompaniment were very likely home-grown.

One can contrast Kimber's harmonies to those of the generation of younger Anglo concertina players in England who began to play after Kimber's passing. Members of this group generally learned concertina on their own with little or no contact with an older generation of players other than perhaps a familiarity with recordings of Kimber or perhaps Scan Tester, but they drew from the aforementioned immersion in western chorded music. They typically incorporate full chords in their playing, often arranged in chordal progressions drawn from that tradition. Musicians like John Watcham and Andy Turner had choral training as children, for example, and sprinkle full chords at will in their playing in what has come to be known as the "English harmonic" style on the Anglo concertina. Alternately, John Kirkpatrick has mentioned a background that approaches chording in a slightly different way, but still attached to western music tradition, using chords available on the melodeon:

> *My views on how to play chords have been largely determined by the fact that I came to the Anglo from the melodeon, and was already conditioned to playing the tune on my right hand and chords on the left. . . . For dance music you need a strong rhythmic vamp, and again influenced by the melodeon, I think a low bass note followed by a high chord sounds best, to give an um-pa effect.*[8]

Digby described his similar experiences as well as those of other players of this post-Kimber time (the so-called Second English Folk Revival of the 1970s and later):

> *It was very difficult to get recordings of Kimber and Tester but there was a wealth of English Country Music, both live and on LP, being played on other instruments, mostly melodeon and fiddle. We "pioneering" Anglo players, like Kimber senior before us, had to ask the question, "How do I get that out of this?" The excellence of some of the melodeon players (Oscar Woods, Bob Cann . . .) is probably why so many Anglo players went for a tune/right, chord/left approach.*[9]

With modern Anglo players like John Kirkpatrick, John Watcham, and Phil Ham, one senses that full chordal accompaniment, usually with bass notes at the lower end, has reached a primacy in playing the Anglo concertina in a way that it hadn't in Kimber's hands. Theirs is a wonderful approach and of course lovely to hear, as well as being the basic starting point for most training in English harmonic-style Anglo playing today. During my younger life I attended various weekend teaching workshops in England and in America from three separate instructors in this style of playing. In each case, nearly the first order of business was handing out a two-page chart full of chords for the Anglo—how to play, for example, an A minor chord both on the push and on the pull. It was usually followed by a basic explanation of the components of a full chord on the left hand: the root of the chord along with third and fifth interval notes make the "pah" preceded by a bass note an octave or so lower for the "oom." The left hand "oom-pah" complements the melody note on the right hand, which is usually the same note as the chord's root, but an octave higher. It is a way of teaching and playing Anglo that is deeply rooted both in notions of western chordal accompaniment and in the mechanics of the popular English melodeon.

Moreover, there is an added element of complexity to modern harmonic Anglo playing on three-row concertinas, relative to that of Kimber. One must remember which chords are appropriate, and then remember how to finger them on the push and the pull on all three rows of the instrument, typically reaching across rows on the left hand to get the right combination of buttons. Then the chosen chords must be fitted to the melody on the right hand, which often requires melody notes to be played at alternate positions off the "home" row to enable the fullest expression of the chord—in other words, the needs of the "best" chord on the left hand trump a simple playing of the melody line on the right. The result can be a lot of muscle memory work in a piece of music.[10] For most, one suspects that the memory work is worth the effort, and it makes a beautiful sound.

But then so did Kimber, although in a much simpler way on a two-row instrument. In considering the difference in styles, recall that he had no formal musical training—to use Neal's term, he was "musically unlettered." Although obviously a very musically gifted person—he took part in hand-bell ringing groups, played the drum in village drum and fife bands, and reportedly also played the tin whistle—he was a home-grown artist who could not read music, and probably could not name chords and their constituent parts. "Oom-pahs" are not prominent in his playing. He typically eschewed full chords within the body of a piece, usually preferring to play two-note chord fragments except at the beginnings and ends of A and B parts. These chord fragments —"partial chords"—mainly served to underpin the *rhythm* of a piece.

The simplest way of playing the concertina, according to most printed tutors of the era, was to play a melody along the row, staying on either the C row for the key of C, or the G row for the key of G. These tutors also mention the octave playing technique, described more below, in which the melody is played separately but concurrently on two sides of the instrument, but with each side an octave apart from the other. Developing the octave style further, William Kimber appended partial chords to the lower octave notes on the left side, to create a rhythmically harmonic sound to accompany the melody on the right hand. As mentioned in the previous chapter, harmonic style playing of this sort has deep roots in England, and was taught in some of the earliest printed tutors for the German concertina, in the 1840s. It is also known that self-taught street musicians were playing in a harmonic manner as early as the 1850s (see pp. 34-35).

In a previous study of archival recordings of late nineteenth- and early twentieth-century Anglo players from around the world, called *House Dance* (2011 and 2022),[12] a key finding was that octave playing was perhaps the most popular way of playing the Anglo concertina for rural house dances of the era. The dance tunes most commonly played at that time were polkas, waltzes, schottisches, and other so-called couples or "ballroom" dances that originated in Central Europe, the original home of the German concertina. The dances were not overly fast, and octaves provided extra volume for concertinas that played at crowded house and barn dances in a time before electronic sound amplification. When German and, later, Anglo-German concertinas were adapted to playing different types of popular music, like Morris dances and minstrelsy tunes, the early octave technique was largely continued. In England, not only Kimber but Scan Tester and Fred Kilroy heavily employed octaves in their playing. Scan Tester learned this skill from his older brother Trayton, who appears to have come to it on his own. It is likely that others came upon octave playing similarly, by invention. In Ireland, Jim Droney, Mary Ann Carolan, and Ella Mae O'Dwyer are three of several recorded octave players of polkas and waltzes, but they all typically played melodies singly (no octave notes) when more rapid-fire reels were being played. Australia's Dooley Chapman played almost entirely in octaves for bush dances, and in South Africa, early players like Stephen Emil (Faan) Harris, Chris Chomse and Hans Bodenstein played in octaves, but added chords.[13] Of the late nineteenth- and early twentieth-century concertina players in Australia who could not master octave playing and just played singly along the row, Dooley Chapman said "They weren't the best, that's for sure."[14]

What might have been the particular attraction to the Kimbers of the two-row Anglo concertina, played in octave manner with partial chords, for use with the Headington Morris ? Certainly, the fiddle, played at the Quarry by Kimber senior and by Frank Cummings before him, would be best imitated on a concertina by playing along the row, simply and melodically in the older Irish style. But Morris dancing, performed outdoors to the ringing of bells strapped to the dancers' feet, needed more volume, which octaves partly delivered. And the dancers required rhythmic emphasis too, which Kimber achieved by dropping out notes on the upbeats to further emphasize the downbeat (footfalls), and by adding partial chords to the remaining downbeats for yet more rhythmic emphasis. As musician Stephen Rowley has observed, it might be that the ability of an Anglo concertina played in that manner to mimic the pipe and tabor was a key inspiration for the Kimbers. The pipe and tabor had been played for Morris dancing at least as far back as the 16th century if not earlier, and has exerted a strong influence to this day on Morris music and dance. As Keith Chandler observed, "the pipe was shrill and the tabour was loud…the accuracy of the melody produced by the pipe was subservient, perhaps even superfluous, to the rhythm produced by the drum."[15] With the pipe played by one hand, and the drum by the other, the parallel with the two-handed, duet-like approach on the concertina is compelling. Kimber's left hand is, in essence, his tabor.[16]

The Morris was danced almost exclusively to the pipe and tabor until the late seventeenth century, when the fiddle began to slowly replace it in court circles. In Oxfordshire, according to Chandler, the pipe and tabor was predominant against the fiddle until it began to recede in the 1830s, but was still used by some sides until the early twentieth century. The fiddle was used at Headington Quarry from the 1840s, but Kimber would have seen pipe and tabor used by other sides all his early life at Morris gatherings. Also, he mentioned that "whittle and dub" player Jack Hall often played at Quarry pubs, as discussed in the last chapter. Sharp noted that they passing of the pipe and tabor was much lamented by oxfordshire dancers, recalling that "many old Morris men have told us that they

Figure 3.2. Pipes and tabors.

1. Tabor and stick, Leafield, Oxon, made c. 1800.
2. Tabor and stick, c. 1850, Deddington, Oxon.
3. Wooden pipe that accompanied No. 1.
4. Pipe, c. 1850, Bampton, Oxon. Manning, 1897, in *Folklore, a Quarterly Review*, vol. 8. The items were placed at Cecil Sharp House in London, but were destroyed during the German bombing of London during World War II.

gave up dancing when the pipe and tabor were superseded by the fiddle, because they found it impossible to dance with the latter instrument." They likely missed the rhythmic drumming of the tabor more than anything else.

The pipe and tabor has seemingly had a long and symbiotic relationship with the Morris in both the music itself and the dance steps. The typical South Midlands Morris dance step is *left foot/ right foot/ left foot/ hop on the left foot*, which sequence is then repeated starting on the right foot. It goes with the typical cadence of the tabor, played 'to the step' of the dancers, which is *tump/ tump/ tump/ pause, tump/ tump/ tump/ pause*.[17] That basic cadence is repeated in many of Kimber's Morris tunes, and it is perhaps a testament to that long symbiotic relationship between pipe and tabor playing with Morris dancers. For example, consider the tune "Rigs o'Marlow," which has three repetitions of that particular beat in its A part. Even a 6/8 jig-time tune like *Bacca Pipes* contains that basic underlying rhythm, although it is danced with a much different set of steps.

Thus it may well be that this ability to add a tabor-like beat to a melody may have been a compelling, if not major, reason that William Kimber junior, and perhaps his father as well, picked up the concertina. Both were dancers and appreciated the importance of a well-established and audible beat. In particular, by carefully watching the lead dancer, a musician could adjust tempo as needed by the dancers, and anticipate dance steps that might need a few more micro-units of time – a 'playing to the step' that was part of the tools of the trade of a good taborer. The slowed beat for Morris capers, where the dancers leap into the air, provides an extreme example. A concertina played in a two-handed manner is effective at this playing to the step in the same way that the pipe and tabor is. Of course, a fiddle player can adjust tempo to the step too, but the left hand of the concertina allowed yet more emphasis to be placed on the beat

As mentioned previously, Kimber typically played *two* adjacent keys on the left hand when hammering out the rhythm, not just one note. Those two notes formed a partial chord consisting of a root note and a third interval above it. This partial chord opened up a new dimension of harmonic accompaniment not available to a tabor. Unlike the finely crafted chords of a typical piano or even melodeon piece, however, Kimber's partial chords were often "unexpected." As Dave Townsend and Andy Turner put it,

> *The unexpected chords are not the result of consciously pursuing a chordal scheme, but of allowing harmonizing notes to follow the melody. . . . In fact the techniques which produce these surprising harmonisations are generally very simple.*[18]

It is as if the partial chords were an unplanned side effect of Kimber's primary goal, a rhythm that was made twice as loud by adding a second note to the 'beat' of the left hand. In Kimber's playing the partial chords are typically not "chosen," in the way that a folksinger might carefully choose chords on his guitar to accompany his singing, but rather are the simple and somewhat mechanical result of adding notes a third interval higher to melody notes played on the left hand. That is, of course, a bit of an oversimplification, as Kimber did much more in the way of placement of chordal sounds than that, but it serves as a starting point.

Contemplating his disarmingly simple keyboard techniques and then learning them are the goals of the remainder of the chapter. Kimber's crisp, simple, and somewhat "quaint" way of playing the concertina is of course not everyone's cup of tea—but it might be yours. Throw away all the chord charts, and let's begin.

Keyboard basics

The musical notation scheme used in this book is shown in Figures 3.3 and 3.4. This numbering scheme is standard for most modern Anglo concertina tutors. The thirty-button concertina has three rows of buttons (Figure 3.3). One of the "discoveries" made that resulted from the musical analysis of Kimber's recordings done for the first edition of this book was that Kimber never seems to have played any buttons from the top row of the thirty-button instrument that he had owned since 1909. He was given that instrument by an appreciative audience at Steinway Hall to replace his earlier two-row instrument, which fell apart during a performance there (see Chapter 2). Musical analysis and a photograph taken of Kimber in 1906 (Figure 1.27) show that he learned on a twenty-button and devised his unique style of playing to fit its keyboard layout. Having developed this two-row, twenty-button playing style early in his life, he appears never to have attempted to change it with his newer three-row, thirty-button concertina, which he obtained at the age of twenty-seven. The buttons on the top row shown in Figure 3.3 are thus not further considered here. Buttons on the "upper" row of the two-row twenty-button C/G instrument are numbered 1–5 and are pitched in the key of C. Those numbered 6–10 are on the "lower" row, which is pitched in the key of G.

The pitches of the various buttons of the two rows are shown in Figure 3.4 in scientific pitch notation where C_4 designates middle C on a piano. The instrument contains all or part of four octaves, ranging from C_3 at the bottom end to C_6 at the top. For each button, the note shown on top is played on the push, and the note on the bottom is played on the pull.

Kimber's techniques on the twenty-button Anglo

Kimber's unique *style*, described earlier as crisp and danceable with sometimes unique harmonies that seem to spring from an older England—all rather subjective descriptors, of course—is produced by employing a number of *techniques* on the keyboard of a twenty-button C/G concertina. He never dictated a summary of those techniques to any of his interviewers, and his only pupil, Reverend Kenneth Loveless, passed away without substantially passing on those techniques to the younger generation of second folk revival concertina players who followed in the late twentieth century. For our part, we initially studied tape recordings of Kimber at a much-slowed speed and slowly pieced together how he fingered things (in recent years, digital "slow-down" technology has greatly improved this process). Reflecting on all that, we offer the following summary list of basic fundamentals, and then present a "basic template" of his playing techniques. That is followed by a discussion of various "finishing touches" he used to add spice to his playing. Kimber of course didn't do all this technical analysis; he played intuitively with experience gained by playing over many decades. The analysis here aims only to teach some background fundamental skills and techniques used intuitively by Kimber, in order for Anglo players to reach

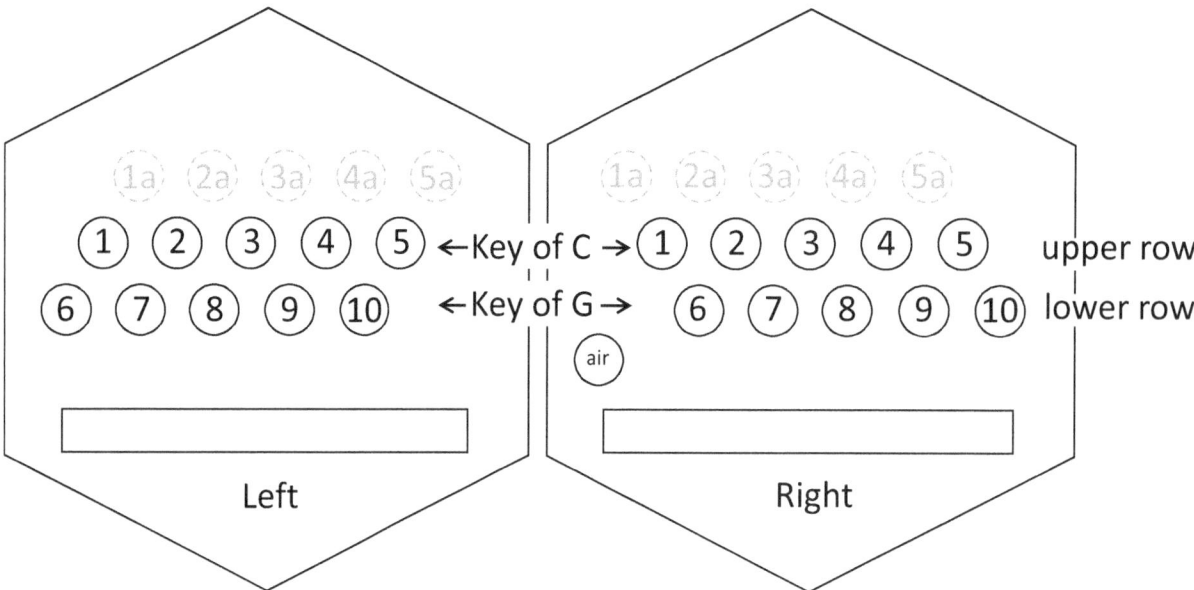

Figure 3.3. Button numbering diagram for the twenty- and thirty-button Anglo concertina. The row at the top, shown in faint dashed lines, represents the top row on a thirty-button instrument, which is absent on the twenty-button model. This top row was completely unused by Kimber, who learned on a twenty-button concertina, and it is thus ignored in this report. The twenty-button has an "upper" row typically pitched in the key of C, with a "lower" row in the key of G.

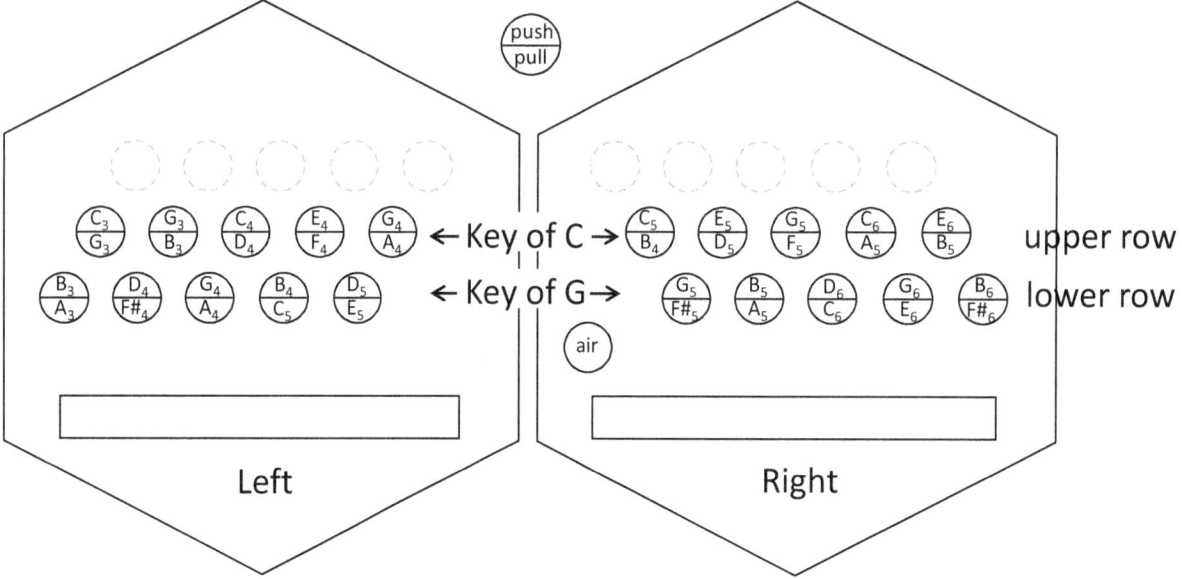

Figure 3.4. The notes of a twenty-button Anglo concertina, shown in scientific pitch notation where C_4 designates middle C on a piano. The instrument contains all or part of four octaves, ranging from C_3 at the bottom end to C_6 at the top. On each button, the note on top is played on the push, and the note on the bottom is played on the pull.

a place where, like Kimber, using his particular playing techniques becomes similarly intuitive.

The Kimber approach involves the following two fundamentals as a starting point. First and foremost, only the twenty buttons of the C and G rows are used (i.e., Kimber plays a twenty-button concertina). The upper row of a thirty-button concertina is never used, with almost no exceptions. Second, the right hand plays the melody, and the left hand plays the accompaniment, with very few exceptions. If the lowest melody notes in a chosen tune drop below the compass of the right hand, then either those few melody notes are transposed an octave higher, or the entire tune is transposed to a different key (typically, from C to G), so that the right hand can play all the melody notes.

A "Basic Template" of Kimber's accompaniment techniques

The following three steps provide a basic framework for designing an accompaniment on the twenty-button concertina and are derived from study of Kimber's technique.

Step 1: Playing in octaves in the key of C. The first step to learning to play in what is essentially a nineteenth-century twenty-button concertina style is to learn to play in octaves, a foundational element to both Kimber's melodic playing on the right hand and his accompaniment on the left.

In octave playing, the left and right hands operate separately, and the instrument is played essentially as if it were a duet concertina. Each hand plays the same melody but an octave apart, with the left hand playing notes an octave below those of the right. The style requires a fair amount of muscle memory to learn, but once learned, this technique becomes completely natural. Kimber of course was mostly playing short bursts of partial chords on the left, rather than playing a complete melody on both hands that is demonstrated in the examples accompanying the discussion of this step, below. The importance of learning to play melodies fully in octaves lies in training the left hand to follow the position of the right. By doing this, the left hand is always in position to *intuitively* lay on a rhythmic beat of an octave-plus-a-third interval partial chord whenever it is needed, without one having to think about it, or to memorize beforehand a particular 'proper' chord and its position in the tune. Kimber uses a much easier, intuitive technique. This will become clearer in the two steps following this one.

The easiest key to learn to play in octaves is that of C major, illustrated in Figure 3.5 and, in audio, by the adjacent QR code. The musical staffs shown in that and in subsequent musical examples and transcriptions in this book employ a dual treble clef staff, with the upper staff (R) for the right hand, and the lower staff (L) for the left hand. The button numbers that overlie the musical notes correspond to numbers on keyboard diagram of Figure 3.3. Button numbers on either staff that have a dash (–) above them are played on the pull, and those without dashes are played on the push. The names of pitches for the notes (A, B, C, etc.) are listed in the space between the two staffs and relate to the keyboard diagram shown in Figure 3.4. Also shown on Figure 3.5 are the solfege equivalents in the key of C (*do-re-mi* etc.).

There are two vertical dashed lines on Figure 3.5. The one on the left highlights the lower limit of the compass of notes on the right hand, and the one on the right gives the corresponding upper limit of notes on the left hand. The area in between

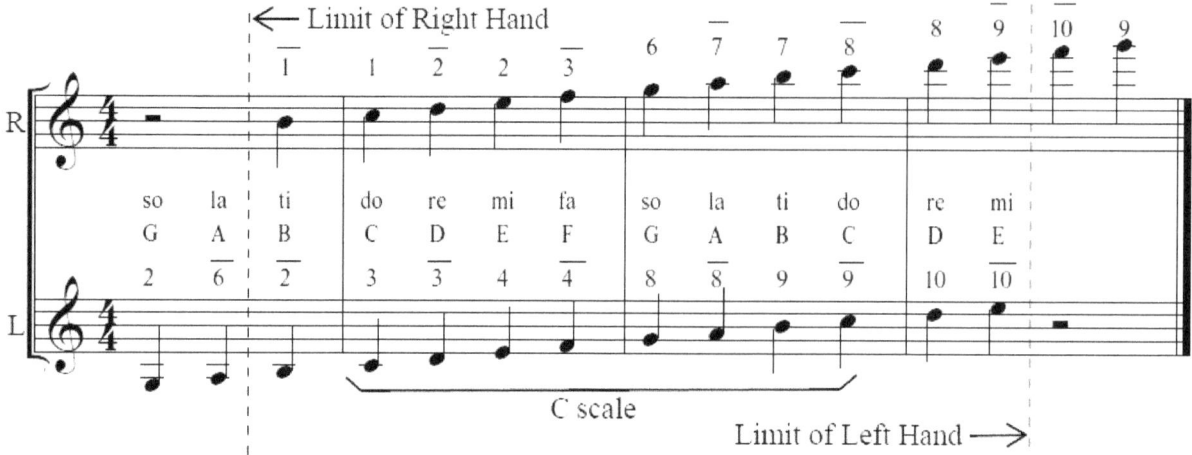

Figure 3.5. The octave scale in the key of C for a twenty-button C/G concertina. The dual treble staffs represent the playing of the right hand (R) on top, and the left hand (L) on the bottom. Button numbers on each hand correspond to those shown in Figure 3.2, and the names of notes (A, B, C, etc.) relate to the keyboard scheme shown in Figure 3.3. Numbers overlain by a dash (–) are played on the pull, and those without the dash are played on the push. The scale is also notated in solfege to show that only one additional note in octaves is available below the lower C (B, or *ti*) and two above the higher C (D and E, or *re* and *mi*). Note that both rows of the concertina are required to be able to play the eight-note scale (*do* to *do*), and that the fingers on each hand trace a figure Z on the buttons while ascending the scale (see Figure 3.5). The vertical dashed lines show the limits of the instrument when played in octaves.

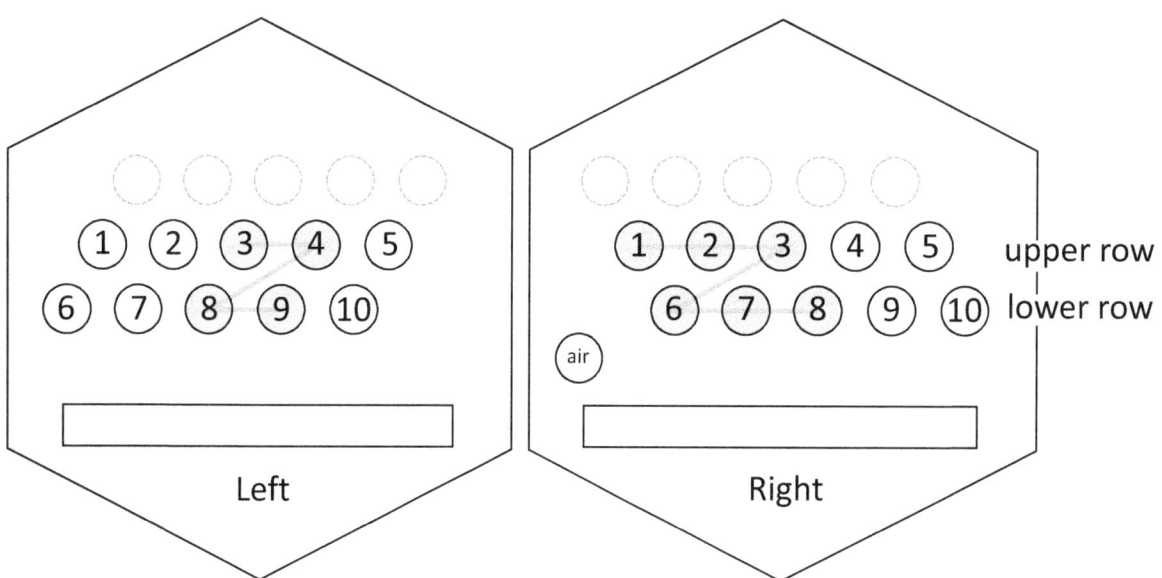

Figure 3.6. The button numbering diagram for the twenty-button Anglo concertina, over which is superimposed Z-shaped grey lines that show the path traveled by the fingers of each hand in playing the ascending C scale in octaves, as detailed in Figure 3.4.

the dashed vertical lines defines the compass for which octave playing in the two-handed manner is possible. Within that zone the basic scale of the key of C (in solfege, *do-re-mi-fa-so-la-ti-do*) is further highlighted with a bracket.

Scale of C in octaves (accompanies Figure 3.5 to left)

Learners wishing to play in the style of William Kimber should commit this basic octave scale in C to muscle memory. It is easiest to learn the scale by playing it just on the right hand first, then just on the left hand, and then playing the two sides in unison. On both hands, the scale ascends from the upper (C) row of the instrument (for *do-re-mi-fa*) then changes to the lower (G) row for *so-la-ti-do*. As can be seen in Figure 3.6, the fingers on each hand trace the letter Z as the scale is ascended. The only "tricky" bit in the exercise comes from the fact that the left hand changes buttons at a different part of the scale than the right; this is the part that requires practice and muscle memory. Once learned well, it becomes second nature. The other key played in octaves on the twenty-button concertina is that of G major. Its fingering is slightly different, as discussed in a later segment.

Once the octave scale in C is mastered, we can turn to one of Kimber's loveliest jigs, *Bacca Pipes*. We'll analyze the A part of this tune, breaking it into the various layers of techniques that Kimber employed to create a finished tune with rhythmic accompaniment. The tune is in the key of D Dorian mode, which means that it uses the same notes as the key of C (i.e., no sharps), but its scale starts and ends on the note D (e.g., *re mi fa so la ti do re*), giving the scale and the tune an odd melancholy sound. The compass of the C octave scale is appropriate for its playing.

Figure 3.7 shows the melody of the A part of *Bacca* Pipes in octaves. It will be optimal if you can learn this melody in full octaves before proceeding. It is a simple tune. The attached recording demonstrates the sound.

Step 2. Adding rhythm. Now for some rhythm (Figure 3.8), done by subtracting off-beat notes from the left hand, while continuing to play the left hand octaves on the downbeat notes. By doing this, Kimber is playing 'to the step,' timing his beats to the footfalls of the dancers. How this subtracting is done depends upon the rhythm inherent in the time signature of melody as well as the player's musical intent in serving the purpose of dancers or listeners. *Bacca Pipes* was danced as a jig over a set of crossed churchwarden smoking pipes that were laid on the floor. It is written in "jig time," which is a time signature of 6/8, with six beats to the measure. The inherent rhythm of jig time emphasizes the first beat of each of two triplets per measure, e.g., "ONE-two-three-FOUR-five-six." Since the "rhythm section" is sequestered by Kimber to the left hand, he only plays the left-hand octave notes on the first beat of each triplet. The other lower octave notes are simply tossed out, as shown in Figure 3.8. *Voilà!* By dropping out the second and third notes of each triplet, you get an instant rhythmic accompaniment, especially if you add some brisk snap to the remaining left-hand downbeat notes. Note that in measure 3 all the left-hand octave notes of one of the triplets have been left in, for a bit of variety, just as Kimber did. Again, it is optimal for learners to be able to play this modified octave rendering of the tune before proceeding. The attached recording demonstrates the sound.

Other examples of tunes in jig time that Kimber plays are *Bonnets So Blue, Constant Billy, Haste to the Wedding, Father O'Flynn, Jockie to the Fair, Laudnum Bunches, The Old Woman Tossed Up in a Blanket, Pop Goes the Weasel,* and *The Willow Tree*. Each of these tunes has its own unique characteristics with variations on the simple rhythmic

Figure 3.7. The A part of *Bacca Pipes* written in octaves.

Figure 3.8. The A part to *Bacca Pipes* written in octaves, but with off-beat notes removed in order to form a basic left-hand rhythmic accompaniment.

Bacca Pipes played in octaves (accompanies Figure 3.7 to left)

Rhythm added to *Bacca Pipes* via subtraction (accompanies Figure 3.8 to left)

accompaniment scheme discussed here. We'll return later to the matter of rhythm and Kimber's accompaniment styles for other dance rhythms (4/4, 2/4, etc.).

Step 3. Adding partial chords. Now we'll add some harmony to *Bacca Pipes*. Kimber's approach to chording on the twenty-button concertina was extremely simple; he typically formed partial chords by adding the next button to the right of each left-hand octave note, which is a third interval up from the starting note. Figure 3.9 shows the octave scale in the key of C major with third intervals added on the left hand; the resulting partial chords are named. Some are major chords (e.g., C, F and G), and others are minor (e.g., Dm, Em, Am, Bm). To understand why some partial chords are major, and others are minor, examine a piano keyboard (left). The white keys represent the diatonic scale of C. If one plays the C scale (white keys only) and adds a third interval note to each note on the scale (e.g., C plus E or E plus G), some of these third intervals involve an interval of three semitones (also called half-steps) yielding a minor chord, and others have four semitones, yielding a major chord. For example, to go from C to E involves moving up two white keys and two black keys and forms a major chord. Going from from E to G involves moving up two white keys but only one black key, and it forms a minor chord with quite a different sound. These chords, both minor and major, are called partial chords because they lack the third note of the chord triad, which is a fifth interval up from the starting note. For example, CE is the partial major chord of C, where CEG represents the full chord (triad).

All that terminology might sound a bit involved, but remember that Kimber wasn't particularly bothered by terminology or theory; he just added a button up from each left-hand octave note (hence, a third interval on a push-pull Anglo keyboard) without over-analyzing it. When that partial chord is combined with the right-hand melody note, the result is a 1-3-1 partial chord (for example, CEC or FAF). With that simple technique in mind, it is an easy task to affix partial chords to *Bacca Pipes* with its octave rhythmic accompaniment, as shown in Figure 3.10. Play this passage now and see if you aren't beginning to feel a little of the Kimber sound coming into your playing, just using this very simple technique. None of the chords are dissonant, although some of the chord "choices" are less comely than others. But with just these three purely mechanical steps, we are perhaps 70% of the way to Kimber's arrangement. For that reason, the application of these three first steps—which are almost always all applied—is here called the "Basic Template."

Returning for a moment to the discussion of the octave technique, it is apparent that Kimber is, for the most part, not "choosing" which chords to play, but rather is playing what harmony the keyboard gives him. The classic octave playing technique is the foundation that controls which partial chords happen. By using octaves in positioning the left hand relative to the right-hand melody, one can apply reasonable chords at will without even thinking about it, in a purely intuitive manner. Differences between Kimber's finished accompaniments and an accompaniment crafted merely with the foregoing "Basic Template" are by exception; Kimber throws in special things at will to spice it up. These can be summed in a list of "Finishing Touches," below.

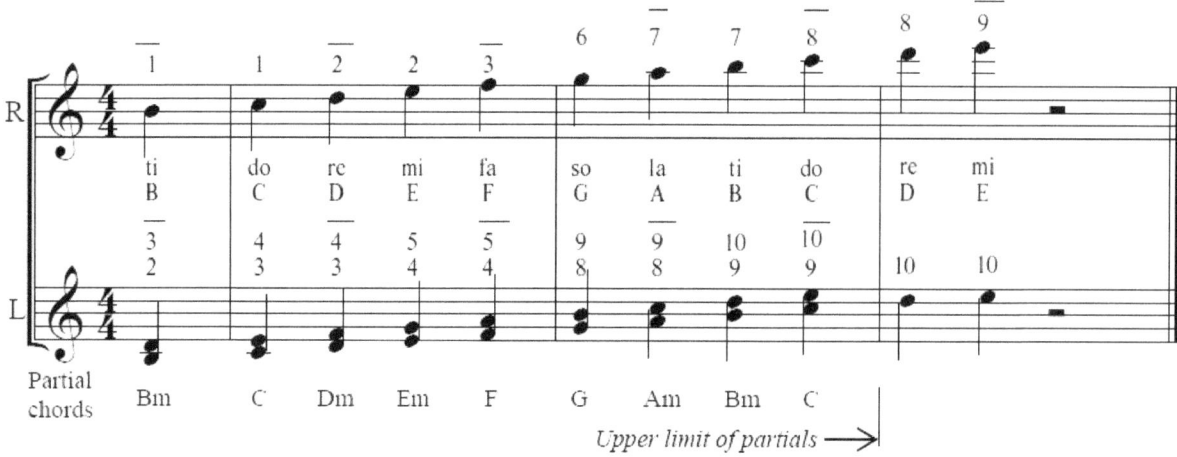

Figure 3.9. Octave scale in the key of C, with partial chords formed by adding the adjacent button to the right of each octave note on the left hand. Depending upon position on the diatonic scale, these added notes are either a major third interval (four semitones) higher, yielding a partial major chord, or a minor third higher (three semitones), yielding a partial minor chord. Partial chords are available as high as the upper C on the lower row.

Figure 3.10. The A part of *Bacca Pipes* with a simple rhythmic accompaniment of partial chords added, an octave down.

"Finishing Touches" to complete the accompaniment

Octave scale in C played with partial chords (accompanies Figure 3.9 to left)

Bacca Pipes played with simple partial chords (accompanies Figure 3.10 to left)

Figure 3.11. Full chord left-hand triads for a twenty-button concertina. Although two full minor chords are shown (Am and Dm), they were not much used by Kimber, although he played partial chord versions of them.

To get from a 70% "nearly there" to the full depth of Kimber's accompaniments, we need to choose from a smorgasbord of "Finishing Touches." These include four additional "optional" steps in which Kimber shaped the sound of the accompaniment, either to make it sound more pleasing to him or to make it more useful to his dancers. Some of these steps also add a bit of variety to repeats of the A or B part. These steps each may or may not be taken, depending upon the needs of the tune and of course upon personal preference. Kimber rarely played the left-hand accompaniment of a tune the same way twice, and the following finishing touches are the ways that he varied it, at will.

Step 4. Bookending the piece with full chords. In almost all tunes, Kimber uses full chords at the beginning and end of major segments (e.g., the beginning and ending notes of the A or B parts). This entails adding fifth interval notes to the two-note partial chords to make them full chords (triads). For example, a left-hand C partial chord (CE) becomes CEG, plus the higher C on the right hand. This is done to place emphasis on the start and finish of a passage, for the dancers. *These are nearly always simple C major (CEG) or G major (GBD) chords,* the fingerings for which are shown in Figure 3.11. The C major chord on the push on the left hand is simply Left 3+4+5 Push, or CEG. The pull C major chord exists on a two-row Anglo only as an anemic partial (Left 9+10 Pull), so it is not included in this chart of triads. When even a bit more emphasis is needed to a C chord, usually at the end of a piece, Kimber often adds an extra octave to the C melody note on the right hand (Right Push 1+4). An example of that may be found at the ends of the A and B parts in *Bean Setting*, in Chapter 4.

For tunes played in the key of G, there is a G major chord on either the pull (Left 1+2+3 Pull; GBD) or push (Left 2+6+7 Push, GBD), or an octave higher on the push at Left 8+9+10 Push, GBD. Two minor chords are also shown on this chart of triads, but Kimber rarely used them.

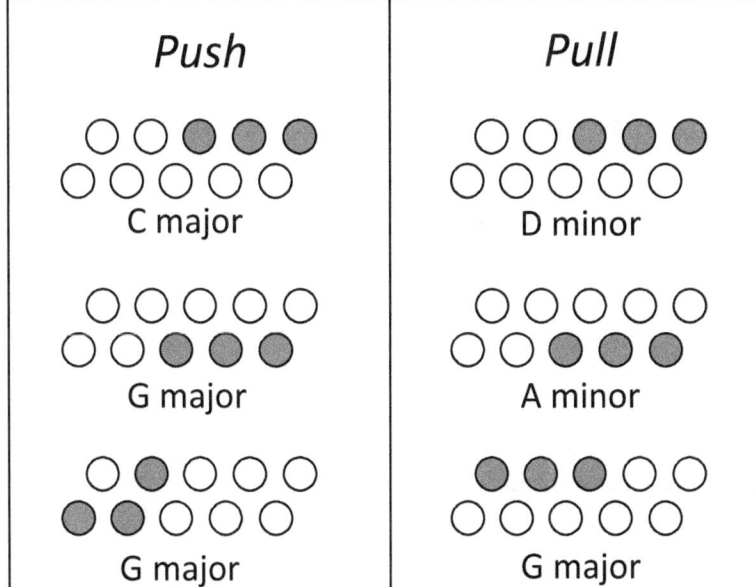

Full triad chords may also be inserted, somewhat sparingly, in the interior of a long passage of partial chords where needed to emphasize a particular part of the melody, although in the interior Kimber usually stuck with two-note partial chords.

Step 5. Chord inversions. In a tune in C major, the right-hand melody note F (Right 3 Pull) is usually accompanied by the F major partial chord on the left hand (FA, or Left 4+5 Pull), which together make the F major partial chord FAF. In many cases Kimber inverts that chord by adding a C and dropping the bottom F (ACF: Left 9+8 plus Right 3 Pull). That may sound complicated, but he merely changes the FA partial (Left 4+5 Pull) to AC (Left 8+9 Pull) while keeping the right-hand melody note F at the same position. The inverted chord sounds a bit exotic and spicy, and Kimber uses the two versions of F (standard and inverted) interchangeably throughout his music. Such inversions form a big part of his unique sound.

He also occasionally inverted the E minor chord, replacing E minor (EGE: EG on the left with E on the right, or Left 4+5 Push and Right 2 Push) with its first inversion (GBE: GB on the left, or Left 9+8 Push; and E on the right, or Right 2 Push). He also occasionally inverted Dm. Examples are shown in Figure 3.12 and 3.15, below.

Bacca Pipes played with Kimber's arrangement (accompanies Figure 3.12 to right)

Step 6. Adding "oom-pahs." Kimber sometimes replaces the first of a pair of accompaniment partial chords with a bass note to the chord, thus giving an "oom-pah" sound (e.g., Figure 3.20, below). He typically used these oom-pahs very sparingly, usually to break up the monotony of a string of rhythmically similar partial chords. Using them too frequently imparts a melodeon-like sound to the accompaniment, which typically was not part of his style. Of course, many of the oom-pah bass notes and triads played on a three-row Anglo by many current Anglo players are not possible on the limited compass of a two-row instrument.

William Kimber playing *Bacca Pipes*, via His Master's Voice, 1948

Step 7. Octave runs. When there is a sequence of rapid notes in a single measure of melody, Kimber sometimes deletes a couple of left-hand partial chords, and instead plays every note of that brief sequence in octaves. This tends to break up the potential monotony of long sequences of rhythmic partial chords (e.g., measure 3, Figure 3.12).

With these finishing touches in mind, we'll go through a few case studies to see how and where Kimber applied them.

Completing *Bacca Pipes*

Having already created a Basic Template version of *Bacca Pipes* (Figure 3.10), let's examine the A part of *Bacca Pipes* notated exactly as Kimber played it (Figure 3.12); this is our final target. The right-hand staff (the melody) is identical, but there are a few noteworthy differences with the Basic Template version, which are listed at the bottom of Figure 3.12. Each of those differences is due to the application of three further "finishing touches." These are as follows, in no particular order.

Application of Step 5. As mentioned earlier, Kimber was very fond of inverting the F chord by replacing FAF (the partial chord FA (Left 4+5 Pull) plus the right-hand melody note F (Right 3 Pull)) with an "inversion" of the F chord ACF (Left 8+9 Pull plus the right-hand melody F (Right 3 Pull)). In effect, there is no "bottom" to the chord, which in its full non-inverted expression would be FACF. As mentioned in the preceding summary of Kimber techniques, the inverted chord sounds a bit exotic and spicy, and Kimber uses the two versions of F interchangeably throughout his music. It constitutes a key element of his unique sound.

Figure 3.12. The A part of *Bacca Pipes* as Kimber played it. The list highlights the finishing touches that were added to the basic template version (Figure 3.10).

Finishing Steps Employed:

Step	Action	Measures where used
4	Add full chord triad at start, finish	Lead-in measure, 8
5	Inversion of F partial chord	1,3,5,7
6	Insert oom-pah couplet	None
7	Substitute octave run to vary rhythm	3

Figure 3.13. The melody line (right hand) for the A part of *Bacca Pipes*, including a comparison of accompaniment chords for (1) "typical" guitar chords for *Greensleeves*, (2) the basic template version (from Figure 3.10), and (3) the Kimber version (from Figure 3.12). The underlined objects are places where Steps 4 through 7 have been applied.

Application of Step 7. In the "basic template" version of *Bacca Pipes* (Figure 3.10), the simple rhythm consists of a very long sequence of rapidly played partial chords punctuated by rests (ONE-two-three-TWO-two-three) that borders on being monotonous. In the third measure of Kimber's version (Figure 3.12), he breaks up this monotony by replacing a pair of partial chords with a simple run of octave notes. Such brief octave runs are a useful device that Kimber frequently employs.

Application of Step 4. As mentioned previously, Kimber was fond of adding grandiose full chords at the beginning and end of both the A and B parts of a piece. These almost certainly served to help the dancers—both Morris and social—know the beginning and end of each main segment, and almost always were either C major or G major chords. *Bacca Pipes* presents somewhat of a conundrum, as the tune is in the key of D Dorian mode. How will Kimber deal with that?

Kimber announces the beginning of the tune with a C major chord (Figure 3.12). It would seem appropriate enough, as the C chord has notes in it which are in the D Dorian scale, although the use of a C chord is not particularly modal in sound. A more interesting chord choice is that inserted at the end: a G major chord. It is a bit jarring to the ears, as we might expect a D minor chord there. Figure 3.13 tabulates the use of full and partial chords in the *Bacca Pipes* jig, in three ways: as 'typically' played on a keyboard or guitar, as played after application of the Basic Template, and then the chords that Kimber actually played. The final chord typically played by a guitarist would be D minor, and indeed the mechanically chosen "basic template" version lands on just that chord. Our brains seem to long for that D minor when hearing that tune in our heads, as we are shaped by years of listening to Ralph Vaughan Williams' *Fantasia on Greensleeves*. One would think that Kimber might play a full triad of a D minor chord here (note that this triad is shown in Figure 3.11 as Left Pull 3+4+5). But he learned the tune long before he ever heard that *Fantasia*, and obviously didn't like the rather weak sound of that pull D minor chord. Instead, he wished for a resounding major chord to signal to his dancers the end of the piece. He used a G major.

We'll discuss a bit further on his chord choices in a summary, below. But before we leave that final G chord, note that in the second ending of the A part, he intentionally inverts the second playing of it, going from a pull G chord (Left 1+2+3 Pull, or GBD) to an *inverted* push G chord (Left 6+7+8 Push, or BDG) The inverted G with its different 'feel' acts as a subtle bridge between the A part and the B part of the tune, as if to remind the dancers that a dancing transition is about to occur. That inversion is intentionally placed, as it requires a change in bellows direction. It is not an essential choice, but rather represents a bit of Kimber's artistry.

Reflecting on Kimber's chord choices

It has been said that Kimber's chord selections are sometimes unusual—part of his unique sound. Less charitably, a guitar player I once knew wouldn't wish to play along with any of these arrangements, calling many of Kimber's chord choices "wrong." That final G major chord in place of a 'typical' D minor chord would seem to be a case in point. As mentioned earlier, Kimber came from a rural village where, in his youth, harmonic playing was mostly absent, and he did not read music. That is not to say that the village was unmusical—far from it. But the age-old musical traditions in the Quarry mainly involved melody instruments like pipe and tabor, tin whistle, and fiddle. Pianos were beyond the financial reach of most, and there was no village band. For that reason, there was not a pervasive playing of chorded music in that environment, with all this entails—no indoctrination into the chord progressions and ending cadences that are so pervasive today in all sorts of modern music, as for example the chords used in Vaughan Williams' *Fantasia on Greensleeves*.

From the foregoing analysis of *Bacca Pipes*, it would seem clear that Kimber's playing developed first and foremost as primarily melodic, with rhythmic partial chord punches on the left hand to support the dance. As has been shown, Kimber's partial chord choices were largely not "choices" at all but were rather the result of adding a third interval note above the left hand octave notes to provide more volume. *The partial chords came with the mechanical technique*; he didn't have to choose them, or understand musical theory, or know about chord progessions and the three-chord trick. The partial chords simply served to punch the beat better than single-octave notes would. The fact that they made a pleasing sound, albeit sometimes unusual, was an added bonus.

There were of course times when Kimber would proactively choose a chord, and even here the choices were unusual. For example, the ending G major chord in *Bacca Pipes*. Why use that chord? He needed a grandiose full chord to give oomph to the ending for the dancers, and the D minor partial didn't have it; it sounded too weak to him. He knew that the G chord (GBD) was good and strong, and had a D note in it, so that may be why he used it.

That G chord in particular did not please my guitar-playing friend; it was 'wrong.' But Kimber's arrangement holds its own and has that certain Kimber charm. And the third interval partial chords that rather mechanically follow the melody line up and down the keyboard have their own take on chord progressions. It produces a charming effect that would rarely occur to many players today, as they search for the 'right' full chords to accompany music in a way that goes smoothly with the chord progressions that are imbedded deeply into our subconscious. Equally unusual is Kimber's use of the inverted F chord (ACF) instead of the expected F (FAC). He used this device (Step 5) very often, so it clearly is no accident; nor does it fill some fingering convenience. He put it in because it sounded nice to him, and now it is a significant part of his style.

Kimber plays each partial chord very briskly, no matter what length the melody note may have. This is of course consistent with the chords' use as a tabor-like drum for the dancers, and that briskness was his bread and butter. There may be another reason as well. The particulars of the fine tuning and temperament of his Jeffries concertina are not known, but our modern concertinas are almost always tuned with equal temperament, a sixteenth century innovation that was largely adopted by learned and church music circles in Britain by Kimber's time in the late nineteenth century. Without straying too far into the weeds, third intervals fine-tuned in this temperament do not sound particularly pleasant when played as long notes—especially those at higher pitch. Those chords played long on a concertina have a beating to their tone that many find unpleasant. Whether Kimber's instrument was tuned that way or not, his characteristic manner of playing partial chords was to play nearly all of them in a staccato fashion, which greatly alleviates the beating problem. In all the scores in this book, the time duration of the left-hand notes is shown as being the same as that of corresponding right-hand melody notes. This is done for

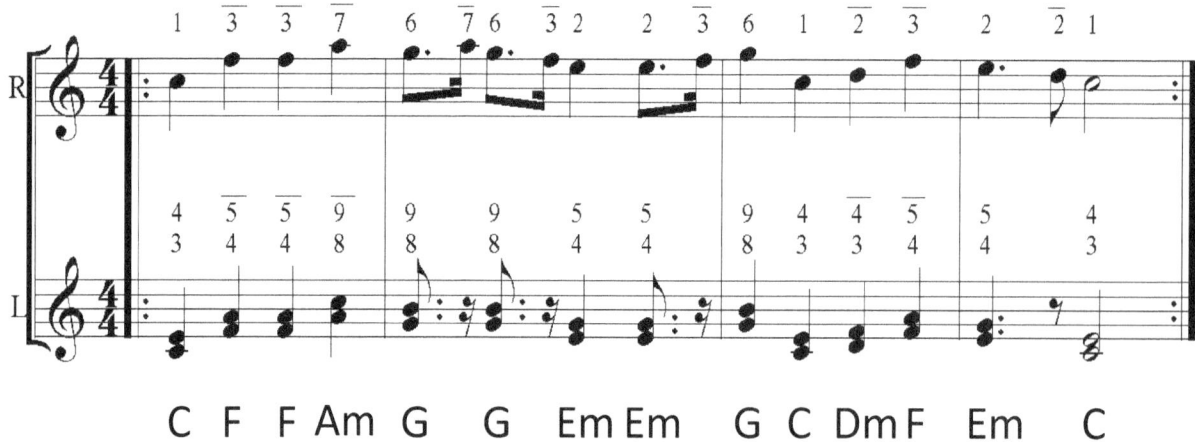

Figure 3.14. The A part of *Country Gardens*, with a simple accompaniment made by using the Basic Template, Steps 1–3. The bottom line shows the names of the partial chords.

Figure 3.15. The A part to *Country Gardens* as Kimber played it. At bottom are listed (1) the chords in a typical guitar arrangement, then (2) the tune with an accompaniment rendered by mechanical application of the Basic Template, and (3) the tune as Kimber played it. Underscored letters on the latter line represent places where Kimber used full chord triads rather than his more usual two-note partial chords (Finishing Step 4). Note that in the final version, Kimber inverts several chords; see text for explanation.

ease in sight reading. Regardless of whether shown on the staff as eighth notes or quarter notes, Kimber played each accompaniment partial chord in a brisk staccato fashion, which is not only an important part of his style and important in supporting the dancers, but easier on a listener's ears.

Playing in C major and 4/4 time: *Country Gardens*

Basic template version of *Country Gardens* (accompanies Figure 3.14 to left)

Each dance tune has a unique rhythm that goes with its time signature. As we've seen, *Bacca Pipes* is a 6/8 jig with a "ONE-two-three-FOUR-five-six" rhythm, which Kimber typically accompanied by playing only on the accented first and fourth beats of each six-beat measure. The accompaniment for tunes in other time signatures like 2/4 and 4/4 similarly accents certain notes, in a manner that varies by dance type. Sharp collected the Morris dance tune *Country Gardens* from Kimber. As early as 1735, when it was published in a flute tutor, it was a song air used for English country dances,[19] and its even, 4/4 cadence is perfectly suited to the smooth walking step of many such dances.

The cadence has a slight accent on the first beat, but the other beats are nearly as strong, just as one might count out successions of four steps while walking. The first line could be sung ONE-TWO-THREE-FOUR, ONE-and-TWO-and-THREE-FOUR-and, ONE-TWO-THREE-FOUR, LONG-and-LONG. Kimber's left-hand accompaniment inserts octave-and-third partial chords at each of the four downbeats in each measure and drops out any upbeat "ands." Using the "basic template" of steps 1 through 3 as discussed earlier in the summary of Kimber's techniques yields the accompaniment shown in Figure 3.14. If you play this simple accompaniment, you can see that as with *Bacca Pipes*, application of the first three technique steps gets you perhaps 70% of the way to a Kimber style; it is quite serviceable and intuitively easy.

Kimber's arrangement of *Country Gardens* (accompanies Figure 3.15 to left)

Application of the "finishing touches" 4, 5, and 6 adds quite a bit of finesse to the basic template version and results in the version that Kimber played (Figure 3.15). Step 4 involves placing the full C chords at the beginning and end of the piece, for the typical strong beginnings and ends. He also adds a fifth interval note to the C partials in measures two and three, thereby constructing a full triad. This probably occurs because it is so easy to do, or possibly he wished to emphasize those notes.

Invoking finishing touch 5, Kimber inverts three chords of the template version (F, Dm, and Em) by dropping out the bottom note of each partial (e.g., the bottom note in the partial FA) and adding a third up from the remaining note (e.g., AC) yielding F_{inv} (AC), Dm_{inv} (FA) and Em_{inv} (GB). Inverted chords are easy to hear because of their 'spicy' aural character, for want of a better term, and easy to spot in the sheet music because the lower note of the left-hand partial chord does not match the (octave higher) melody note on the right hand; the chord is hence "rootless." As mentioned earlier, Kimber liked the peculiar sound of inversions and used them extensively.

William Kimber playing *Country Gardens* via His Master's Voice, 1948

Finally, Step 6 is represented by the bass note G in the third measure, which creates an oom-pah C chord in the first half of that measure. It breaks up what would otherwise perhaps be a monotonous group of partial chord beats. Two characteristics of this finished accompaniment are notable:

(1) Kimber's final chosen chords (partial and full) are nearly identical to the mechanically inserted chords of the "basic template" version, which indicates that his chord choices are mostly dictated by the mechanics of adding third intervals to the diatonic keyboard, not as intentional chording "choices" *per se*.

(2) Kimber's chords in both the template and finished version are in places decidedly more minor in feel than those typically played by, say, a folk guitar player (compare the chord lists on Figure 3.15). Those extra Am and Em chords—dictated by the diatonic keyboard—are a big part of Kimber's less than orthodox sound, and they, along with the inverted chords, give the accompaniment an earthy quality, where standard arrangements (e.g., Sharp's and Grainger's piano arrangements) sound a bit sweet.

Although Cecil Sharp carefully and accurately transcribed Kimber's playing of the melody (his original notation is shown in Figure 3.16), he seems to have paid little attention to Kimber's chords. Given the "sweet" and major chord tendency of Sharp's piano arrangement of this piece (and later, that of Percy Grainger), Sharp may not have regarded Kimber's earthy harmonies highly. He certainly never mentioned them in his writings. In any event, it was easy to have them turned off while he notated Kimber's playing; all Sharp had to do was to ask that Kimber play the right hand only while Sharp transcribed the basic melodies.

Figure 3.16. Cecil Sharp's 1906 transcription of *Country Gardens* from William Kimber's playing. From the Vaughan Williams Memorial Library, EFDSS, London.

Playing in octaves in the key of G

So far, the examples given have been in the key of C major or its Dorian mode cousin. Playing in octaves in the key of G major introduces a few minor complexities, and before we continue exploring dance rhythms in the key of G, it is necessary to say a few words about them.

Octave scale in G (accompanies Figure 3.17, next page)

The octave scale in the key of G is shown in Figure 3.17. As was the case in Figure 3.5, the two dashed lines show the limits of the keyboard that can be played duet-like in two-handed octaves in the key of G. Unlike the octave scale in C, there is not a complete string of notes that can be played from *do* to *do* in that manner. It is only possible to play *mi-fa-so-la-ti-do-re-mi-fa-so-la* using both hands. Although this appears at first glance as a non-starter, many tunes can be fully played within this restricted compass. Even when a tune extends beyond that compass, for example higher to *ti* or *do*, there are two ways Kimber would typically accommodate that extended upper range. The first would be to go on playing that high *ti* and *do* as single notes, as shown at the right in Figure 3.17. In the quickness of playing, the lack of an occasional octave note is not particularly noticeable. A second method would be to employ an octave jump at that point, dropping the scale immediately down a full octave, as shown in Figure 3.18. There is a corresponding octave jump shown on the lower end of the compass as well. This octave jumping was often employed by Kimber, and the average listener will either not notice it, or at most might think that the octave jump is part of the written melody. Examples of such jumps are discussed further later.

Octave Scale in G employing octave jumps (accompanies Figure 3.18, next page)

When playing the ascending G scale in octaves (starting at the lower *do* at Right 3 Push, Left 5 Push, Figure 3.18), the place along the upper row where the fingering moves from the top row to the bottom row (between the E and the F#) is different than was the case in the key of C. The key of G requires an F sharp, which is not to be found on the upper row of either hand (the key of C has no sharps). Thus, the fingering of the octave scale drops from the top to the lower row after the E (Right 3 Push, Left 4 Push) is played, avoiding the F natural and reaching down to the lower row for the F#. When the octave scale in C is played, the F natural is played in the upper row, so the drop down occurs just *after* it is played in that case.

Octave scale in G with partial chords and octave jumps (accompanies Figure 3.19, next page)

Adding partial chords to the G octave scale is fairly straightforward, with two exceptions (Figure 3.19). In the upper part of the G scale *when including partials*, the octave jump is required two steps earlier (after *fa* rather than after *la*), because the third intervals needed for the partials push up and out of left-hand range two notes earlier than is needed for the octave scale alone. Finally, at the left-hand partial chord Dm (D at Left 3 Pull plus F# at Left 7 Pull), the needed F# is not to be found on the C row, and in this case the third interval F# is found on the lower row at Left 7 Pull. These octave jumps and the partial chord with the F# may seem a bit complicated, but in practice they are only rarely encountered in Kimber's playing.

Minstrel rhythm: *Getting Upstairs*

There were at least two American minstrel tunes in the Headington Quarry Morris repertoire at the end of the nineteenth century. *Getting Upstairs* was collected by Cecil Sharp from Kimber, and *Buffalo Gals* was collected by Mary Neal's colleague Clive

Figure 3.17. The scale of G major in octaves, for the twenty-button concertina. The vertical dashed lines delimit the extent of the keyboard in which octaves are possible using both hands in the key of G. Outside of this zone octaves are possible, but both notes are played on the same hand, making fingering awkward, and Kimber typically avoided that.

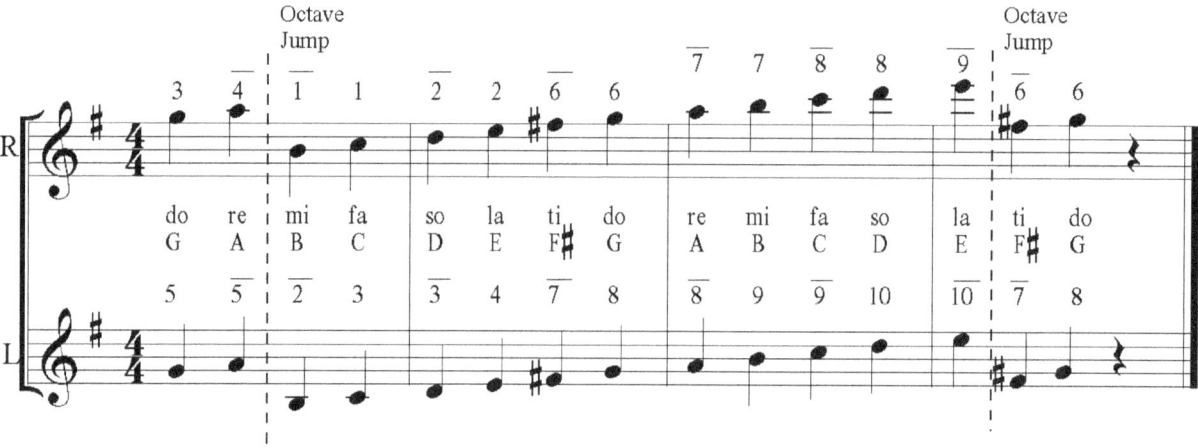

Figure 3.18. An octave scale in the key of G major, with octave jumps at the vertical dashed lines. The sharps on the individual F notes are shown for clarity.

Figure 3.19. Octave scale in the key of G with third interval partial chords and octave jumps. Sharps on the F notes are shown for clarity.

Carey from dancer Joe Trafford. *Getting Upstairs* originated with early American minstrel performer and collector T. D. "Daddy" Rice, who may in turn have obtained the tune from an enslaved source.[20] We can say with some precision when *Getting Upstairs* reached England, because the London *Times* reported in its edition of February 2, 1839, that "By late London papers before us, we perceive that Rice has found out a new way to please John Bull. The popularity of 'Jim Crow' [the song and dance *Jump Jim Crow*] seems to be eclipsed by 'the new fancy song' of '*Sich a gittin up stairs*.'" The minstrel craze was all the rage in England for nearly half a century, and beyond the obvious racial caricatures that are today reviled, a key element was the extremely lively, fresh and invigorating music. Early nineteenth-century English and American popular music before the minstrels was mainly an exercise in a 4/4 beat with an emphasis on the downbeat (ONE-two-THREE-four). The minstrels captured a new beat, taken from African American slave culture, that emphasized the upbeat (one-TWO-three-FOUR). That beat was largely a byproduct of the plantation banjo, carried by enslaved Africans to the American South. Just as the rhythms of ragtime, jazz, and the blues shook global popular music in the early twentieth century, minstrel music had a similar widespread appeal in the nineteenth. It was different, exotic, exciting and new.

Getting Upstairs with Kimber's arrangement (accompanies Figure 3.20, below)

William Kimber Playing *Getting Upstairs* via His Master's Voice, 1946

Cecil Sharp collected the tune from Kimber, but other Morris groups of the time also had it. Kimber's arrangement (Figure 3.20) is only slightly different than a "basic template' arrangement using just Steps 1–3, so only his finished version is shown here. The A part of Kimber's version, true to the tune's minstrel origins, has two passages that emphasize the upbeat rhythm. It might be sung: one-TWO-three-FOUR / ONE-and-TWO-and-THREE-and-FOUR-and / one-TWO-three-FOUR / ONE-and-TWO-and-THREE. It is easy to imagine heavy chords from plantation-style four-string banjos on the upbeats of measures one and three. In those measures the offbeat rhythm is achieved by inserting oom-pahs (Finishing Step 6). The bass notes are low single notes, whereas the succeeding partial chords are louder and relatively shrill two-reed partial chords, yielding the emphasized offbeat rhythm on the second and fourth beats. Measures 2 and 4 are played in a more standard 4/4 fashion, with sixteenth-note runs where only the downbeats are given left-hand octave-and-a-third interval partial chords. Kimber ends the A part with a low G major chord, as per "finishing step" 4.

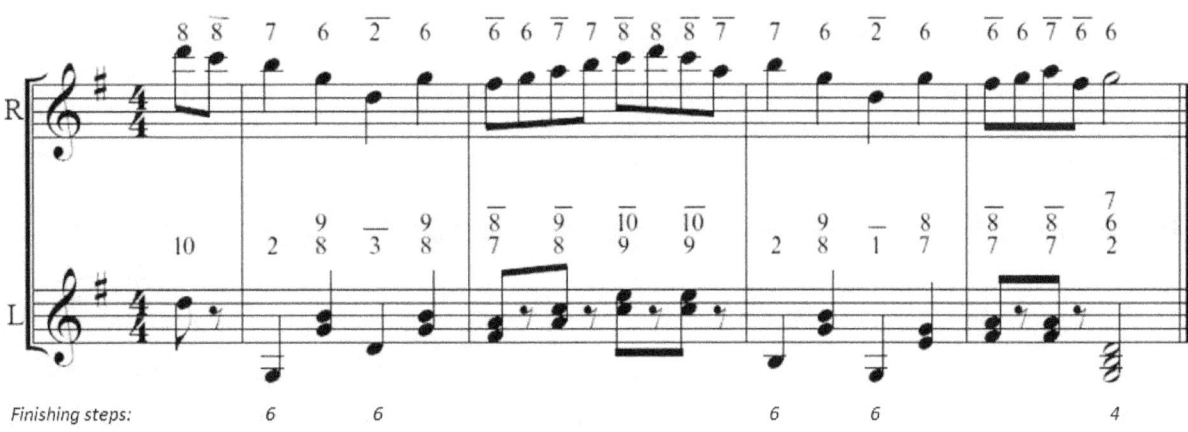

Figure 3.20. The A part of the minstrel tune *Getting Upstairs*, as Kimber played it.

Playing a schottische: *Over the Hills to Glory*

Kimber recorded several schottisches, which like *Country Gardens* are 4/4 but present a rhythmic variation that suits the schottische dance. Typically, they are played a bit more slowly and the first and third beats are accented heavily, with the second and third beats receiving slightly less emphasis: ONE-and-TWO-and-THREE-and-FOUR-and. *Over the Hills to Glory* is a typical schottische, and its basic template version is shown in Figure 3.21, in which steps 1–3 are already applied to the left hand. The melody could be sung ONE-and-TWO-and-a-THREE-and-FOUR-and/ ONE-and-TWO-and-a-THREE-and-FOUR-and, etc. Accordingly, Kimber places all four downbeats in each measure of the accompaniment but emphasizes the first and third beats more than the second and fourth. He drops out all of the upbeat "and-a" notes on the left hand to frame the driving rhythm. The result is a drumming four-beat step similar to that of *Country Gardens*, but with the first and third beats heavily accented. The partial chords and the rhythm of the basic template version sound reasonable for a first pass, although the opening two D major partial chords at the entrance sound a bit awkward.

Basic Template version of *Over the Hills to Glory* (accompanies Figure 3.21 to right)

Figure 3.22 displays the same tune, but in Kimber's finished version. In this schottische, with its very driving rhythm, he wants a loud and pulsating left hand and achieves it by inserting *many* more full chords than is typical of his playing ("finishing step" 4 on steroids). Starting with the first measure, he places an oom-pah bass G followed by a pull G major chord in the first two beats (an oom-pah, as per finishing step 6), then in the rest of that measure adds the normal partial chord but with an added fourth interval note below (hence DBG at Left 7-8-9 Push), which forms an inverted G major triad that is an octave higher than the previous normal G chord. He could as easily have played the normal version of that higher G chord, GBD at Left 8-9-10 Push, but as mentioned in step 5, he often preferred inverted chords. Then the second measure starts with a pair of full C chords (Left 3-4-5 Push) that are again fashioned by just adding another button up to the usual partial chord Left 4-5 Push. In the first beat of the third measure, as well as the second beat of the fourth measure, he substitutes another inversion (FA, or Left7-8 Pull) to what would otherwise be played as DF (Left 3-7 Pull) in the Basic Template version (Step 5). A few more full C and G chords round out the last two measures. All and all, the string of full chords gives a rousing effect.

Over the Hills to Glory with Kimber's accompaniment (accompanies Figure 3.22 to right)

There are a lot of modifications in the finished Kimber version (Figure 3.22) versus the basic template version (Figure 3.21), and the overall intent of the finishing touches seems clearly to provide a driving, pulsating rhythm of full chords to this schottische. Had that not been the case, perhaps the accompaniment might have resembled the basic template more closely. Other schottisches recorded by Kimber include the *Keel Row, Nae Good Luck About the Hoose,* and *Moonlight Schottische*.

A concertina lesson from Kimber: *Princess Royal*

A tune like *Getting Upstairs* is played high on the compass of the twenty-button concertina. Using as high a pitch as possible was something that Kimber clearly valued, as it cut though crowd noise and was thus favored by the dancers. There is a snippet of one of the recordings that Theo Chaundy made of Kimber in 1956 where Kimber himself relays a verbal lesson about how he approaches his playing regarding

William Kimber Playing *Over the Hills to Glory* via His Master's Voice, 1946

Figure 3.21. The A part of *Over the Hills to Glory*, Basic Template version (Steps 1–3).

Figure 3.22. The A part of Kimber's version of *Over the Hills to Glory*.

pitch.[21] It is worth reviewing, as it marks the only time when Kimber is recorded discussing how he plays. He speaks of teaching someone named David (possibly David Chaundy, Theo's son, who had learned to Morris dance at Oxford in the late 1940s) how to play a version of the Morris tune *Princess Royal* in the key of A minor:

> *As I was trying to tell David, he starts on one octave* [E at Right 2 Push, on the C row], *but he can't play it.*

Example A of Figure 3.23 shows "David's" way of playing the tune, according to Kimber. Continuing the lesson, Kimber then plays a single high E, at Right 9 Pull on the G row, an octave higher in pitch but still in the same key, saying:

Example A: How David played *Princess Royal* (accompanies Figure 3.23A to right)

> *That's where I start. That saves me a lot of <u>this</u>* [he opens and closes the bellows back and forth a few times].

Here Kimber is making the point that higher notes use less air, and that playing as high (treble) as possible allows a crisper and less air-intensive way of playing. Kimber then plays two measures of the A part as "David" would play them (Figure 3.23, part A).[1] He then says:

Example B: How Kimber played *Princess Royal* (accompanies Figure 3.23B to right)

> *But I don't start that* [low]. *I go for the easiness of the bellows, you see?*

Kimber then played the first two measures as he himself would play them (Figure 3.23, part B).

> *Quite a different method altogether, you see? . . . As I told him, I don't want so much of this* [Kimber plays the lowest C on the instrument, Left 1 Push then Left 1 Pull several times]. *I don't want that . . . I don't play like that. I don't want that* [because it is too low]. *. . . Treble. That's what the dancers want.*

He then played a full version of *Princess Royal*, a full octave higher than "David's" version (see the full score, p. 188). As Kimber mentioned, playing higher notes takes less air, so there is less bellows movement. But the real reason appears to be that the dancers like it, no doubt because it is easier to hear over crowd and street noise.

---

[1] The last note of both measures in this Example A is the note A, which should have been a continuation of the downward progression down the A minor scale, e.g., E-D-C-B-A. Instead, the A on both hands moves up an octave. The reason for this is clear to anyone who tries the music out on a two-row concertina. Had Kimber continued to go down the scale, his right hand would run out of buttons, forcing him to play both A notes on the left-hand side. It was a nearly inviolable rule for Kimber that he keeps the melody completely isolated on the right hand, forcing him to jump an octave like this every now and then. In practice it is not as noticeable to the ear as it might seem.

Figure 3.23. Kimber in his "lesson" contrasts two sets of the beginning measures of *Princess Royal*. Example A is as "David" would play it. Example B, an octave higher, is as Kimber would prefer it. Transcribed from a 1956 recording of Kimber by Theo Chaundy, available at the website of Folk Arts Oxford, www.merryville.uk.

Comparing Kimber with modern players: *Constant Billy*

Before leaving the topic of Kimber's unique techniques and style, it is appropriate to consider just how different his twenty-button keyboard approach is from that of more modern Anglo players, who nearly all use thirty-button, three-row instruments. As mentioned earlier, most modern players, who began to play long after Kimber had passed away, tend to apply full chords to the left-hand accompaniment, more or less like that of a melodeon with its oom-pah accompaniment. The use of full chords and a bass line usually needs the full three rows of the concertina, as was mentioned at the beginning of this chapter.

Consider the first four measures of the tune *Constant Billy*, as played by the well-known and masterful American player Bertram Levy, who wrote an extensive and influential tutor for the Anglo concertina in 1985 (Figure 3.24, Example A. Levy played the tune in the key of C, seemingly a simple choice. That key may have been chosen because it would seem simplest for instructional purposes. His accompaniment consists of a string of oom-pahs with full chords and an attractive "walking bass" line. Those beautiful chords and the walking bass line cause added complexity, however. In Levy's hands the melody has to leave the right hand and enter the left hand in measures 3 and 4, violating the "right-hand-melody, left-hand-

Figure 3.24. The A part of *Constant Billy*, contrasting two styles of playing it. Example A, as played by Bertram Levy in 1985 on a three-row Anglo concertina, from his *The Anglo Concertina Demystified*. Example B, as Kimber played it on a two-row concertina.

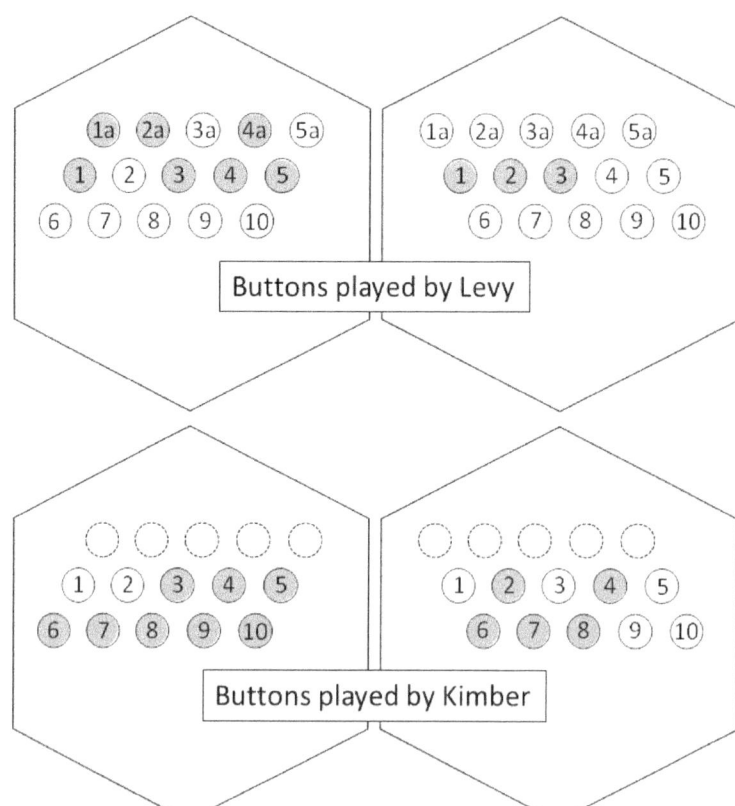

Figure 3.25. Comparison of buttons employed while playing the first four bars of *Constant Billy*, Bertram Levy and William Kimber versions.

Example A: Levy's arrangement of *Constant Billy* (accompanies Figure 3.24A to left)

Example B: Kimber's arrangement of *Constant Billy* (accompanies Figure 3.24B to left)

William Kimber Playing *Constant Billy* via His Master's Voice, 1948

accompaniment" dictum that Kimber almost never broke (the missing melody notes on the right hand of Levy's arrangement are visible as rests on the right-hand staff in measures 3 and 4). Kimber's version (Figure 3.24, Example B) is in the key of G, which, when played in the octave manner, allows the entire melody to fit on the right hand. As discussed earlier, he also preferred a more treble (higher) pitch so that the tune could be better heard by dancers. Moreover, where Levy makes extensive use of the top row of notes on a thirty-button concertina, Kimber's playing only requires the notes of the bottom two rows, as shown in the keyboard diagram comparison of Figure 3.25.

Making this pleasing progression of oom-pah chords with its bass line is an important goal in Levy's accompaniment and was a hallmark of his playing at the time of release of his tutor. It is a hallmark as well of many accomplished Anglo players of the last half century, many of whom were heavily influenced by melodeon players. To get that walking bass line and its accompanying full chords to fit, the note A in measure 3 not only drops off the right hand (normally it would be played as Left 5 Pull) but is played instead on the *push*, on the third row (Left 4a Push). This change enables an A minor chord to be inserted. The overall effect of the melody and oom-pah accompaniment is pleasing to the ear, but it comes at a cost. Moving that melody note to the left hand in order to accommodate a chord means changing the "normal" in-out flow of notes on the right hand as well as an extra need to remember to use a button on the third (top) row. This makes demands on muscle memory that exceed those of Kimber's simpler, two-row-only, melody-on-right-hand-only approach. Kimber's accompaniment follows the lower octave notes on the left hand in a simple, largely intuitive way, much like it did in the accompaniment of *Bacca Pipes*, discussed earlier. He did toss in two oom-pah pairs in the third measure, but only to break up a long string of partial chords. It is also worth noting that Levy's bass notes are played at a leisurely full quarter note (crotchet) length, whereas Kimber's accompaniment notes are typically much shorter in duration.

Which version is more pleasing to the ear depends entirely on the listener, though most modern players choose to play in the melodeon-like highly chorded manner of Levy. But one senses that pleasing a listener was not Kimber's immediate goal; keeping the dancers moving in time was. The accompaniment of a string of oom-pahs employed by Levy gives the tune a somewhat vertical, up-down feel (as if DOWN-up-DOWN-up-DOWN-up-DOWN), whereas Kimber's accompaniment made by his partial chords imparts a strongly lateral "moving" rhythm (as if ta-DUM-ta-DUM-ta-DUM-ta-DUM). In the Headington Quarry version of the Morris dance, the dancers are in constant motion throughout the A part, and Kimber's rhythm fits that motion perfectly. In the B part, the dancers stand still as they rap their sticks together. It is there that Kimber employs an uncharacteristic string of oom-pahs (see *Constant Billy* in the transcriptions, p. 133). The oom-pah rhythm nicely fits the part of the tune in which the dancers are standing in place.

The precise accompaniment rhythm of a piece is a *choice* made by the musician, not something that is completely inherent to the melody line or the dance style. Kimber was a master of rhythm when playing for the dancers, something that came from his long experience with both dancing and playing for the Morris. He was known to keep a close eye on his dancers when playing, anticipating their needs. His rhythm choices were unerringly in synch with the needs of the dance.

Summary

The exercises in this chapter are an attempt to lay out a basic template of techniques that Kimber used in fashioning left-hand accompaniment, including both rhythm and partial chords. As we have seen, about 70 to 80% of his style is due to relatively simple mechanical techniques that fit the confines of the twenty-button concertina—the "basic template"—and the remainder, where his real artistry lay, includes application of many other optional "finishing touches", techniques that further shaped his rhythmic and harmonic accompaniment, either to impart a bit of rhythmic spark or to obtain a particular feel for the harmony. In the rest of this volume, transcriptions are presented of all his recorded tunes, demonstrating his accompaniment style in detail.

It has been widely reported that Kimber once told Kenneth Loveless, then his pupil, that his father William Kimber senior had once instructed him: "These are the notes that you play, and you don't play any others."[22] That dictum applies fairly well to the right-hand melody line of his tunes. He typically did not vary the melody much if at all during several repeated playings of a tune during a single recording, nor in repeated recordings of a tune over time. However, his father's admonishment clearly does not refer to the left-hand accompaniment. Kimber widely employed subtle changes to his accompaniments, even in repeated renderings of a tune in one playing. If we consider the basic template discussed here as his accompaniment framework technique, then he would insert various finishing touches, or not, at will during the repetitions of the piece. In particular, he would often drop in an oom-pah chord when needed to break up the monotony of long strings of partial chords; insert chord inversions to spice up the sound; add in full chords where required for extra oomph; and pop in simple octave runs to replace partial chords whenever the spirit suited him. These many small and subtle changes are not well captured in the transcriptions of this volume, because for most of the transcriptions only one playing of each tune is transcribed. But once the basic tune is mastered, the subtle variations in accompaniment can be readily heard on his recordings and replicated by anyone studying his style.

Kimber was a unique musician, and one senses that we shall not see his like again. With his "unlettered" background he was able to apply rather mechanical partial chords that although natural on the two-row instrument would not necessarily occur to or be preferred by many other musicians today. The effect, as mentioned earlier in this chapter, might be said to have a certain quaintness, or to sound of a different era. However quaint and ancient sounding, it is hoped that the preceding pages show that his techniques are quite accessible and easily learned. There is much to ponder in Kimber's playing, and we hope this tutorial helps any Anglo concertina player use those techniques to expand beyond Kimber's recorded repertoire.

[1] Roger Digby, 2000, "A Review of *Absolutely Classic: The Music of William Kimber*," December 2000, concertina.net.

[2] Simon Pipe, 2014, "Morris Dancing Luminati—Out in Force." Adapted from an article published in *Morris Matters* magazine, July 1999.

[3] Andy Turner, 2021, "Double Lead Through," a post on his blog, *Squeezed Out*, at www.squeezedout.wordpress.com.

[4] Dave Townsend and Andy Turner, 1999, "Stylistic Characteristics of William Kimber's Anglo-Concertina Playing," in the booklet of the CD *Absolutely Classic: The Music of William Kimber*. EFDSS CD03, London, p. 56.

[5] Anonymous, "The Music of a Village," *The Musical World* (London), April 4, 1885, pp. 221-22.

[6] Frank Kidson and Mary Neal, 1915, *English Folk-song and Dance,* Cambridge: Cambridge University Press, p. 132.

[7] Roger Digby, personal communication, May 30, 2023.

[8] John Kirkpatrick, 1973, "How to Play the Anglo, Part 3," *Concertina Newsletter*, no. 13 (July). Reprinted in Gary Coover, 2021, *The Anglo Concertina Music of John Kirkpatrick,* Honolulu: Rollston Press.

[9] Roger Digby, personal communication, May 30, 2023.

[10] For a more detailed discussion of such muscle memory, with examples, in the piece *Lumps of Plum Pudding* as played by the brilliant player John Watcham, see Dan Worrall, 2021, "Review of The Anglo Concertina Music of John Watcham," Review Section, *The Concertina Journal*, https://www.concertinajournal.org/reviews/.

[11] Keith Chandler, 1993, *Ribbons, Bells, and Squeaky Fiddles: The Social History of Morris Dancing in the English South Midlands, 1660-1900*, Hisarlik Press, Enfield Lock, Middlesex UK, p. 180.

[12] Dan Worrall, 2011 and 2022, *House Dance: Dance Music Played on the Anglo-German Concertina by Musicians of the House Dance Era,* Honolulu: Rollston Press, 291 pp.

[13] *Ibid.*

[14] Dooley Chapman, 2005, *Your Good Self* (CD), Chris Sullivan's Australian Folk Masters, CS-AFM-001.

[15] Keith Chandler, 1993, p. 174.

[16] Stephen Rowley's "Morris Music, a History," on YouTube via the Morris Federation, discusses the link between Kimber's concertina playing for Morris dance and its pipe and tabor predecessors: https://www.youtube.com/watch?v=j-YjGVFe0Vo.

[17] Keith Chandler, 1993, p. 174.

[18] Townsend and Turner, *ibid.*

[19] Frank Kidson, 1907, contribution on John Playford to J. A. Fuller Maitland, 1907, *Grove's Dictionary of Music and Musicians*, vol. 3, as quoted online at https://www.mustrad.org.uk/articles/kid_txt2.htm.

[20] See online discussion of 2010 at http://mudcat.org/thread.cfm?threadid=37741Such a Getting Upstairs.

[21] The Chaundy tapes are all available online on the site www.merryville.uk as part of the "Back to the Quarry" project of Folk Arts Oxford.

[22] Kenneth Loveless, 1974, sleeve notes for the LP The *Art of William Kimber*, Topic Records 12T249.

William Kimber, ca. 1925. Courtesy of the Vaughan Williams Memorial Library.

A Note on the Transcriptions of Chapters 4-8

Chapters 4-8 contain transcriptions of all of Kimber's recorded tunes, including both Morris and social dance music. Beginning in 1935 and extending into 1948, Kimber made a series of audio recordings of most of the tunes transcribed here. These audio recordings all include both melody and accompaniment, as do the transcriptions made from them. A few tunes are taken directly from Sharp's early handwritten notation, in those cases where there are no audio recordings of Kimber playing them. Sharp notated the melodies of many of Kimber's tunes while studying the dance steps. When Sharp notated these tunes, Kimber seems to have played just the right-hand parts, which would produce the melody notes without the chordal accompaniment. Hence, those particular tunes are transcribed below as melody only.

The transcriptions are made for the Anglo concertina. They are displayed with two stacked treble staffs, the upper one for the right hand (the melody) and the lower one for the left hand (the accompaniment). Numbers displayed above each staff refer to the buttons of the instrument and are numbered as per the fingering diagram shown in Figure 3.3, Chapter 3. Button numbers accompanied by a bar indicate that they are played on the draw of the bellows, and those without bars are played on the push.

Each of the transcriptions records a single time that the tune was played by Kimber in an audio recording. In most cases the first time that Kimber played through the tune was used for the transcription, neglecting the extra "first to yourself" playing of the A part that was usually present. This extra playing of the A part was used at the tune's beginning to get the dancers ready to perform.

These transcriptions were produced over the period 1994 to 2024 using various technologies. The first were made by slowing cassette tape recordings to half speed, which produced a slowed recording that is an octave lower in pitch – a difficult way to transcribe tunes, to be sure. In more recent decades the advent of digital technology allowed slowed digital recordings in original pitch; we used Roni Music's "Amazing Slow-Downer" software but there are other programs that work as well. The handwritten transcripts were transferred to digital scores using MakeMusic's "Finale" software. Midi files – digital audio representations of the scores – were produced from the digital scores and were used in checking for transcription accuracy. They are also useful for providing a quick audio representation of melodies, so they were translated into mp3 audio files and are included via QR codes that are placed alongside the description of each transcription, in chapters 4 through 8. QR codes linking to original recordings of Kimber are included where available and out of copyright. For obvious reasons, the recordings of Kimber are always to be preferred for learning purposes, but the learner may find the digital audio representations of the transcriptions useful for getting the 'gist' of a melody and accompaniment where the actual recording of Kimber is not available. Adjustment of the tempo of all recordings may be readily done using slow-down software.

Laudanum Bunches, digital audio of the transcription

William Kimber playing *Laudanum Bunches* via His Master's Voice, 1948

[1] Theo W. Chaundy, 1959, "William Kimber: a Portrait," *Journal of the EFDSS*, vol. 8, no. 4, p. 209.

William Kimber's Morris cap, from ca. 1912. Presented by the Headington Quarry Morris Dancers in 2023 to their current musician, Andy Turner. Photo courtesy of Andy Turner.

Figure 4.1. William Kimber taking a break during a Morris street dance, ca. 1950s. Image courtesy of the Vahan Williams Memorial Library.

Chapter 4. The Headington Morris Dance Tunes

Cecil Sharp recorded the tunes and dance steps of twenty-one Headington Morris dances from William Kimber and published most of them over the period 1907–1911 in his *Morris Book*, volumes 1 (eight dances) and 2 (eleven dances); an additional two tunes were notated by Sharp but were not included in the Morris books. In the first part of this chapter, each of these tunes is described and categorized, and the second part contains detailed transcriptions of all 21 tunes. In Chapter 5, other mostly non-Headington Morris dances recorded by Kimber are discussed. The recordings used for transcribing most of the Headington dances are found in the 1975 Topic LP of Kimber's earlier audio recordings, entitled *The Art of William Kimber*, but most of these same recordings were also included in the 1996 EFDSS CD, *Absolutely Classic: The Music of William Kimber*. Transcriptions included in chapters 5-8 come both from those two CDs but also from a number of other sources, listed in the Discography at the back of the book. All the sound files of Kimber's playing included as QR codes below are from *The Art of William Kimber* via a Topic Records YouTube site.

Headington Morris dance types

The twenty-one tunes included in this chapter were used for five types of Morris dances, as noted by Sharp in his *Morris Book*, volumes 1 and 2. Many of these dances are illustrated in various online videos made of the modern Headington Quarry Morris Dancers, to which the reader is referred.

Stick dances in the Headington tradition utilize painter sticks of about 17 inches in length carried in the right hand or both hands. Sharp noted five of them: *Bean Setting, Constant Billy, Hunting the Squirrel, Rigs o' Marlow*, and *Rodney*.

Handkerchief dances utilize two white handkerchiefs carried by each dancer, originally almost long enough to reach the ground when dancers' arms were hanging down by their sides. The handkerchiefs are waved, tracing patterns in the air. Sharp noted seven of these dances: *Blue-Eyed Stranger, Country Gardens, Double Set Back, Getting Upstairs, Haste to the Wedding, The Twenty-Ninth of May*, and *The Willow Tree*.

In **corner dances**, the opposite corners of the side of six men dance sequentially in pairs. Sharp noted three at Headington: *How D'ye Do, Sir?, Laudnum Bunches*, and *Trunkles*.

Morris jigs are solo dances that showcase the skills of the individual dancer. They can be in "jig time" (6/8) but are as likely to be in 4/4 time. Sharp noted five of these: *Bacca Pipes, Jockie to the Fair, Old Mother Oxford, Old Woman Tossed Up in a Blanket*, and *Shepherd's Hey*.

Step dances are typically hornpipes or reels danced in pubs but sometimes are part of Morris street events. Typically, these reels involve three, four or six men. One that was noted by Sharp in his *Morris Book* is the *Headington Morris Reel*, danced to the old tune *Soldier's Joy*. This and other step dances played by Kimber are noted in chapter 8 of the present work.

Figure 4.2. Headington Quarry Morris men at practice, ca.1898–1899. Courtesy of Vaughan Williams Memorial Library and the Morris Ring Photographic Archives.

Tune sources and explanation

The first melodies transcribed by Sharp at Sandfield Cottage on the day after Boxing Day in 1899, according to Sharp, include: *Laudnum Bunches, Bean Setting, Constant Billy, Blue-Eyed Stranger*, and *Rigs o' Marlow*.[1] He recorded three others in 1905–1906 to round out the selection for his *Morris Book*, volume 1: *Country Gardens, Trunkles*, and *How D'ye Do, Sir?* At this early stage in Sharp's study of the Morris, he and Mary Neal both considered the dance as representing the survival of some "primitive religious ceremonial."[2] Sharp researched the Headington tunes in the first volume of his *Morris Book*, however, and found that most were either eighteenth-century country dance tunes or old song airs, with the exception of *Shepherd's Hey*, *Trunkles* and *Bean Setting*, for which he could find no antecedent sources.

Since that time, similarly recent sources have been found for twenty of the twenty-one Headington dance tunes notated by Sharp from Kimber's playing. Only *Bean Setting* has defied research into its pre-Headington origins. Four represent old song tunes, fifteen are country dances, and one is an American minstrel song. Thus, if the Headington *dances* are indeed ancient—not a given assumption among modern scholars—then the tunes for the most part are not. Most reach back into the late eighteenth century, with a few reaching slightly earlier into the late seventeenth century, and one is of mid-nineteenth century origin. For comparison, it would be as if a modern popular dance competition displayed on television in the year 2024 used tunes from late nineteenth-century ballroom dance as well as early twentieth-century ragtime and the early jazz era: out of living memory, but not so long ago. Although Sharp thought that *Bean Setting* might be a relic primeval dance, its company among a group of mostly eighteenth-century dance tunes—as well as its fairly typical walking pace, like that of many country dances—suggest otherwise.

William Kimber playing *Bacca Pipes* via His Master's Voice, 1948

Bacca Pipes: Digital audio of the transcription

Bacca Pipes (Morris jig; p. 128). The *Bacca Pipes* jig is a version of *Greensleeves*, which had its origin in a London broadside ballad of 1580 by the name of *A Newe Northen Dittye of ye Ladye Greene Sleves*. Shakespeare knew the tune, as it is mentioned in *Falstaff* and *Mistress Ford*. It appears in the seventh edition of *Playford's Dancing Master* (1686) as *Greensleeves and Pudding Pies*, and in Walsh's *Compleat Country Dancing Master* (1718) under the same title.[3] The tune was popular as a London military slow march in the sixteenth and seventeenth centuries and has been much adopted for various purposes in the nineteenth and twentieth.

Kimber's melody and chord choices for Bacca Pipes are discussed at length above, in Chapter 3. The Headington title referred to the dance steps rather than the tune; it was danced over a crossed pair of churchwarden pipes (Figure 4.3). Kimber had a special recollection of dancing this jig:

> *The best that I can remember as I enjoyed most was when we danced before King Edward and Queen Alexandra and the rest of the royal family at Chelsea Polytechnic Hospital. It was a grand day and it turned out a success with me and the students from the Polytechnic. It was a good affair; it turned out lovely.*
>
> *But after it was over, we went to the Marquee. I sit with Mr. Sharp and two more ladies, and on my right was the King and Queen Alexandria. After we'd had tea King Edward turned to me. He said, "I've no doubt, Kimber. . . ," he said, "that I've seen your father dance at Oxford when I was at Christ Church." I said, "I know you have, your Well then after that, Mr. Sharp gave a lecture at the Mansion House . . . and there was a most brilliant sight, I can tell you. I remember dancing Jockey to the Fair and the Shepherd's Hey and the Bacca Pipes, and the applause over them Bacca Pipes I don't think I shall ever forget.*
>
> *There was two gentlemen there who badly wanted these pipes for souvenirs. I said, "Well, the pipes don't belong to me. There's Mr. Sharp, if he says you can have them, you can have them. I've done with them, I've danced over them, that's all I can do." But anyway, they bid one against another for these two clay pipes till they got to a pound each. One had one, and the other had the other, and they gave the two sovereigns to Mr.*

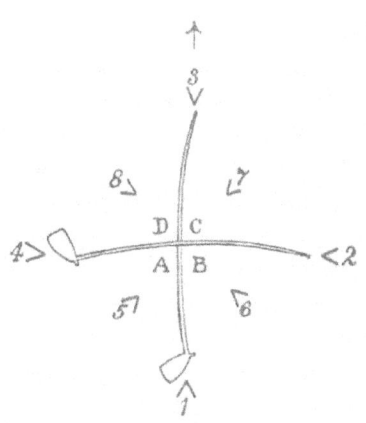

Figure 4.3. Crossed churchwarden pipes and the steps for the Bacca Pipes jig. From Cecil Sharp's *Morris Book*, volume 1.

Sharp. But after it was over Mr. Sharp said to me, "Well Kimber, I never danced the pipes. You danced the pipes; this money must be yours. So, I had the two sovereigns. I give me mate one as has danced with me, and I had the other meself. So that was the end of that one! [4]

Bean Setting (stick dance; p. 130) was transcribed from a 1946 studio recording by Kimber and was included as a Headington dance in Sharp's *Morris Book,* volume 1. It is traced back only to the Headington Quarry version that Sharp took from Kimber's playing, published as a pianoforte piece in Sharp and Macilwaine's *Morris Dance Tunes* (1909–1913), and from Clive Carey's version taken from Joseph Trafford, the latter published in Mary Neal's *Esperance Morris Book*, volume 2, in 1912. The dance appeared at the Corn Exchange performance organized by Percy Manning in 1899.

William Kimber playing *Bean Setting* via His Master's Voice, 1946

The third and fourth measures of the B part nicely illustrate the 'Z' pattern in fingering of both hands as the scale is ascended, with a transition from fingering placement on the middle (C) row to the lower (G) row (see discussion of Figure 3.6 in Chapter 3). It also shows Kimber's use of an inverted F partial chord in the first and last notes of the fourth measure; this favored sound is frequent in much of his playing. Note the use of an added octave note on the right hand when playing the note C on the right hand (e.g., the last measures of both the A and B parts). Kimber sometimes did this for special emphasis at the beginning or end of a phrase.

Bean Setting: Digital audio of the transcription

Figure 4.4. Headington Quarry Morris men, October 9, 1916. Courtesy of the Headington Quarry Morris Dancers.

William Kimber playing *Blue-Eyed Stranger* via His Master's Voice, 1946

Blue-Eyed Stranger: Digital audio of the transcription

Blue-Eyed Stranger (handkerchief dance, p. 132) was transcribed from a 1946 studio recording by Kimber and was included as a Headington dance in Sharp's *Morris Book,* volume 1. The tune is a variant of the Scottish song *The Mill, Mill, O* in *Orpheus Caledonius* (or, *A Collection of the Best Scottish Songs*) of 1725, according to Sharp, who transcribed a version of it in 1909 from a Hereford gypsy fiddler named John Locke. It was called *The Peacock* in Smollett Holden's *Collection of Irish Airs* (Dublin, 1806).

Like most of Kimber's tunes, it is in the key of C, and in the A part the melody dips briefly into the left hand. The tune starts with a bit of a squawk, made with a B grace note that slides into and slightly overlaps the high C that forms the first beat, making for a slight dissonance. Kimber sprinkles such effects into several of his pieces, adding spice for the listener. In the accompaniment, he uses an oom-pah pair or two, but then returns to his more usual partial chords.

William Kimber playing *Constant Billy* via His Master's Voice, 1948

Constant Billy: Digital audio of the transcription

Constant Billy (stick dance, p. 133) was transcribed from a field recording of Kimber in 1956, made by Theo Chaundy at Chaundy's home in Oxford; its dance steps were published in Sharp's *Morris Book,* volume 1. It is a version of a country dance tune of the same name in *Playford's Dancing Master Volume 3* of 1726, according to Sharp. An even earlier version is in *Walsh's Compleat Country Dancing Master* of 1718. Its origin was apparently as an early eighteenth-century Scottish song, *How Shall We Abstain from Drinking*, included in the eighteenth-century *Airs and Melodies of the Highlands of Scotland*. A version with Welsh words was published by Edward Jones in his *Bardic Museum* of 1802 and republished by John Parry in 1833 as *The Ashgrove*.[5] In Sharp's time it was in use with several south Midlands Morris sides, including Bampton, where Percy Manning recorded the tune with the following lyrics:

Oh, my Billy, my constant Billy!
When shall I see my Billy again?
When the fishes flies over the mountains
Then you'll see your Billy again.[6]

Country Gardens (handkerchief dance; p. 134) was transcribed from a 1948 studio recording of Kimber and was included as a Headington dance in Sharp's *Morris Book,* volume 1. The tune was included in Thomas Walker's *Quaker's Opera* in 1728 as *Country Garden*, and was used in 1740 as the tune for the song *The Vicar of Bray* as well as for a number of songs of political satire of that era.[7] However venerable, the tune must have sounded quite fresh to Percy Grainger, who took the tune from Sharp's notes and arranged it for the piano and orchestra. When asked his opinion of Grainger's new work, Kimber commented: "He didn't add anything. He murdered it. You couldn't dance to it!"[8] Sharp collected these lyrics from Kimber:

William Kimber playing *Country Gardens* via His Master's Voice, 1948

> *Old woman, if you please,*
> *Will you come along with me*
> *Into my fine country gardens?*

In the transcription of this tune we have written out all the repeats of the various parts (excepting the extra A part added as a "once to yourself" for the dancers to ready themselves) to give the reader a taste of the subtle variations made by Kimber in playing the entire piece. The changes from the first to the repeated version of the A, B, and C parts are minor; an inserted oom-pah here, an extra chord note there. But even such subtle changes can help make the listening more pleasant.

Country Gardens: Digital audio of the transcription

Double Set Back (handkerchief dance; p. 138) was transcribed from a 1946 studio recording by Kimber and was included as a Headington dance in Sharp's *Morris Book,* volume 2. The tune appears to be a version of the hornpipe *Morning Star*, which appeared in several nineteenth-century Scottish and English musicians' manuscripts.[9] This tune provides a good example of his typical accompaniment method, consisting almost entirely of partial chords on the left hand.

William Kimber playing *Double Set Back* via His Master's Voice, 1946

Double Set Back: Digital audio of the transcription

William Kimber playing *Getting Upstairs* via His Master's Voice, 1946

Getting Upstairs: Digital audio of the transcription

Getting Upstairs (handkerchief dance; p. 140) was transcribed from a studio recording of 1935, and its corresponding dance was included in Sharp's *Morris Book,* volume 2. It originated with early American minstrel performer and collector T. D. "Daddy" Rice, who may in turn have obtained the tune from an enslaved person in the southern USA.[10] The *London Times* reported in its edition of February 2, 1839: "By late London papers before us, we perceive that Rice has found out a new way to please John Bull. The popularity of 'Jim Crow' [the song and dance *Jump Jim Crow*] seems to be eclipsed by 'the new fancy song' of 'Sich a gittin up stairs.'" Nineteenth-century lyrics were collected by the Bluegrass Messengers, who use the tune in a current bluegrass setting:

> *On a Suskyhanner raft I come down de bay,*
> *And I danc'd, and I frolick'd, and fiddled all de way.*
> *Sich a gitting up stairs and a playing on the fiddle*
> *Sich a gitting up stairs I never did see*
>
> *Trike he to and heel—cut de pigeon wing,*
> *Scratch gravel, slap de foot—dats just de ting.*
> *Sich a gitting up stairs, &c.*

The song is also an American children's song and was collected by Cecil Sharp in Appalachia. The typical modern lyrics were included on the Ashley Hutchings Topic LP *Son of Morris On*:

> *Some likes coffee, some likes tea*
> *Some likes a pretty girl, just like me*
> *Such a getting upstairs and a playing on the fiddle*
> *Such a getting upstairs I never did see.*

Headington Morris dancer Joseph Trafford claimed to Clive Carey that another minstrel tune, *Buffalo Gals*, was once a part of the Headington Quarry dance repertoire, and he provided the commonly known melody of it to Carey.[11] Sharp notated neither the tune nor the dance. It may have been that that minstrel tune, written about brothel women in Buffalo, New York, was a bridge too far for Sharp.

Haste to the Wedding (handkerchief dance; p. 142) was transcribed from a 1946 studio recording by Kimber and was included as a Headington dance in Sharp's *Morris Book,* volume 2. The tune appeared in the pantomime *The Elopement* in 1767, and a version was included in Thompson's *Compleat Collection of 200 Favourite Country Dances*, published in London in 1783.[12] By 1840 it was used during the wedding of Queen Victoria and Prince Albert, and became popular across England as well as rural Ireland, where it was often played at wedding dances in the late nineteenth century. [13]

William Kimber playing *Haste to the Wedding* via His Master's Voice, 1946

Kimber's playing includes three types of triplets: undotted, dotted, and reverse dotted. As most are dotted, the other two types serve to spice up the rhythm. The transcription here is written out to include repeats (AABB), so that one may examine the very subtle changes between the two playings of each part. All these variations are on the left hand; the melody typically never changes in his playing.

Haste to the Wedding: Digital audio of the transcription

Headington Morris Reel (step dance) was transcribed from a 1948 studio recording by Kimber and was included as a Headington dance in Sharp's *Morris Book,* volume 2. This step dance was danced to the tune *Soldier's Joy.* That tune is discussed, and its transcription is included in Chapter 8, p. 292).

Figure 4.5. Left to right: Harry Kimber, Bob Turrell, Arthur Kimber, and Kenneth Loveless. Courtesy of the Morris Ring Photographic Archives.

How D'Ye Do, Sir?: Digital audio of the transcription

How D'ye Do, Sir? (corner dance; p. 145). We have no audio recording of Kimber playing this tune, but Sharp's pianoforte version of the tune (Sharp and Macilwaine's *Morris Dance Tunes* (1909–1913) and his dance instructions in the *Morris Book*, volume 1, originated with Kimber. For that reason, only the melody line is shown in the transcription here. Clive Carey also transcribed a version taken from Joseph Trafford, the latter published in Mary Neal's *Espérance Morris Book*, volume 2, in 1912.

Sharp thought this tune to be a version of the country dance *Blowzabella, My Bouncing Doxie*, which appeared in d'Urfey's *Pills to Purge Melancholy*, in 1719,[14] and as a tune for flute called *Blousy Bella* in a 1708 manuscript by Buononcini in the British Museum. The tune was picked up in a number of country dance tune books in the late eighteenth century, including Wright's *Compleat Collection of Celebrated Country Dances* of 1740.[15]

Sharp notated the tune from Kimber at the Espérance Club on May 25, 1906, but in the key of F, which almost certainly was not how it was played by Kimber. Most likely, Kimber whistled or sang the tune to Sharp, so the key was somehow transposed in transmission. Of the two keys Kimber commonly used on his concertina (G and C), the key of C best fits the compass of the tune, so that is how it is presented here. The first three notes of the tune (C, G, A) could all be played on the C row (in order, right hand Push 4, Push 3, and Pull 4), but Kimber's usual chording and his typical playing of the C scale in a Z pattern (see Chapter 3) would indicate that he would play these entry notes on the G row, as shown in the transcription (in order, right hand Pull 8, Push 6, and Pull 7).

Although there is no recording of Kimber's full playing of the piece, perhaps the most likely accompaniment – as befitting the "basic template" methodology of Chapter 3 – would have started with a left hand Pull 10+9 on the first note, a rest during the second melody note, and a Pull 9+8 on the third note. A workable accompaniment would be to use the basic template for both A and B parts in this simple tune (using left hand partial chords on the first and third beats). Adding a bass note or an octave run every now and then, as per the "finishing touches" list, would nicely add some variety and interest to the accompaniment, and adding a full C chord at the end is a given.

William Kimber playing *Hunting the Squirrel* via His Master's Voice, 1946

Hunting the Squirrel: Digital audio of the transcription

Hunting the Squirrel (stick dance; also known as *Hunt the Squirrel*; p. 146) was transcribed from a 1946 studio recording by Kimber and was included as a Headington dance in Sharp's *Morris Book*, volume 2. The tune dates back to a version published in the *Playford Dancing Master*, fourteenth edition of 1709. Clive Carey transcribed the same tune and dance from Joseph Trafford, with the title *Drawback*,[16] but *Hunt the Squirrel* appears to be the older name and is the name used by Kimber. It is a very simple and engaging tune.

Jockie to the Fair (Morris jig; p. 148) was transcribed from a 1948 studio recording by Kimber and was included as a Headington dance in Sharp's *Morris Book,* volume 2. The tune appears in Skillern's *Twenty-Four Country Dances for the Year 1780*, and it was widely popular in England, Scotland and Ireland. Thomas Hardy mentioned the tune several times in his 1874 novel *Far from the Madding Crowd*.[17]

There are three parts. The slowed down capers of the C part allow a grand belting out of full chords; note how Kimber artfully places some octave notes in among them for a break in the pattern. The transcriptions approximate this grand tempo by slowing the tempo to half speed, but in practice the timing is adjusted to the speed of the leaping dancers. After the slow capers, Kimber inserts an incomplete measure (3/8) and the pace then increases markedly.

William Kimber playing *Jockie to the Fair* via His Master's Voice, 1948

Jockie to the Fair: Digital audio of the transcription

Laudnum Bunches (corner dance; p. 152) was transcribed was transcribed both from a studio recording of 1948 and from a field recording of June 10, 1957 recorded by Theo Chaundy. The latter was made with the Headington Morris side dancing outside the Mason's Arms pub in Headington Quarry, when Kimber was 85. The tune is a version of *Balance a Straw*, which was included in Rutherford's *Compleat Collection of 200 Country Dances* of 1760.[18]

The tune's dance steps were published in Sharp's *Morris Book* volume 1. As Kimber played it in 1948, it has an unusual makeup of parts played, after a 'once to yourself' of the A part, AABBBAABBBAACCCAACCC. The Headington Quarry side dances with 'bunched' handkerchiefs, held in the hand at all four corners. The title may have suggested 'bunches' of poppies, from which laudanum was derived. The tune's unusual rhythm moves alternately uses normal dotted triplets (with the first note dotted) and inverted dotted triplets (where the second note is dotted, and the first note shortened). The full chords used during the C part are particularly fine and enjoyable to play.

William Kimber playing *Laudanum Bunches* via His Master's Voice, 1948

Laudanum Bunches: Digital audio of the transcription

William Kimber playing *Old Mother Oxford* via His Master's Voice, 1948

Old Mother Oxford (Morris jig; p. 154) was transcribed from a 1948 studio recording by Kimber and was included as a Headington dance in Sharp's *Morris Book,* volume 2. It appears to be a version of a Sheffield song titled *The Jovial Cutlers*, thought to date back to 1780 or 1790. It is often known as *Old Mrs. Wilson*.[19] Kimber did not play many grace notes, but included an unusually high number of them in this piece, shown in the transcription as thirty-second notes tied to double dotted sixteenths.

Old Mother Oxford: Digital audio of the transcription

Old Woman Tossed Up in a Blanket: Digital audio of the transcription

Old Woman Tossed Up in a Blanket (Morris jig; p. 158) was transcribed from a field recording of 1956, by Peter Kennedy at Kimber's home in Headington; its dance steps were published in Sharp's *Morris Book*, volume 2. It is a version of the 1688 song of rebellion, *Lillibulero*, and it appears in Henry Playford's *Musick's Hand-maid* of 1689. Its tune is possibly of earlier Irish origin. It appears in R. M. Levey's *First Collection of the Dance Music of Ireland* (1858).[20] The three-part tune is interesting for its rhythmic variations between dotted and normal triplets. William Kimber's lyrics are:

> *Oh, there was an old woman tossed up in a blanket*
> *Ninety-nine miles beyond the moon,*
> *It's under one arm she carries a basket,*
> *Under the t'other she carries a broom.*
> *Old woman, old woman, old woman cried I,*
> *Oh wither, oh wither, oh wither so high,*
> *I'm going to sweep cobwebs beyond the skies,*
> *And I shall be back with you by and by.*

Rigs o' Marlow (stick dance; p. 160) was transcribed from a 1946 studio recording of Kimber and was included as a Headington dance in Sharp's *Morris Book,* volume 2. Sharp pointed out in his *Morris Book* that *Rigs o' Marlow* was a version of the ancient Irish *Rakes of Mallow*, found in collections of Irish airs dating back as far as 1720. It appeared in John Johnson's *Choice Collection of 200 Favourite Country Dances*, vol. V (1751). Johnson's *Compleat Tutor of Guitar* (ca. 1725) called it *The Rakes of Marlow*, apparently for the village of Marlow, Buckinghamshire; the original tune refers to the Irish village of Mallow, near Cork.[21] The Headington side sang:

William Kimber playing *Rigs O'Marlow* via His Master's Voice, 1946

> *When I go to Marlow Fair*
> *With the ribbons in my hair*
> *All the boys and girls declare*
> *Here comes the rigs of Marlow.*[22]

Kimber's playing of this tune is very upbeat and jaunty, with unusual (for Kimber) right-hand triads added for emphasis. The rhythm of the B part is subtly different from the A; the reversely dotted triplets are easily missed. It is a very enjoyable tune to play and one of the easier ones to learn.

Rigs O'Marlow Digital audio of the transcription

Rodney (stick dance; p. 161) was transcribed from a 1946 studio recording by Kimber and was included as a Headington dance in Sharp's *Morris Book,* volume 2. It is a variant of the eighteenth-century country dance tune *To Rodney We Must Go* published in Aird's *Selection of Scotch, English and Irish Airs*, volume 7, in 1788. The title refers to the British naval officer George Brydges Rodney (1718–1792), hero of the Battle of Saintes (1782).[23] Sharp thought there was a slight connection with the Irish tune *Rodney's Glory*. The tune has a light and airy feel and is one of those tunes that seem to go on effortlessly and endlessly. Nonetheless, it is a short tune and easily learned.

William Kimber playing *Rodney* via His Master's Voice, 1946

Rodney: Digital audio of the transcription

William Kimber playing *Shepherd's Hey* via His Master's Voice, 1948

Shepherd's Hey: Digital audio of the transcription

Shepherd's Hey (Morris jig; p. 163) was transcribed from a 1948 studio recording by Kimber, and the dance was included in Sharp's *Morris Book,* volume 1. Sharp recorded the lyrics at Ducklington:

> *I can whistle, I can play*
> *And I can dance The Shepherds' Hey.*

It can be found as an *Easy Air—Shepherd's Hey* in Thomas Dixon's unpublished manuscript of 1798, from Lincolnshire,[24] as well as in an anonymous early nineteenth-century manuscript in Staffordshire.[25] It was (and is) popular with various Oxfordshire Morris teams as a solo jig. Its brevity makes it an ideal choice as a first tune to learn in the Kimber style.

Figure 4.6. William Kimber playing for the Headington Quarry Morris dancers at Sandfield Cottage in 1949. Vaughan Williams Memorial Library.

William Kimber playing *Trunkles* via His Master's Voice, 1946

Trunkles: Digital audio of the transcription

Trunkles (corner dance; p. 164) was transcribed from a 1946 studio recording by Kimber, and the Headington Quarry dance was noted by Sharp in his *Morris Book,* volume 1. Michael Heaney has shown that *Trunkles* derives from the 1769 "Trincalo's Reel," composed during a Shakespeare jubilee for a production of *The Tempest.* The much-modified Morris version of the tune was and is danced to throughout the south Midlands.[26]

The Twenty-Ninth of May. The tune *The Twenty-Ninth of May* (handkerchief dance; p. 166) was transcribed from a 1946 studio recording by Kimber, and an earlier melody version was notated by Sharp from Kimber's playing at the Cumberland Market in 1907.[27] It is not included in Sharp's *Morris Book*. According to the Traditional Tune Archive, the melody and title are from the opera *The Reprisal*, first performed in London in 1757. It is found in the copybook of fiddler William Clark, 1770. The title "The Twenty-Ninth of May" came from a different tune and was named for the day Charles II came back to England, returning to the crown after the English Civil War. That name has nevertheless stuck to the Kimber version of the tune and the Headington dance.

William Kimber playing *The 29th of May* via His Master's Voice, 1946

The 29th of May: Digital audio of the transcription

The Willow Tree (handkerchief dance; p. 168). The melody and dance steps of *The Willow Tree* were notated by Sharp from Kimber in April 1908, and earlier in 1897 by Percy Manning at Bampton.[28] It was not included in Sharp's *Morris Book*. The transcription was made from a 1956 recording at Kimber's home by Peter Kennedy. The tune is accompanied by the following lyrics:

The Willow Tree: Digital audio of the transcription

> *Once they said my cheeks were red*
> *But now they are drawn and pale*
> *When I like a silly girl*
> *Believed his flattering tale.*
>
> *He said that he'd never deceive me,*
> *And I like a silly believed he,*
> *When the moon and the stars so brightly shone*
> *Over the willow tree.*

In the A part, the dancers sing in a "foot up," followed in the B part by a weeping movement where they lean halfway over and bring the handkerchiefs to their eyes in a mock gesture of weeping.

[1] Chaundy, 1959, p. 206.

[2] Cecil Sharp and Herbert C. Macilwaine, 1991 (reprint), *The Morris Book, volumes 1–5, 1911–1924*, Letchworth Garden City, Hertfordshire: The Hive Printers, p. 11.

[3] A. L. Lloyd and Rev. Kenneth Loveless, 1974, notes to accompany *The Art of William Kimber*, Topic LP 12T249.

[4] William Kimber, as recorded by Peter Kennedy in 1951, *William Kimber Talking*, an interview of William Kimber with Maud Karpeles at Kimber's home, December 4, 1951, Folktrax CD 383, track 15.

[5] *Ibid.*

[6] Percy Manning, 1897, "Some Oxfordshire Seasonal Festivals, with Notes on Morris Dancing in Oxfordshire," *Folk-Lore, Transactions of the Folk-Lore Society*, vol. 8, p. 321.

[7] Lloyd and Loveless, 1974.

[8] Chaundy, 1959, p. 209.

[9] Traditional Tune Archive entry for *Double Set Back*, www.tunearch.org.

[10] See online discussion of 2010 at http://mudcat.org/thread.cfm?threadid=37741 Such a Getting Upstairs.

[11] Clive Carey Collection, Vaughan Williams Memorial Library, www.archives.vwml.org/records/CC/1/535.

[12] Thoughts on Dance: Come Haste to the Wedding, https://www.dancehistoryalive.com/blog/2014/07/come-haste-to-the-wedding/.

[13] Chris Droney, speaking of his grandfather's time as a musician, as interviewed in 2013, in Dan M. Worrall and James J. Branch, 2023, *Chris Droney of Bell Harbour and the Tradition of the Concertina in North Clare,* Honolulu: Rollston Press, p. 99.

[14] Sharp and Macilwaine, 1907, *The Morris Book,* vol. 1.

[15] Traditional Tune Archive entry for *Blowzabella*, www.tunearch.org.

[16] Clive Carey manuscripts, Vaughan Williams Memorial Library.

[17] Traditional Tune Archive entry for *Jockey to the Fair*, www.tunearch.org.

[18] Traditional Tune Archive entry for *Balance a Straw*, www.tunearch.org.

[19] Mainly Norfolk: English Folk and Other Good Music, www.mainlynorfolk.info, entry on *The Jovial Cutler.*

[20] Traditional Tune Archive entry for *Old Woman Tossed Up in a Blanket*, www.tunearch.org.

[21] Lloyd and Loveless, 1974.

[22] Cecil Sharp and Herbert C. Macilwaine, 1991 (reprint), *The Morris Book, volumes 1–5, 1911–1924.*

[23] Traditional Tune Archive entry for *To Rodney We Must Go*, www.tunearch.org.

[24] Village Music Project, Thomas J. Dixon manuscript, www.village-music-project.org.

[25] Traditional Tune Archive entry for *Shepherd's Hey*, www.tunearch.org.

[26] Michael Heaney, 2023, *The Ancient English Morris Dance*, Oxford: Archaeopress, p. 220.

[27] Vaughan Williams Memorial Library, ref. CJS2/10/1515.

[28] Manning, 1897, p. 321. Also, *English Folk Dance and Song*, EFDSS, London, v. 8, p. 210.

"Ye Olde Headyngton Dancers," from the Oxford Review, May 16, 1899. Image courtesy of the Vaughan Williams Memorial Library, EFDSS.

Transcriptions:
The Headington Morris Dances

Bacca Pipes

HEADINGTON MORRIS JIG

Bacca Pipes

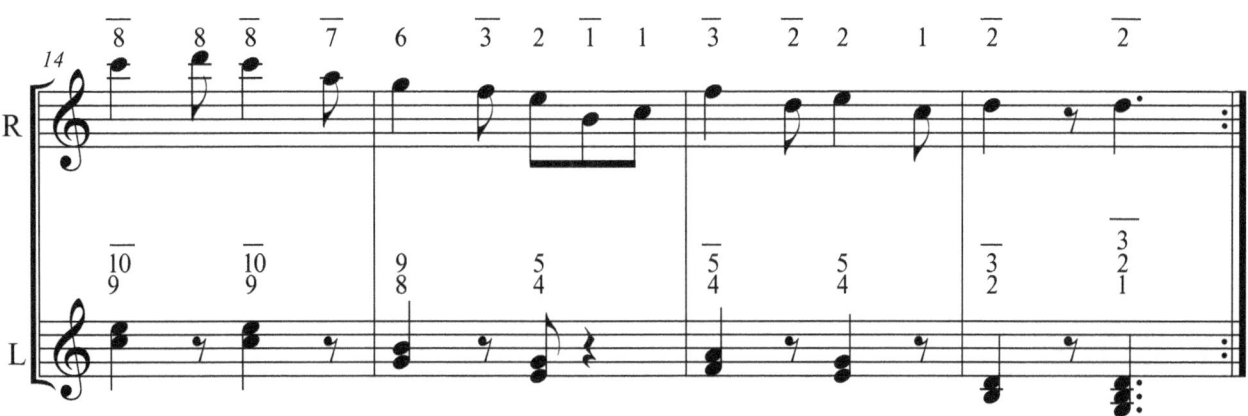

Bean Setting

HEADINGTON MORRIS STICK DANCE

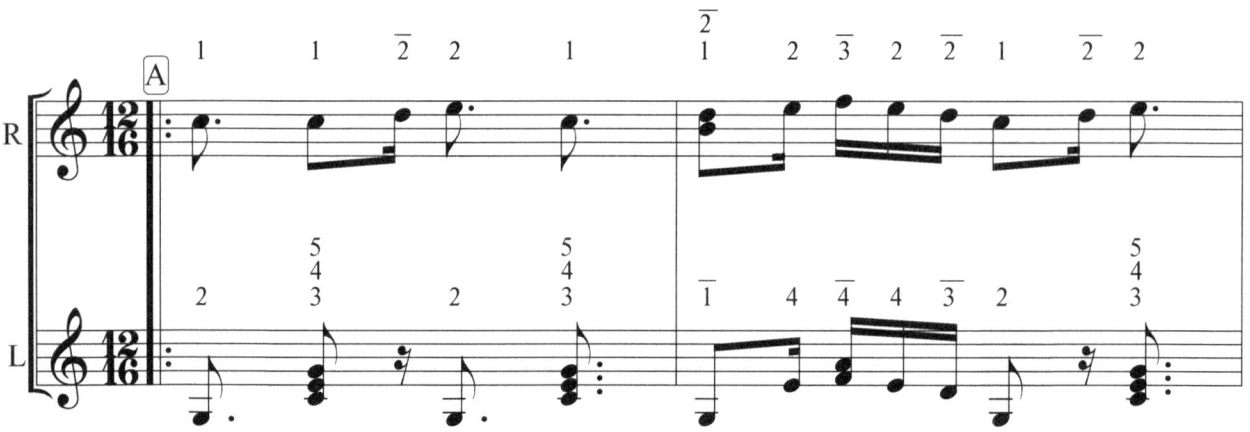
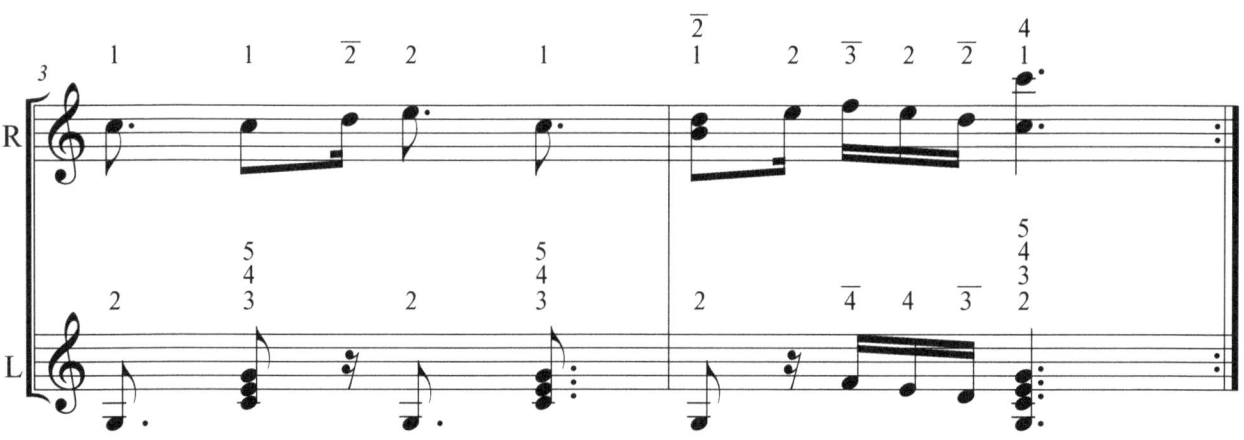

Bean Setting

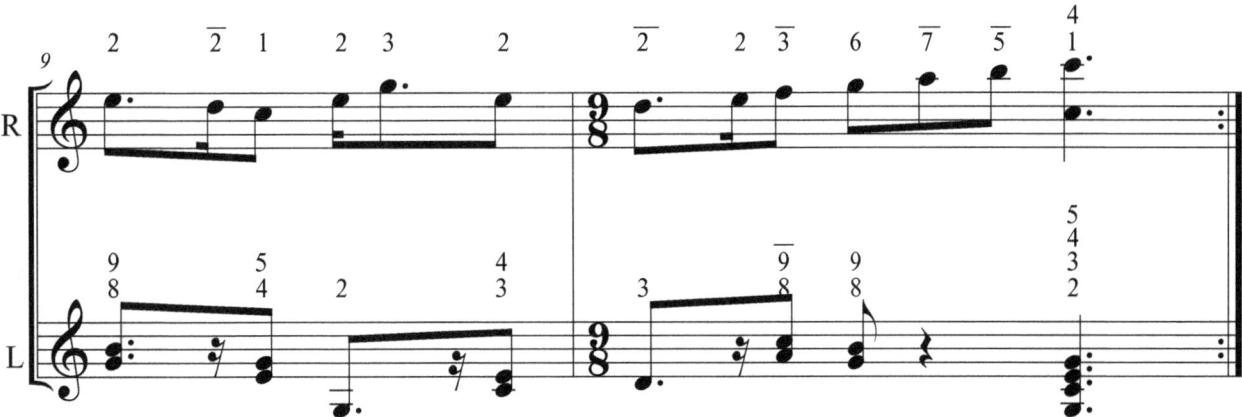

Blue-Eyed Stranger

HEADINGTON MORRIS HANDKERCHIEF DANCE

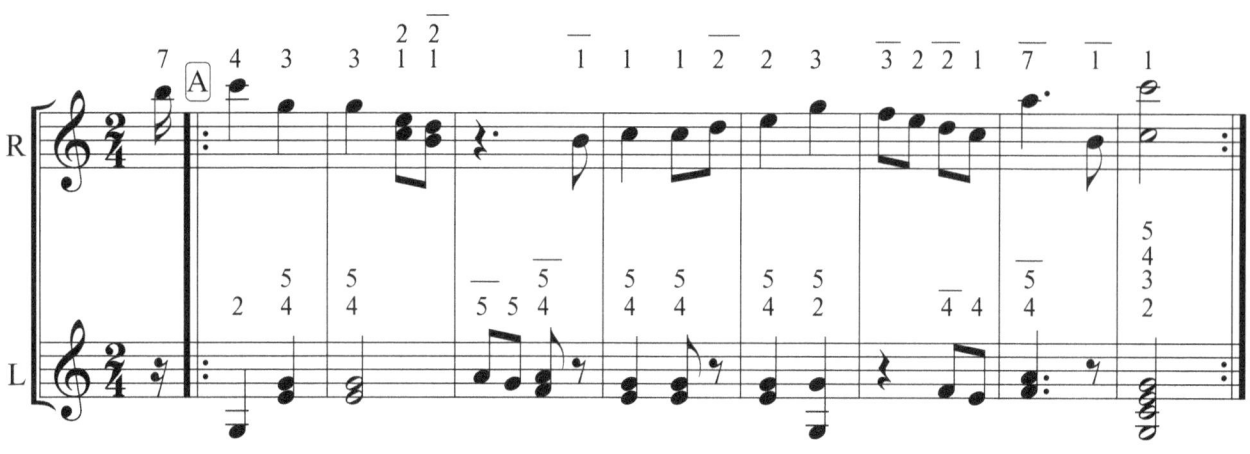
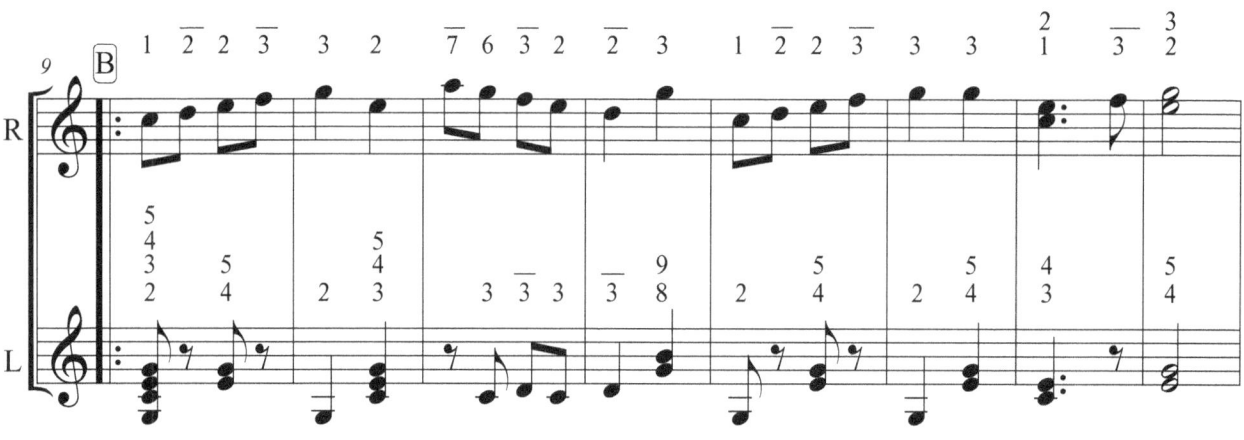

Constant Billy

HEADINGTON MORRIS STICK DANCE

Country Gardens

HEADINGTON MORRIS HANDKERCHIEF DANCE

Country Gardens

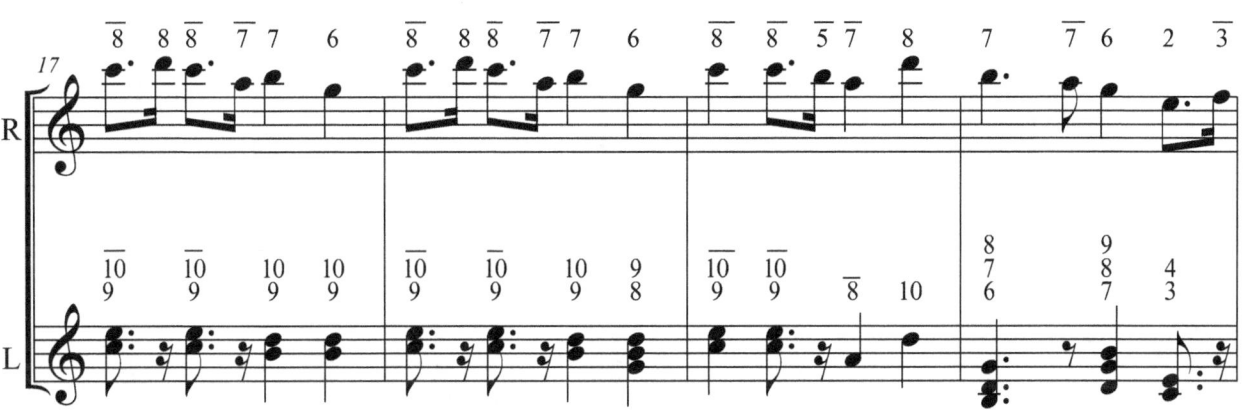

Country Gardens

Country Gardens

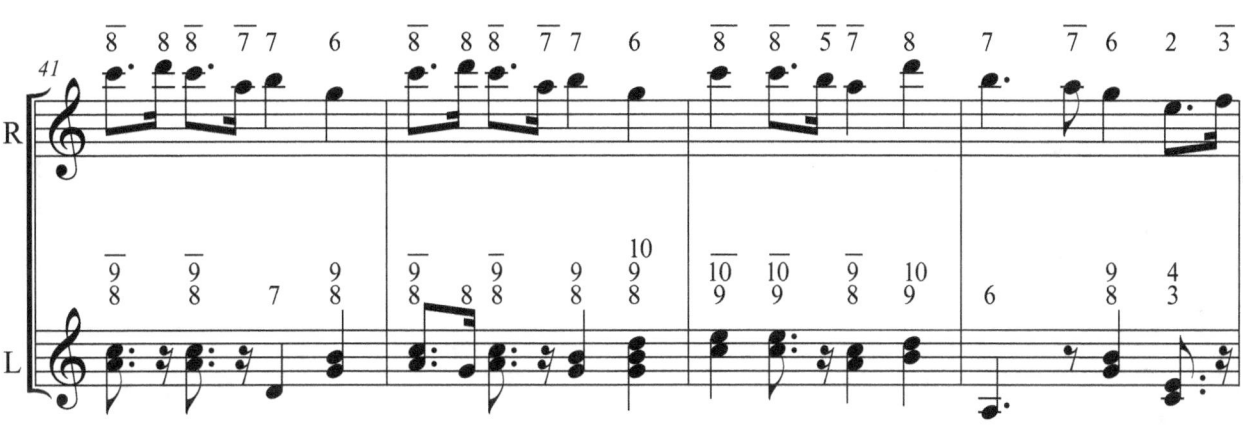

Double Set-Back

HEADINGTON MORRIS HANDKERCHIEF DANCE

Double Set-Back

Getting Upstairs

HEADINGTON MORRIS HANDKERCHIEF DANCE

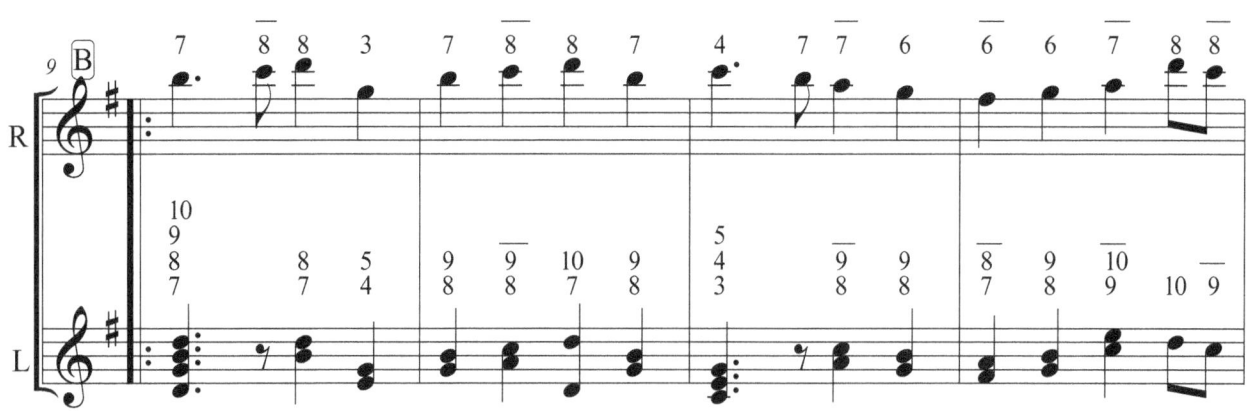

Getting Upstairs

141

Haste to the Wedding

HEADINGTON MORRIS HANDKERCHIEF DANCE

Haste to the Wedding

Haste to the Wedding

How D'Ye Do, Sir?

HEADINGTON MORRIS CORNER DANCE

Hunting the Squirrel

HEADINGTON MORRIS STICK DANCE

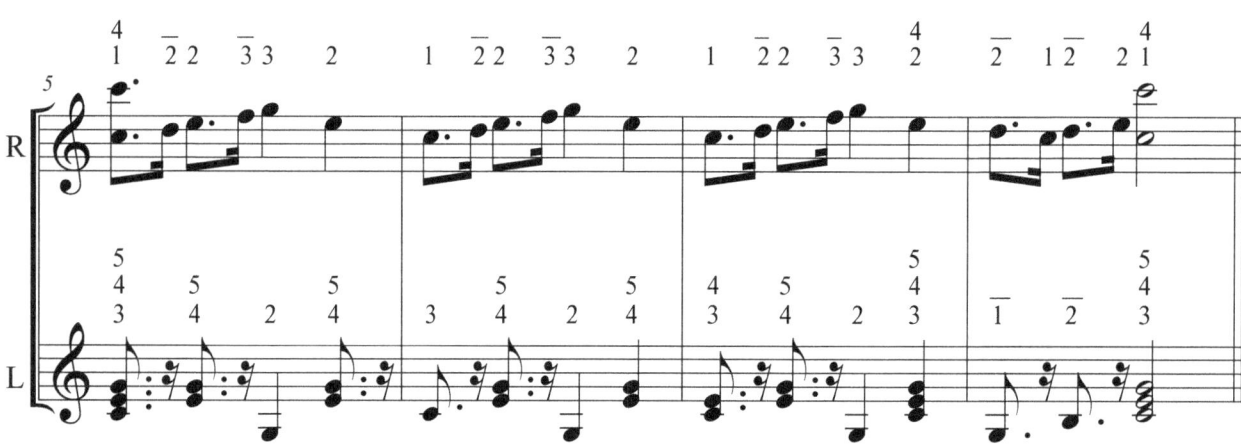

Hunting the Squirrel

147

Jockie to the Fair

HEADINGTON MORRIS JIG

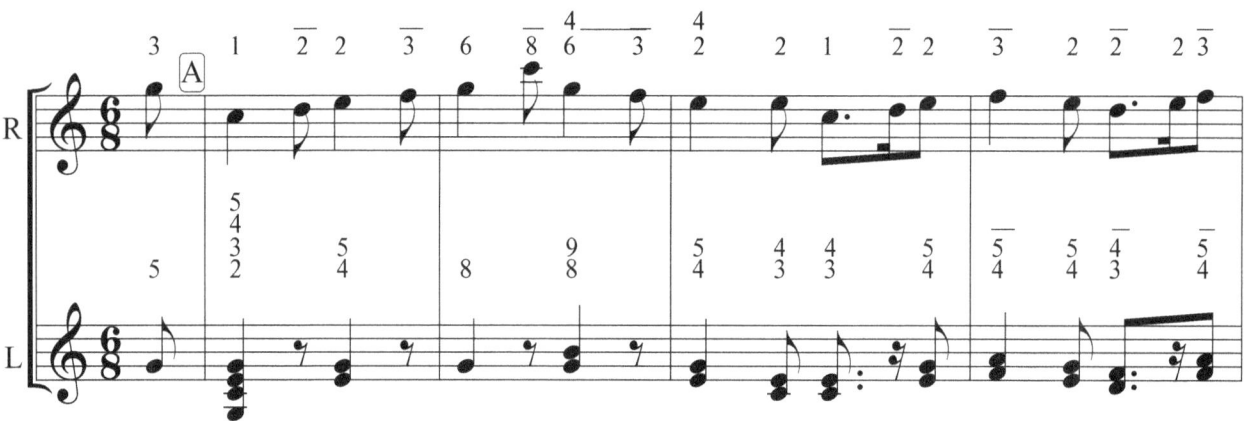

Jockie to the Fair

Jockie to the Fair

Jockie to the Fair

Laudnum Bunches

HEADINGTON MORRIS CORNER DANCE

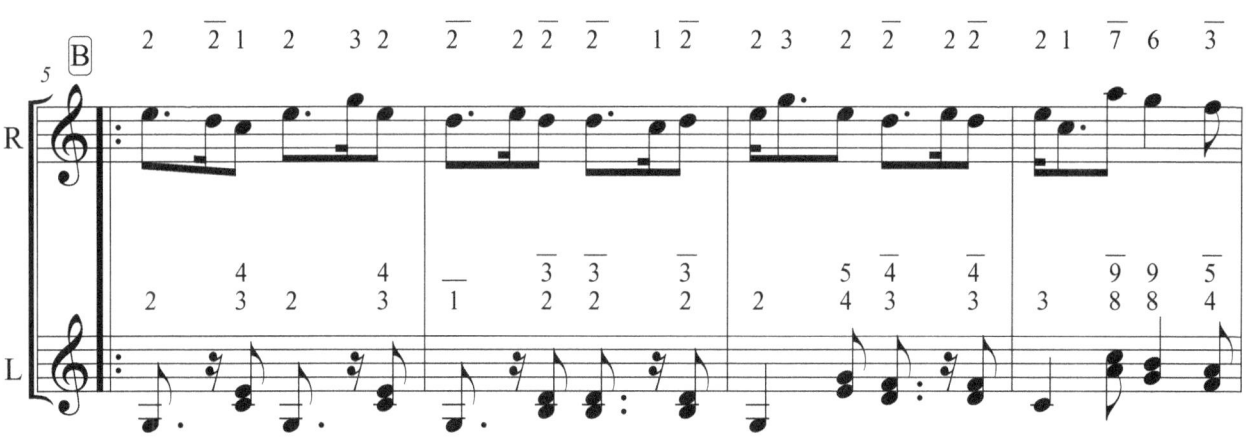

Laudnum Bunches

Old Mother Oxford

HEADINGTON MORRIS JIG

Old Mother Oxford

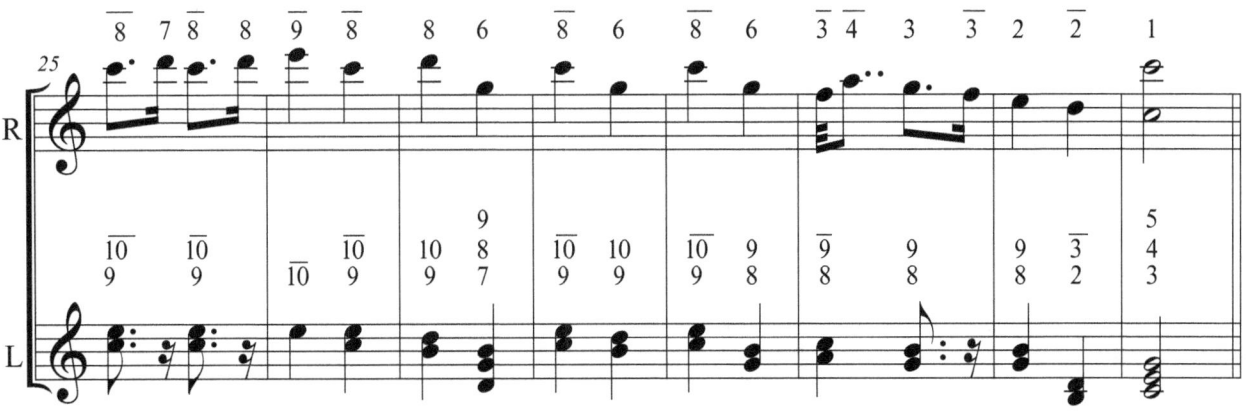
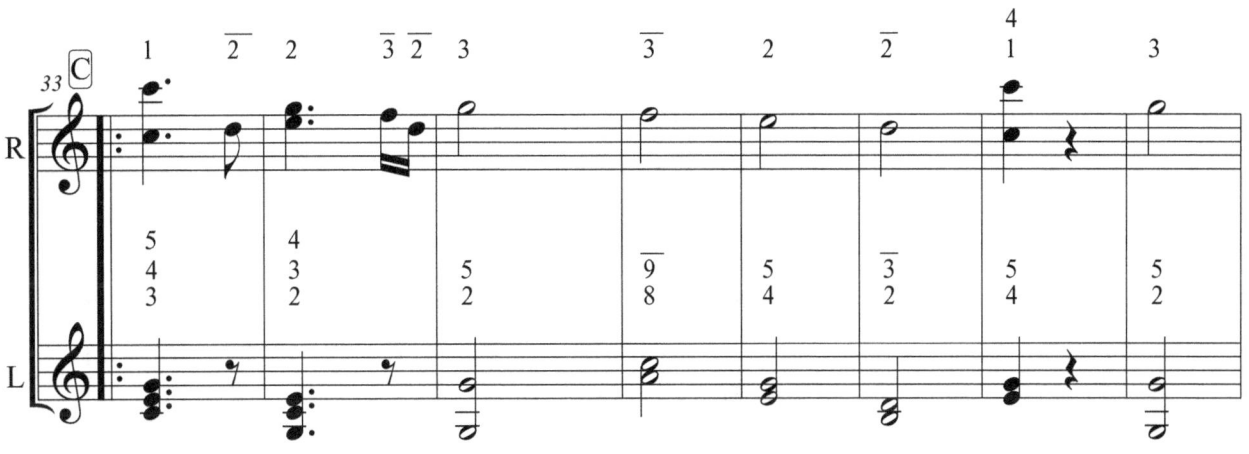
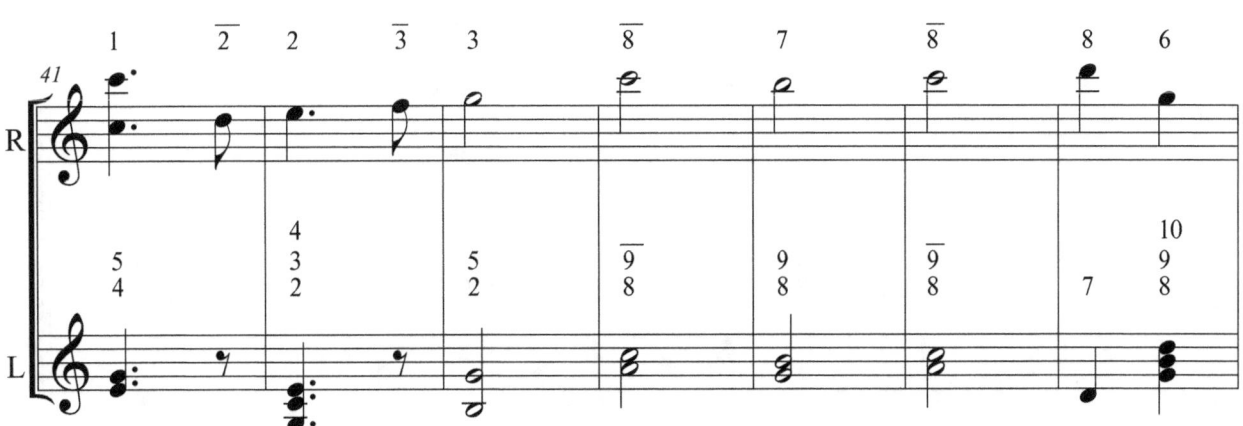

Old Mother Oxford

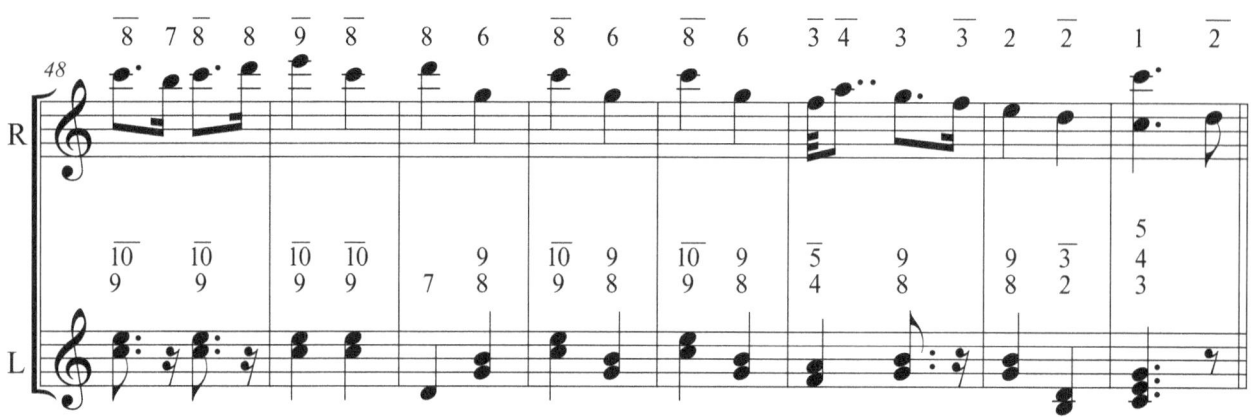

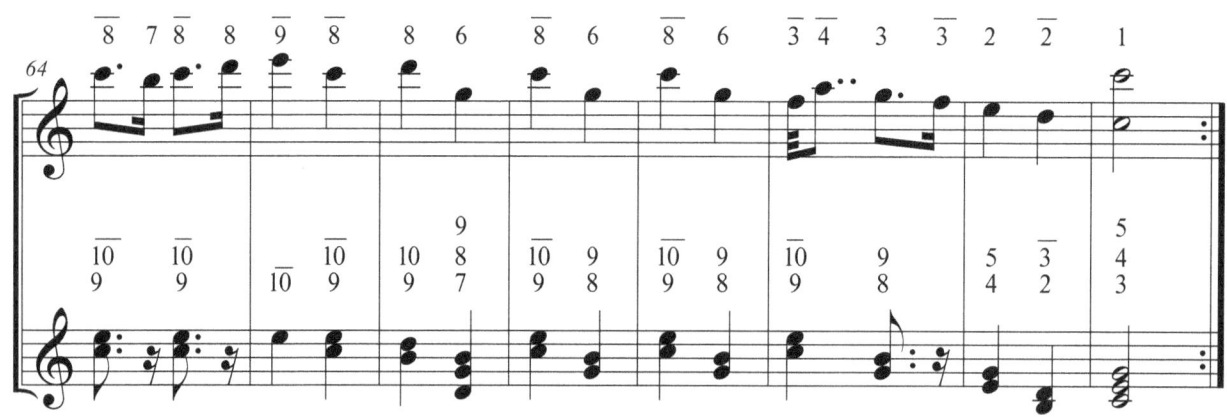

William Kimber and Arthur Kimber, Royal Albert Hall, London, 1950. From the Vaughan Williams Memorial Library.

The Old Woman Tossed Up In a Blanket

HEADINGTON MORRIS JIG

The Old Woman Tossed Up In a Blanket

Rigs O'Marlow

HEADINGTON MORRIS STICK DANCE

Rodney

HEADINGTON MORRIS STICK DANCE

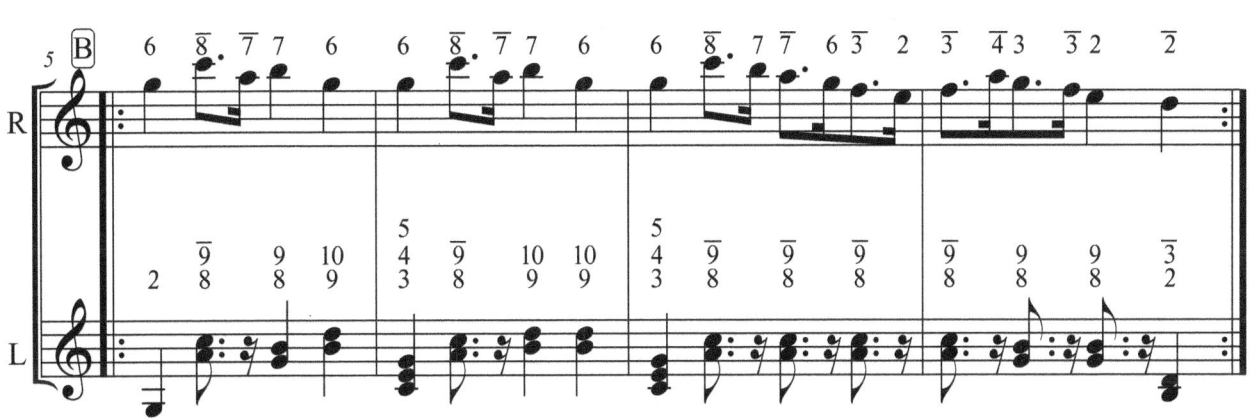

Shepherd's Hey
HEADINGTON MORRIS JIG

Trunkles

HEADINGTON MORRIS CORNER DANCE

Trunkles

The Twenty-Ninth of May

HEADINGTON MORRIS HANDKERCHIEF DANCE

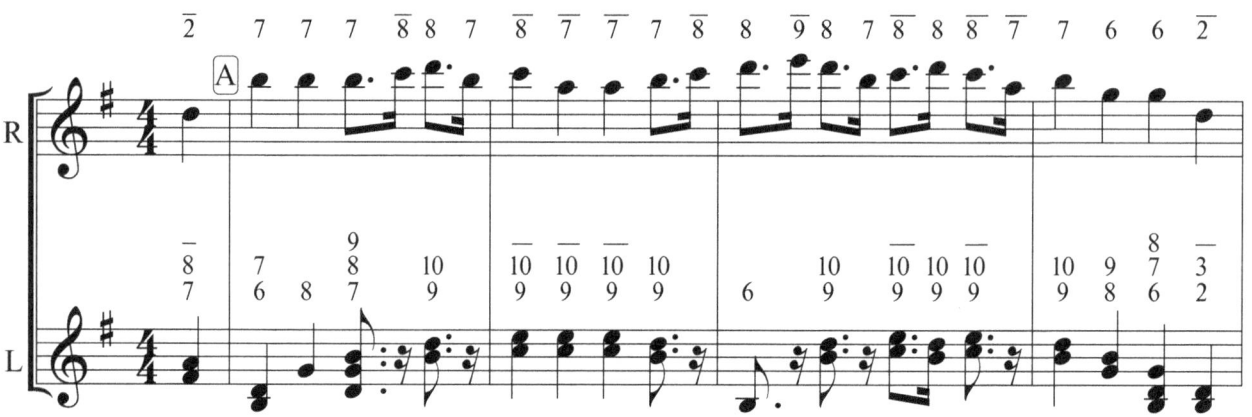

The Twenty-Ninth of May

The Willow Tree

HEADINGTON MORRIS HANDKERCHIEF DANCE

The Willow Tree

Figure 5.1. William Kimber playing for Morris dancer, ca. 1940s. Image courtesy of Vaughan Williams Memorial Library.

Chapter 5. Other Morris Dance Tunes

The nine tunes in this chapter were recorded by William Kimber at various times during his later life but were not among the Headington dances that Sharp noted and included in his *Morris Book* of 1907–1911. Eight of these tunes and their associated Morris dance steps were included by Sharp in the *Morris Book*, but were ascribed to other traditions. One other tune (*Morris On*) was recorded by Kimber only in the 1950s and is not mentioned by Sharp.

That Kimber knew these tunes attests to his long participation in teaching and playing for Morris dance, both with Sharp in the early years of the English Folk Revival and in later years as part of activities of the EFDS and later, EFDSS, as well as for groups like the Oxford University Morris. These tunes would also have been useful when the Headington Quarry Morris men joined the Morris Ring, in 1949. At that time they learned several new dances from other Morris traditions that were part of the Ring.

Tune sources and explanation

Bonny Green Garters: Digital audio of the transcription

Bonny Green Garters (Bampton handkerchief dance; p. 178). Kimber was recorded playing this tune for the Headington Quarry Morris dancers on June 10, 1957, outside the Mason's Arms public house in the Quarry. It is considered a Bampton dance and was collected by Sharp at Bampton for his *Morris Book*, volume 3. Kimber's version is a variant of the tune collected at Bampton by Percy Manning in 1897.[1] It has similarities with a number of Irish and English jigs of the eighteenth and nineteenth centuries, such as the *Rollicking Irishman* (from *Kerr's Merrie Melodies*, 1880) and the country dance *Yorkshire Lasses*

(Perth: John Miller, 1799).² Kimber gave the lyrics to Sharp (by letter, in 1908) as:

First for the stockings and then for the shoes
And then for the bonny green garters
A pair for me and a pair for you
And a pair for they that come after.

These lyrics are the same as those collected by Manning.

The accompaniment of this tune is classic Kimber, with left hand partial chords as well as the occasional oom-pah or octave run, and with full chords at the ends of phrases. Those full chords involve the right hand as well, as seen at the ends of the A and B parts. The tune was played by Kimber for his dancers at a relaxed pace and is a fairly easy arrangement to learn. The rhythm throughout consists of dotted triplets followed by undotted triplets. In the last half of both measures 5 and 6, which repeat phrases of measures 1 and 2, note the substitutions of short octave runs for the partial chords of measures 1 and 2. Once the tune is learned – at its basic level it is quite intuitive – all sorts of these 'finishing steps' variations will occur to the learner.

Figure 5.2. William Kimber playing for the Oxford University Morris Men, 1954, Oxford. Photographer David Welti. Vaughan Williams Memorial Library.

Brighton Camp (Eynsham; p. 180). This country dance and Morris tune appear in a manuscript of a Dr. Rimbault, ca. 1770, from an unpublished manuscript of 1797 in the collection of Frank Kidson, and from T. Skillern's book *Twenty-Four Country Dances for the Year 1799*. William Chappell dates the tune to 1758, when there were military encampments on the southern coast of England watching for an expected French invasion, although there are Irish claims to the tune as well.³ *Brighton Camp* is also known as *The Girl I Left Behind Me*. It was commonly found throughout the Cotswolds, including Eynsham, Adderbury, and Bampton in addition to Headington. Kimber was recorded playing this tune for the Headington Quarry Morris dancers on June 10, 1957, outside the Mason's Arms public house in the Quarry. It and the accompanying follow-up tune at that performance, *Cock o' the North*, are Eynsham handkerchief dances that were collected by Sharp for his *Morris Book*, volume 3.

Brighton Camp: Digital audio of the transcription

Cock O'the North: Digital audio of the transcription

Cock o' the North (Eynsham; p. 182). Kimber was recorded playing this tune for the Headington Quarry Morris dancers on June 10, 1957, outside the Mason's Arms public house in the Quarry. It and the tune that immediately preceded it at that performance, *Brighton Camp*, are Eynsham handkerchief dances that were collected by Sharp for his *Morris Book*, volume 3. The tune dates at least as far back as Playford's *Dancing Master* books (1674 and 1686), under the name *Jumping Joan*, and was a regimental quick march for the Gordon Highlanders.[4]

Manchester Harnpipe: Digital audio of the transcription

Manchester Hornpipe (The Fool's Jig, Bampton; pp. 274, 288). Kimber was recorded playing *Manchester Hornpipe* for the Headington Quarry Morris dancers on 10 June 1957, outside the Mason's Arms public house in the Quarry. It is a Bampton solo Morris jig, danced typically by the fool to the *Manchester Hornpipe*, and was collected there by Sharp for his *Morris Book*, volume 3. *Manchester Hornpipe* (also known as *Rickett's Hornpipe*), popular throughout the British Isles with printed versions dating at least as far back as the ca 1823 music manuscript of Joshua Gibbons of Lincolnshire, and *Kerr's Merrie Melodies* of 1880.[5] The tune is also a classic step dance tune, so its transcription is placed in Chapter 8, p. 288.

Morris On: Digital audio of the transcription

Morris On (p. 184) is a former Headington Morris processional dance. William Kimber's playing of the tune was recorded by Peter Kennedy at Kimber's home in Headington Quarry in 1956, and Kennedy reports that an earlier recording of Kimber playing the tune was made in 1946.[6] The basic melody was transcribed by Peter Kennedy and Maud Karpeles for the *Journal of the English Folk Dance and Song Society* in 1958.[7] Mary Neal published a version of *Morris On* from Berkshire Morris dancers in *The Espérance Morris Book* of 1910, but that dance used the tune *Brighton Camp*, not Kimber's tune. Kimber's version of the tune was made popular by the Ashley Hutchings LP *Morris On* of 1972. There appear to be no known antecedents for the tune prior to Kimber's version; it does not appear in Sharp's *Morris Book*.

Morris Off: Digital audio of the transcription

Morris Off (p. 186) was recorded from William Kimber's playing by Peter Kennedy at Kimber's home in Headington Quarry in 1956. Sharp collected the same tune in 1906 from Morris dancers at Redditch and published it in the first edition of his *Morris Book,* volume 1. In a later edition he withdrew it and another Bidford Morris dance (*Shepherd's Hey*), fearing that both may have been inauthentic. According to Peter Kennedy, *Morris Off* is a version of the tune *Moresques* from Arbeau's *Orchésographie* (1588) that was introduced to the Bidford Morris Dancers by d'Arcy Ferrars in 1888.[8] Mary Neal published the tune in *The Espérance Morris Book* of 1910, without mentioning its source. In 1949 Maud Karpeles notated the basic melody from Kimber's playing. According to her account, Kimber claimed that he learned the tune from his father while still in the cradle.[9] That claim is possible, assuming that William Kimber senior perhaps learned it from dancers at Bidford. The tune as played at Headington Quarry was accompanied by a processional Morris dance that took place at the end of a performance event.[10]

Figure 5.3. Oxford University Men's Morris dancing on Broad Street, Oxford, May Morning, 1931. William Kimber is playing concertina. Photo courtesy of David Rogers, Chris Sheffield, and the Oxford City Morris.

Princess Royal (p. 188) is a tune that is widespread among Cotswold Morris sides. Sharp noted versions from Abingdon (handkerchief dance) as well as Bampton, Bledington, and Longborough (Morris jigs). There are versions in both major and minor keys. A major key version contained in Ashley Hutchings's 1972 LP *Morris On* is perhaps the most widely heard today, but Kimber played a version of it in the key of A minor that that is somewhat similar to that played at Bampton. He recorded it in Theo Chaundy's house in Oxford in 1956, as part of a concertina lesson (see discussion, Chapter 3).[11] The dance is apparently not a part of Headington Quarry tradition. The tune is said to have been composed by the Irish harper O'Carolan around 1725, although others ascribe the tune a British origin.

Princess Royal: Digital audio of the transcription

Swaggering Boney (p. 191) is a Longborough corner dance, included by Sharp in his *Morris Book,* volume 4; Sharp notated the corresponding tune from the singing of Henry Taylor, who had danced with the Longborough side during the jubilee of 1887. At Theo Chaundy's house in Oxford in 1956, Kimber recorded a version of the tune used at Longborough.[12] It was not a part of the traditional Headington Quarry dance repertoire. The tune is older than its titular association with Napoleon Bonaparte. It appeared as *The Runner* in Playford's *Dancing Master* of 1694 but later became popular all over England under the name *Swaggering Boney*.[13]

Swaggering Boney: Digital audio of the transcription

Young Collins: Digital audio of the transcription

Young Collins (p. 193). Kimber was recorded playing *Young Collins,* from the Bledington Morris tradition, for the Headington Quarry Morris dancers on June 10, 1957, outside the Mason's Arms public house in the Quarry.[14] The Bledington version of the tune—similar to Kimber's recorded version—was published in the *Journal of the EFDSS* in 1934.[15] Sharp transcribed the tune from the playing of a Mr. Stagg in 1906, from William Hathaway at Cheltenham in 1907, and from Charles Benfield at Bould (near Bledington) in 1909.[16] Other versions were danced at Longborough, Oddington, and Sherburne. The Longborough version of the tune was published by Sharp in the *Morris Book,* volume 4, although the tune is significantly different than that used at Bledington and by Kimber.

[1] Percy Manning, 1897, "Some Oxfordshire Seasonal Festivals, with Notes on Morris Dancing in Oxfordshire," *Folk-lore, Transactions of the Folk-Lore Society*, vol. 8, p. 320.

[2] Traditional Tune Archive entry for *Bonnie Green Garters*, www.tunearch.org.

[3] Traditional Tune Archive entry for *Brighton Camp*, www.tunearch.org.

[4] Traditional Tune Archive entry for *Cock o' the North*, www.tunearch.org.

[5] Traditional Tune Archive entry for *Manchester Hornpipe*, www.tunearch.org.

[6] Peter Kennedy, liner notes to Folktrax CD 382, *William Kimber (Anglo concertina)*.

[7] *Journal of the English Folk Dance and Song Society*, vol. 8, 1958, p. 211.

[8] English Folk Dance and Song Society, 1963, liner notes by Peter Kennedy in *William Kimber*, EFDSS LP 1001.

[9] Maud Karpeles' manuscripts, at Vaughan Williams Memorial Library, MK/1/4/5359A Morris Off.

[10] *Journal of the English Folk Dance and Song Society*, vol. 8, 1958, p. 211.

[11] William Kimber, 1956, *Princess Royal*, as recorded by Theo Chaundy, www.merryville.uk, Chaundy collection tape 3.

[12] William Kimber, 1956, *Swaggering Boney*, as recorded by Theo Chaundy, www.merryville.uk, Chaundy collection tape 4.

[13] Traditional Tune Archive entry for *Swaggering Boney*, www.tunearch.org.

[14] Merryville.uk online website, http://merryville.uk/young-collins-bledington-dance.

[15] Dance and Tune Index (DT84671), Vaughan Williams Memorial Linrary.

[16] *Young Collins* Morris, Vaughan Williams Memorial Library, and Traditional Tune Archive entry for *Young Collins*, www.tunearch.org.

William Kimber and William "Jinky" Wells with the Bampton Morris dancers in the procession opening the International Festival of Folk Dance, 1935. Image courtesy of the Vaughan Williams Memorial Library, EFDSS.

Transcriptions:
Other Morris Dances

Bonny Green Garters
BAMPTON MORRIS DANCE

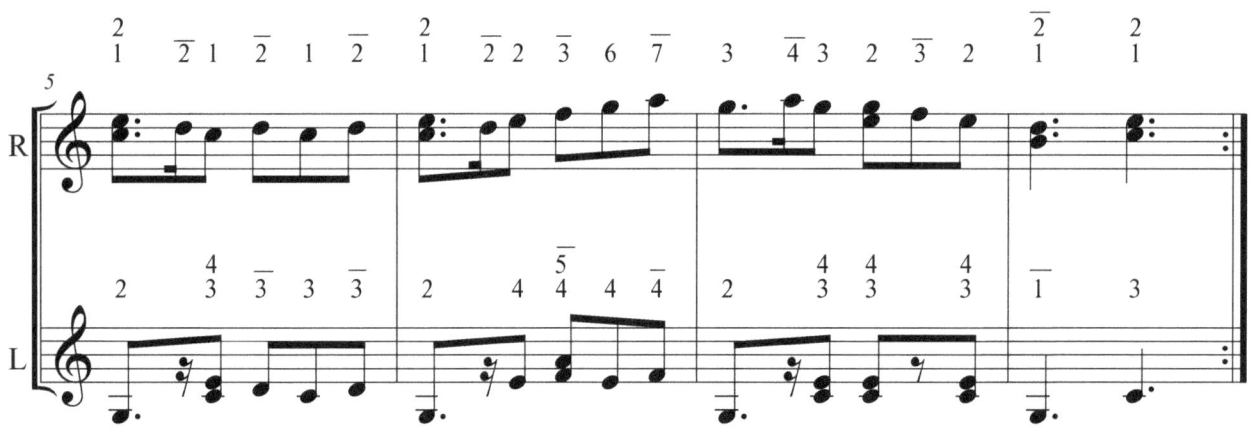

Bonny Green Garters

179

Brighton Camp
EYNSHAM MORRIS DANCE AND COUNTRY DANCE

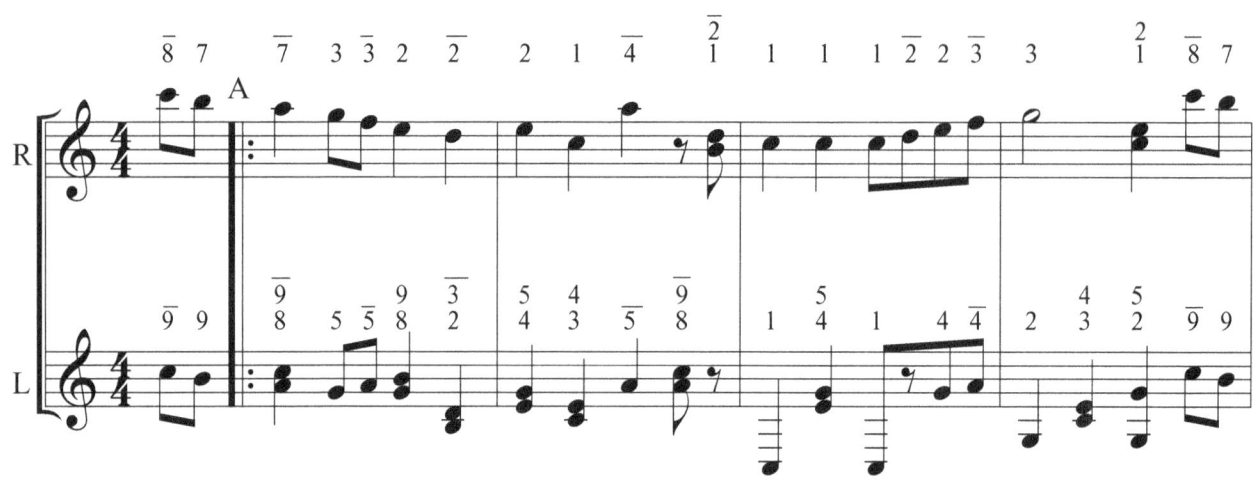
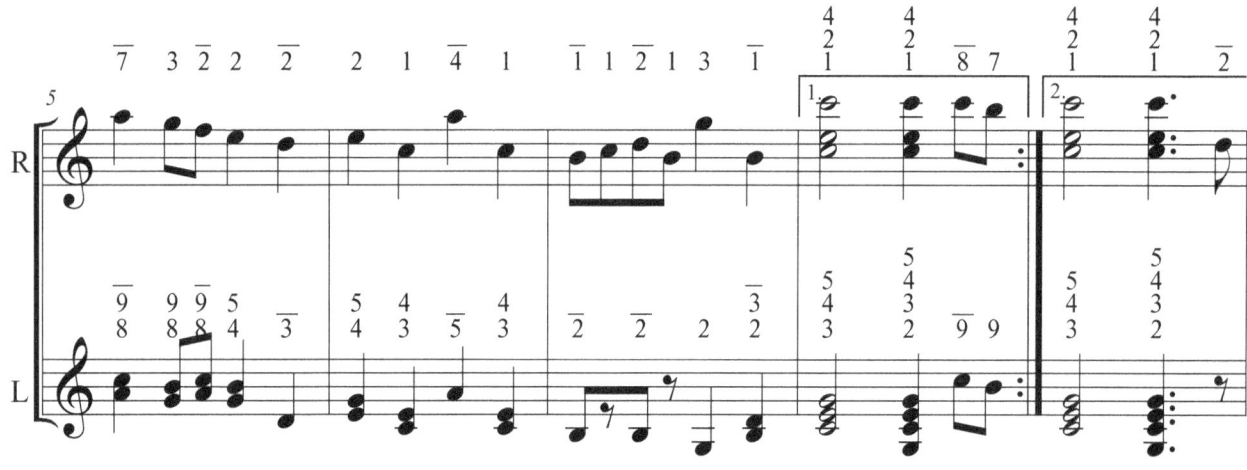

Cock o' the North

EYNSHAM MORRIS DANCE AND COUNTRY DANCE

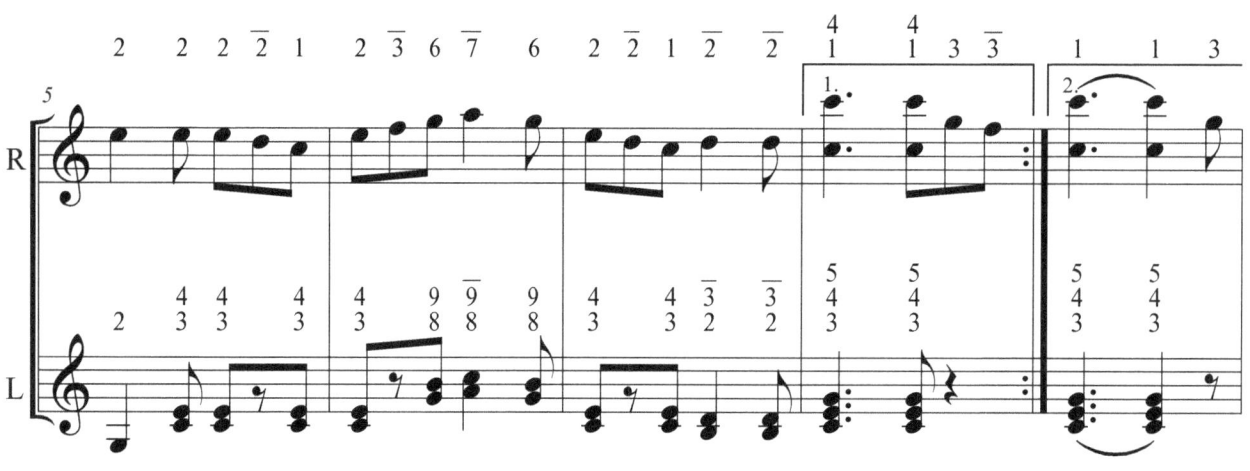

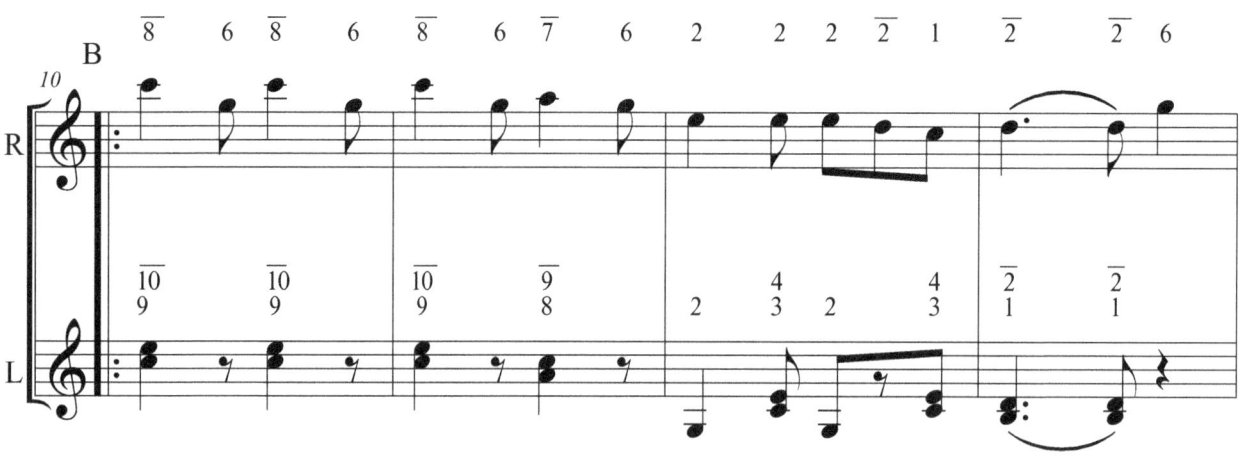

2 Cock o' the North

183

Morris On

HEADINGTON MORRIS PROCESSIONAL DANCE

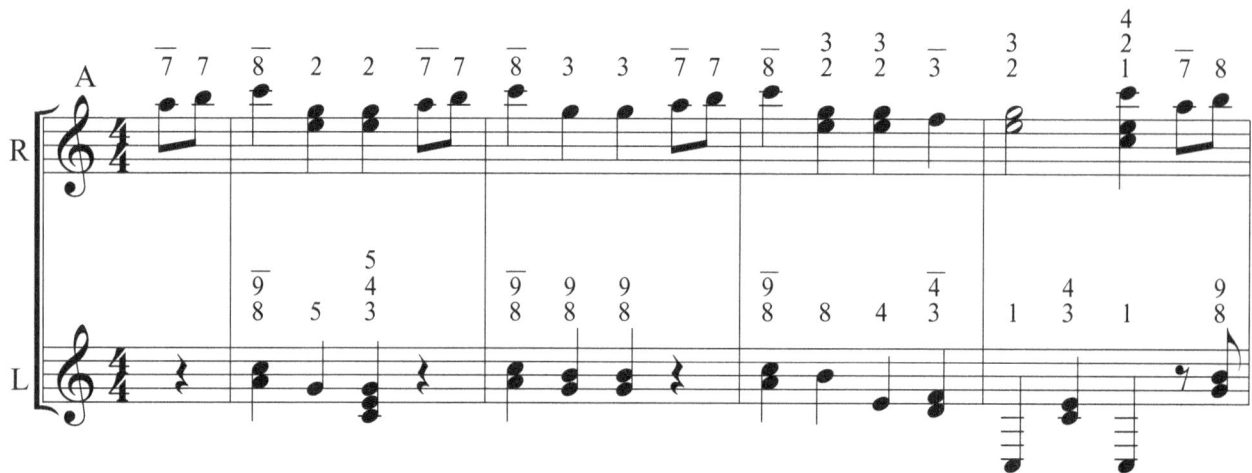

Morris Off

BIDFORD MORRIS DANCE

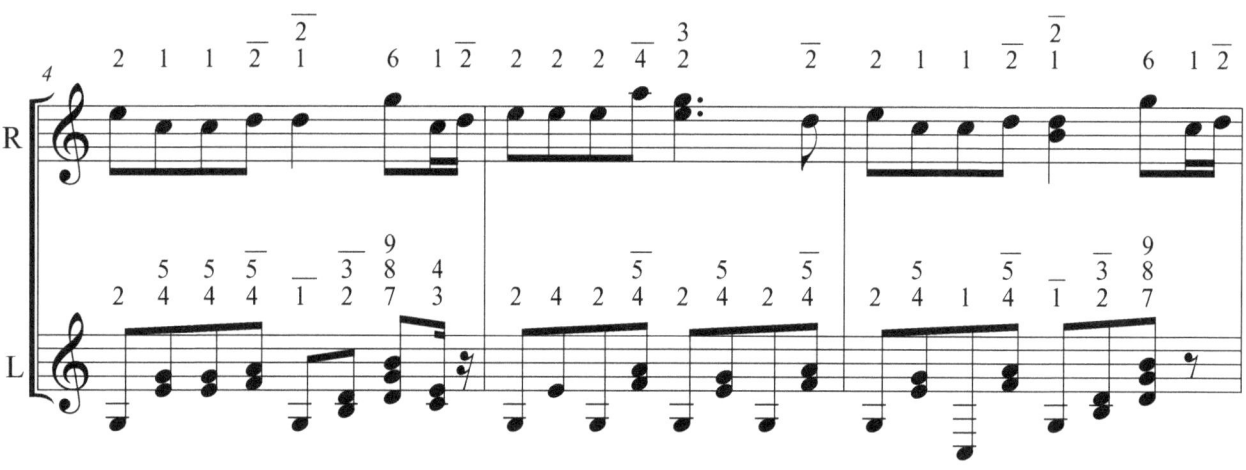

Morris Off

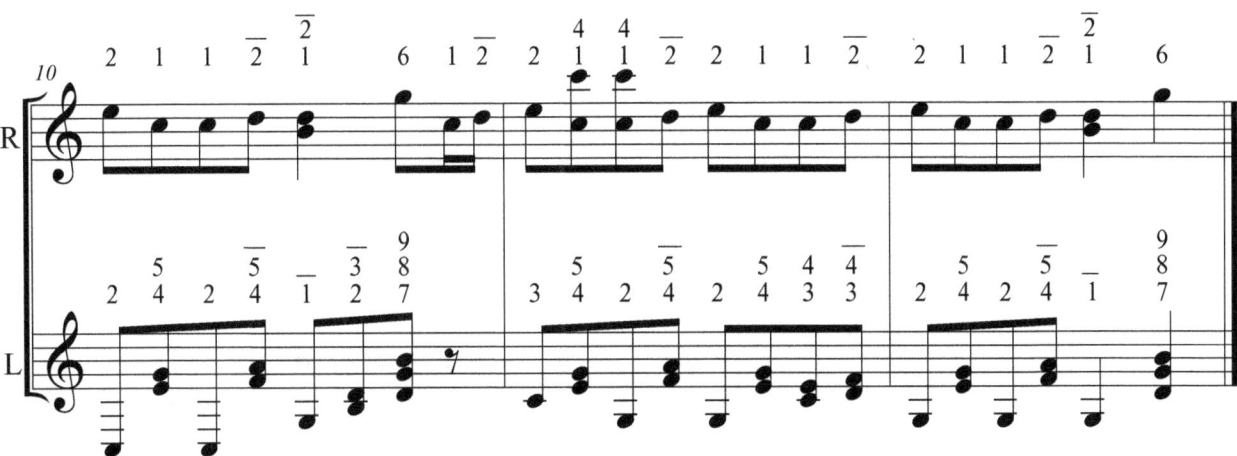

Princess Royal

BAMPTON MORRIS DANCE

Princess Royal

Princess Royal

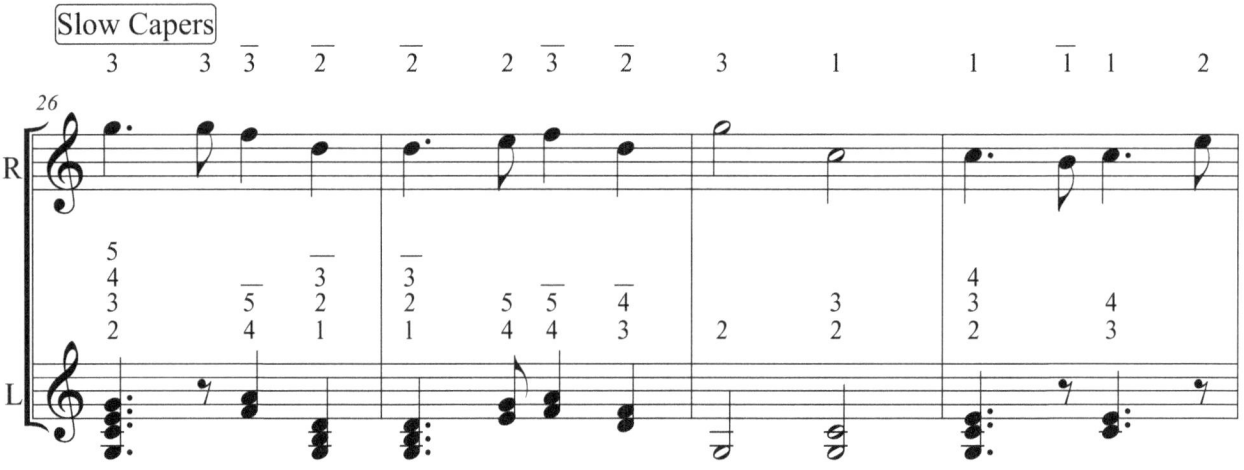

Swaggering Boney

LONGBOROUGH MORRIS DANCE

William Kimber and William "Jinky" Wells, Bampton, 1951. Image from Reg Hall.

Young Collins
BLEDINGTON MORRIS DANCE

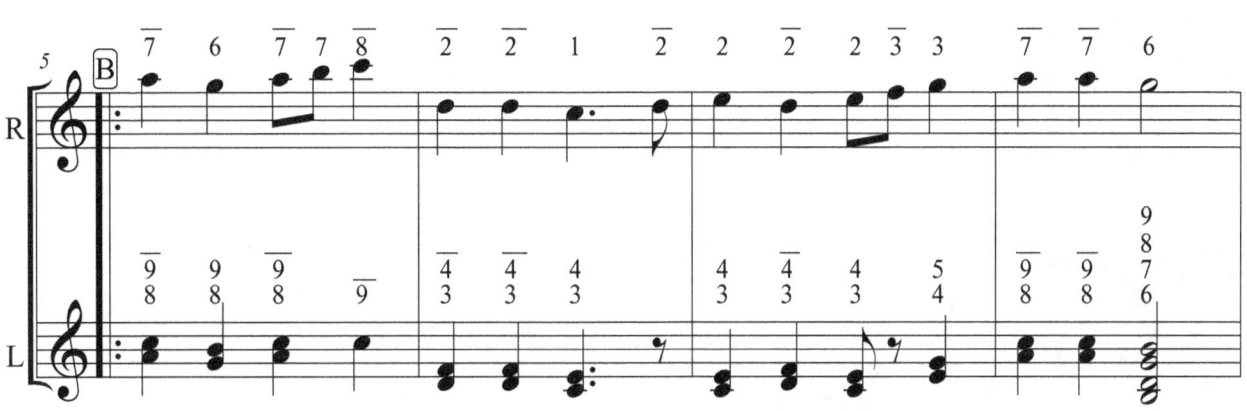

Figure 6.1. A round country dance performed during a Stratford-upon-Avon EFDS summer school, ca. 1912, a year after Sharp published his *Country Dance Book*. Photo from Warwickshire county records.

Chapter 6. Social Dance Part I: Country Dance Tunes

Social dances formed a large part of various Quarry village festivities. These social dances were of course different than the (all male) Morris dance displays, and were more communal than step-dancing in pubs. What were the dances at these village social events? And to which tunes? Two basic types of community social dancing existed in England in the late nineteenth-century countryside: the older country dances, which had by then been long on the wane, and the newer so-called ballroom dances (including square forms like quadrilles, and couples dances like the waltz, polka, schottische, galup, etc.), which were in the ascendancy; these latter dances are discussed in Chapter 7. It seems clear for reasons discussed later that Kimber, in the years before he met Sharp, played somewhat more for quadrilles and couples dances than he did for country dances. However, after he met Sharp, he began to be associated with Sharp's revival of country dance, which was continued with the EFDSS over the next half century. That association resulted in Kimber adding to his repertoire of country dance tunes.

As was discussed in Chapter 4, most of the tunes for the Headington Morris dances originated as eighteenth- and even seventeenth-century country dances, the dances for which had for the most part disappeared by Kimber's time, but the tunes were remembered by village musicians. Country dance, having originated in England

Figure 6.2. A longways country dance at a Christmas party in Wessex, from Thomas Hardy's *The History of the Hardcomes*, in *Harper's New Monthly Magazine*, March 1891.

sometime before 1500[1] and having been further popularized from 1651 by John Playford in various editions of *The Dancing Master,* was at its peak popularity in the high society English ballroom throughout the eighteenth century. As dance historian P. J. S. Richardson noted,

> *In its early days the Country Dance had several forms. There was for instance the Round . . . one of the very oldest of our dances. There was the Square-Eight form . . . and there was the Longways dance such as "Greensleeves." Gradually this later form displaced the others in popularity. . . . In the Longways Country Dance there were two parallel lines— the men in one and the ladies in the other—and by the end of each figure the leading couple passed down the line one place. . . . They were described as "longways for as many as will," and could be danced by any number of couples in excess of two.*[2]

With the arrival of the waltz from central Europe in about 1815, and the quadrille in about 1816, the popularity of country dance in urban areas began to wane. The introduction of the waltz, with its characteristic close contact between dancers, caused widespread pearl-clutching in polite society, but when the polka arrived in England in 1844, it tended to legitimize the earlier waltz in those upper-crust urban ballrooms, and both dances rose in popularity as the older country dances faltered. By the middle of the nineteenth century, country dance was more likely to be found in the countryside, in small villages. By then, most villages had only a few remaining country dances that they continued to employ at festive occasions; quadrilles and couples dances were more prominent.[3]

By 1909 Cecil Sharp had published *The Morris Book,* volumes 1 and 2, and he then changed his attention somewhat from processional dance to social dance, recognizing that the old country dance form was disappearing rapidly from the countryside. He collected eighteen surviving country dances in villages from Devonshire, Derbyshire, Surrey, and Warwickshire from 1907 through 1909, and published *The Country Dance Book*, Part 1, in 1909.[4] All the dances were longways. None of these published field-collected dances originated from sources in Headington Quarry.

Given the prominence of the Quarry's Morris dances in Sharp's collection, notated from Kimber's music and dance steps, it seems a bit odd that Sharp didn't have any dances from his old friend in his book.

It apparently wasn't for want of trying. On April 17, 1908, in Oxford, during the period of 1906–1908 when Sharp was conducting his field research for *The Country Dance Book*, Sharp notated three tunes from Kimber that were characterized as country dance tunes: *Hilly-go Filly-go*, *Off She Goes*, and *The Triumph*, or *Step and Fetch Her*. (He later notated a fourth "country dance" from Kimber in 1914, *Over the Hills to Glory*, but this tune is perhaps better known as a ballroom dance, schottische/polka, and is included in Chapter 8.) He didn't record any steps from Kimber for those several tunes.[5] From this we can assume that country dance in the Quarry—before the Edwardian Folk Revival started by Neal and Sharp—was not in a healthy state, and that as was the case in the rest of the country, ballroom dances (quadrilles as well as couples dances like waltzes, polkas, and schottisches) had largely pushed out country dances from social dance settings. Of the country dance tunes notated from Kimber in 1908, only one (*The Triumph*) found its way into Sharp's *Country Dance Book*, but with dance steps and tune taken from concertina player William Ford of Lew Trenchard, Devonshire, in 1907—one of the first country dances that Sharp collected.[6]

Because Sharp did not use any of Kimber's country dance tunes in his country dance book, we can assume that they were not commonly danced in the Quarry by the early twentieth century. There are audio recordings of Kimber playing *The Triumph* and *Hilly-go Filly-go*, and they are included in the transcriptions that follow, but there are no existing audio recordings of him playing *Off She Goes*. The transcription here of that tune is from Sharp's notes from Kimber's playing and consists of the unaccompanied melody line (right hand) only.

Kimber made audio recordings of five more country dance tunes late in his life during the period 1946–1956: *Bonnets So Blue, Pop Goes the Weasel, The Ribbon Dance, The Quaker's Wife,* and *Double Lead Through*. The first three of these tunes and dances are contained in Sharp's *The Country Dance Book,* Part 1, but not sourced to Kimber. Most of these seem to have been learned by Kimber during the period of his participation in teaching at EFDS and later EFDSS summer festival events, at first with Sharp, until Sharp's death in 1924, and then for several decades with the EFDSS at summer schools during festivals. Certainly Kimber played concertina for those country dances, as he recalled in an interview with Peter Kennedy and Maud Karpeles in 1956:

Kennedy: [What are the] names of the [other, non-Morris] dances you used to do?

Kimber: The names? The polkas? There was one, *Little Polly*—I likes a girl with a blue frock on . . .

Here Kennedy had to steer Kimber away from the obviously more popular couples dances (e.g., the polka) to the country dances that he and the EFDSS were more interested in:

Kennedy: And the country dances?

Kimber: Ah, well, they be in the book [Sharp's *The Country Dance Book,* Part 1].

Maud Karpeles: Up sides and down the middle?

Kimber: *Step and Fetch Her* [The Triumph], *Pop Goes the Weasel, Ribbon Dance, Quaker's Wife*—all them. *Bonnets So Blue* that's one of my favorites.

Kennedy: *Hilly-go Filly-go?*

Kimber: "Hilly-go Filly-go all the way. I shall never forget the day when I was on the railway." I used to play them. I used to have some fine fun.[7]

It should also be noted that Kimber made audio recordings of three other tunes for which the titles were included in *The Country Dance Book,* Part 1 (*Brighton Camp, Haste to the Wedding,* and *Hunting the Squirrel*), but he played these primarily for Morris dances (see Chapters 4 and 5). Kimber's versions of *Brighton Camp* and *Hunting the Squirrel* are distinctly different from those used in Sharp's country dance book. None of Sharp's versions of these three dances published in that book came from Kimber.

Figure 6.3. A country dance in a small Australian village in North Queensland, ca. 1910. They are performing a round dance in a rural setting, which is more evocative of what Quarry dances might have resembled than the fancier setting of Figure 6.1. Image from the Oxley Library, State Library of Queensland.

Sharp seems to have found slim pickings for collecting country dances in the field, because after 1909 he changed his focus to retrieving and rehabilitating country dances from John Playford's dance books of the late seventeenth and early eighteenth centuries. Those ancient, retrieved dances were published in *The Country Dance Book,* Parts 2 through 6 (the last two after Sharp's death). One of the dances published there with its tune was *The Twenty-Ninth of May.* Kimber recorded a tune of that name, used for a Morris dance, but the tune is completely different from Sharp's published version.

Two other country dance tunes audio-recorded by Kimber, *Double Lead Through* and *The Quaker's Wife,* do not appear in Sharp's *Country Dance Book,* Part 1. Sharp notated the melody of *Double Lead Through* from Kimber at Oxford in 1908 as a "country dance" tune,[8] and Clive Carey noted the (longways) steps to *Double Lead*

Through from James Rooke in Sussex in 1912,[9] but somehow the tune didn't find its way into Sharp's book. Kimber made an audio recording of the tune in a studio in 1946. *The Quaker's Wife* (also, *Merrily Kissed the Quaker's Wife*) is a widespread country dance tune and is different from the Morris tune of that name associated with Bampton. Peter Kennedy recorded it from Kimber's playing at Headington in 1956.

Tune sources and description

Bonnets So Blue: Digital audio of the transcription

Bonnets So Blue (p. 206 was recorded from Kimber's playing at Headington Quarry by Peter Kennedy in 1956. Sharp notated the tune from four separate sources before 1909, none of them Kimber, and placed it with its dance in *The Country Dance Book*, volume 1. The tune, according to Frank Kidson and Mary Neal in their *English Folk-Song and Dance* (1915) can be traced back at least as far as the mid-nineteenth century to a Surrey fiddler named Hammond. The tune was used not only for country dance but also for Morris dance in Bucknell, Oxfordshire, where it is a solo jig dance, and to a manuscript owned by William Winter from Somerset.[10] As discussed earlier, it is likely that Kimber learned the tune during the Edwardian era Folk Revival.

William Kimber playing *Double Lead Through* via His Master's Voice, 1946

Double Lead Through (p. 208) is a tune for which Kimber made a studio recording in 1946, from which this transcription was made. There is some confusion over it, because Sharp recorded a tune of this title from Kimber in 1908 that was actually the tune *Hilly-go Filly-go*.[11] Maud Karpeles recorded a longways country dance called *Double Lead Through,* but it is not clear from her dance notes which tune she intended it to accompany.[12] The tune originated in the French opera *La Fille de Madame Argot*, released in 1872 with music composed by Charles Lecoq.[13] Among English traditional players there are no records of versions of this tune older than that of Kimber.

Double Lead Through: Digital audio of the transcription

Hilly-go Filly-go (p. 212) is a 6/8 jig that was recorded from Kimber's playing by Peter Kennedy in 1956, and appeared on the 1963 EFDSS LP, *William Kimber*.[14] It was notated much earlier as a "country dance" tune by Sharp from Kimber's playing (Kimber later made an audio recording of a different tune under that title, as mentioned previously). Peter Kennedy included the tune in his *Fiddler's Tune Book* of 1951. It is also known as *King of the Cannibal Isles* and the *Nottingham Swing*, and in Scotland is danced to the *Cumberland Reel*. It is said that the tune was composed as the third set of a quadrille called *The Two Rivals* by John Charles White, who ran a music shop in Bath in the early nineteenth century. [15] White published a large number of both quadrilles and country dances.

Hilly-Go Filly-Go: Digital audio of the transcription

For those fortunate enough to find a copy of the 1963 LP – the only place a recording of Kimber playing this tune is to be found – you may notice that the second playing of the A part is wildly different than that of this transcription (which merely repeats the A part). The short story is that Kimber botched the second playing of the A part, first time through, and got temporarily lost. He likely hadn't played the tune in years, and was being peppered with requests from Peter Kennedy, and was not given a second take. He realized his mistake, however, and in the second time through of the complete tune on that recording he got it perfectly. Mistakes like that in his recorded playing are rare, and it is amazing that his playing was typically so spot on in recordings like this one, made in the 1950s when he was in his eighties and was playing old social dance tunes that he had not likely played for many years.

Off She Goes (p. 215) is a 6/8 jig that was notated by Sharp from Kimber's playing in Oxford in 1908 under the name 'Country Dance,'[16] but it is commonly known today as *Off She Goes*, by which it is more popularly known.[17] There is no extant audio recording of William Kimber playing it. It is thought to have originated in the late eighteenth century and was widely popular throughout England, Scotland, Ireland and North America. It appears in *Henry Thompson's Twenty-Four Country Dances for the Year 1805*, among many other tune books of that century.[18] The transcription is from Sharp's notes of a session with Kimber on April 17, 1908. Sharp noted the tune in the key of G, and transcribed only the notes of the unaccompanied melody (Kimber's right hand). It is very unlikely that Kimber played it precisely as written by Sharp because the next to the last measure has a C#, which is not found on a two-row CG Anglo concertina. In 1908, Kimber still had his earlier two row Anglo (he received the three row Jeffries in 1909, as discussed in Chapter 2), so there is no chance that he could have played that C#. He would likely have substituted a B or an E for that note. Other Anglo players made similar substitutions when faced with missing notes. Certainly, Scan Tester from Sussex and Dooley Chapman from New South Wales, Australia, both of whom are Anglo players from an earlier era, are known to have done that. Sharp, however, may have already known this widespread tune and simply inserted the usual C# to the melody when he notated it from Kimber.

Off She Goes: Digital audio of the transcription

Pop Goes the Weasel (p. 216) was recorded by Peter Kennedy and Maud Karpeles in 1951 from Kimber's playing. Kennedy queried Kimber on the dance steps for this country dance, to which Kimber replied, "It's in the book," meaning Sharp's *The Country Dance Book,* volume 1.[19] From this we can comfortably assume that Kimber only learned it during the Folk Revival, as part of his playing for country dances for the EFDSS. Sharp notated the dance steps to this tune in four different localities, none of them Headington.[20] Kimber's lyrics to it are:

Pop Goes the Weasel: Digital audio of the transcription

> *Every time the tide goes out*
> *And the monkey's on the table*
> *Every time the tide goes out*
> *Pop goes the weasel.*

According to the Traditional Tune Archive's notes, a "weasel" was a metal tool used by English hatmakers, and to "pop" means to pawn an item. Versions of the tune are as old as one in the *Essex Manuscript* of 1830, and another version was published in London in 1853. It became very popular in North America not only as a dance tune but as a trick fiddle tune.[21]

The Quaker's Wife: Digital audio of the transcription

The Quaker's Wife (p. 219), also known as *Merrily Kiss the Quaker's Wife*, was audio recorded by Peter Kennedy in 1956 from Kimber's playing. It has a long association with country dance, dating to Rutherford's *Choice Collection of Sixty of the Most Celebrated Country Dances*, published in London in 1750.[22] It is not in Sharp's *The Country Dance Book*, nor did he notate it from Kimber. As with *Pop Goes the Weasel* and *Hunting the Squirrel*, it is possible that Kimber learned it during or after the Folk Revival.

The Ribbon Dance: Digital audio of the transcription

The Ribbon Dance (p. 220) was audio recorded by Peter Kennedy in 1956 from Kimber's playing. The dance of that name was included by Sharp in *The Country Dance Book*, volume 1. Because Sharp did not notate a version of the tune from Kimber, it is likely a tune that Kimber learned during the revival years. The dance was performed with ribbons around a maypole as well as in a country dance. Kimber's remembered country dance steps were:

Cross hands, back-to-back. Walk 'round her passing back-to-back; now you're doing a dos-si-dos. The top couple join hands [and] galop down the middle between two lines. Now then, both galop back. Top lady and gent turns outward and walk [the] length of the line; all follow behind your lines. You form one arch, pass under the arch. Walk up to the top of the line . . . repeat as desired. Now that's nothing more than the Ribbon Dance. [23]

The Triumph: Digital audio of the transcription

The Triumph (p. 222) was notated by Sharp from Kimber's playing at Oxford in 1908, with the subtitle *Step and Fetch Her*.[24] It was a popular and very widespread country dance and tune. English musician and composer Dave Townsend has counted ten separate versions of the tune that Sharp notated from 1907 to 1909 from sources in Devon, Somerset, Oxfordshire, Derbyshire, Gloucestershire, and Warwickshire.[25] The music and dance were first published in 1790 and introduced in London ballrooms that year, and quickly spread across England, Scotland, and the United States. Christopher Walker, professor of dance at the University of Wisconsin in Madison, observed:

The initial [twenty-four bar] dance was uninteresting. Three years later a different publisher gave a second 'The Triumph' dance that included an unusual, showy figure in which two men lead the woman between them up the set three abreast, with the men's inside hands joined and held up to form an arch above and behind the woman's head. This 'Triumph' figure caught the public's fancy, and it became the signature figure of the dance.[26]

Sharp's *Field Notes* give the following lyrics, taken from Kimber:[27]

> *Step and fetch her*
> *Step and fetch her*
> *For she is a pretty little girl*
> *Don't you tease her*
> *Try to please her*
> *For she is a pretty little girl.*

Sharp also notated the tune *Over the Hills to Glory* from Kimber as a country dance but it has been more commonly used as a ballroom dance—variously, a polka or a schottische—so it is listed in the following chapter. As Sharp did not eventually use it as a dance in his *Country Dance Book*, it seems more likely that it was mostly danced as a ballroom dance in Kimber's day.

[1] David Sutcliffe, 2023, *Cecil Sharp and the Quest for Folk Song and Dance: A New Biography,* London: Ballad Partners, p. 307.

[2] P. J. S. Richardson, 1960, *Social Dances of the Nineteenth Century,* London: Herbert Jenkins, p. 46.

[3] Alan Winston, n.d., English Country Dance and Its American Cousin: History and Comparison, online at www-ssrl.slac.stanford.edu/~winston/ecd/history.htmlx.

[4] Cecil Sharp, 1909, *The Country Dance Book* Part 1, London, Novello.

[5] Chloe Elizabeth Middleton-Metcalfe, 2019, *An Introductory Bibliography of Traditional Social Folk Dance,* Vaughan Williams Memorial Library, EFDSS, table 4.4, Dance List.

[6] Christopher Walker, 2001, "'The Triumph' in England, Scotland and the United States," *Folk Music Journal*, vol. 8, no. 1, p. 23.

[7] William Kimber, as interviewed by Peter Kennedy and Maud Karpeles, at Merryville, Headington Quarry, December 4, 1951. Folktraxx 383, *Kimber Talking*. The former Folktrax website is now administered by Loomis House Press.

[8] Cecil Sharp, 1908, *Double Lead Through*, from William Kimber's playing, VWML CJS2/10/1656.

[9] Clive Carey, 1912, *Double Lead Through*, VWML CC/1/541.

[10] The Traditional Tune Archive, www.tunearch.org, entry for *Bonnets So Blue*.

[11] Dave Townsend, 2021, *Complete Dance Music from the Sharp Collection*, volume 1, Serpent Music, p. 68.

[12] Vaughan Williams Memorial Library, Maud Karpeles manuscripts, MK/1/1/4509 Dance, 'Double Lead Through.'

[13] Andy Turner, 2021, 'Double Lead Through,' *Squeezed Out* blog, www.squeezedout.wordpress.com/2021/03/.

[14] English Folk Dance and Song Society, 1963, *William Kimber,* London: EFDSS, LP 1001.

[15] The Traditional Tune Archive, www.tunearch.org, entry for *Hilly-go Filly-go*.

[16] Cecil Sharp, *Country Dance*, Vaughan Williams Memorial Library archives, Folk Tunes 1657. Also see discussion, Dave Townsend, 2021, *Complete Dance Music from the Sharp Collection*, volume 1: Serpent Music, p. 68.

[17] Cecil Sharp, *Country Dance*, Vaughan Williams Memorial Library archives, Folk Tunes 1657. Also see discussion, Dave Townsend, 2021, *Complete Dance Music from the Sharp Collection*, volume 1, Serpent Music, p. 68.

[18] The Traditional Tune Archive, www.tunearch.org, entry for *Off She Goes*.

[19] William Kimber as recorded by Peter Kennedy in 1951, Folktrax 382, track 32.

[20] Chloe Elizabeth Middleton-Metcalfe, 2019, p. 38.

[21] The Traditional Tune Archive, www.tunearch.org, entry for *Pop Goes the Weasel*.

[22] Dave Townsend, personal communication, February 2024.

[23] William Kimber as recorded by Peter Kennedy in 1951, Folktrax 383, track 33.

[24] Cecil Sharp, *The Triumph*, Vaughan Williams Memorial Library archives, Folk Tunes 1655. Also see discussion, Townsend, 2021, p. 68.

[25] Townsend, 2021, p. 88.

[26] Walker, 2001, p. 4.

[27] Cecil Sharp, *Field Notes*, in the Cecil Sharp manuscript collection at the Vaughan Williams Memorial Library.

A Jeffries Anglo concertina (not William Kimber's). Image courtesy of Roger Digby.

William Kimber, 1946, Stratford-on-Avon summer festival. From the Vaughan Williams Memorial Library.

Transcriptions:
Country Dance Tunes

Bonnets So Blue

COUNTRY DANCE

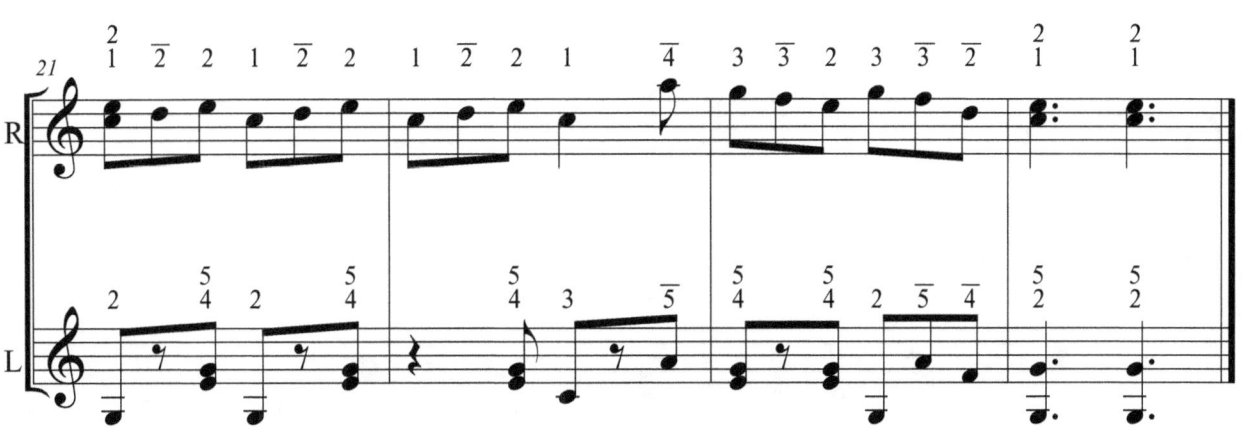

Double Lead Through

COUNTRY DANCE

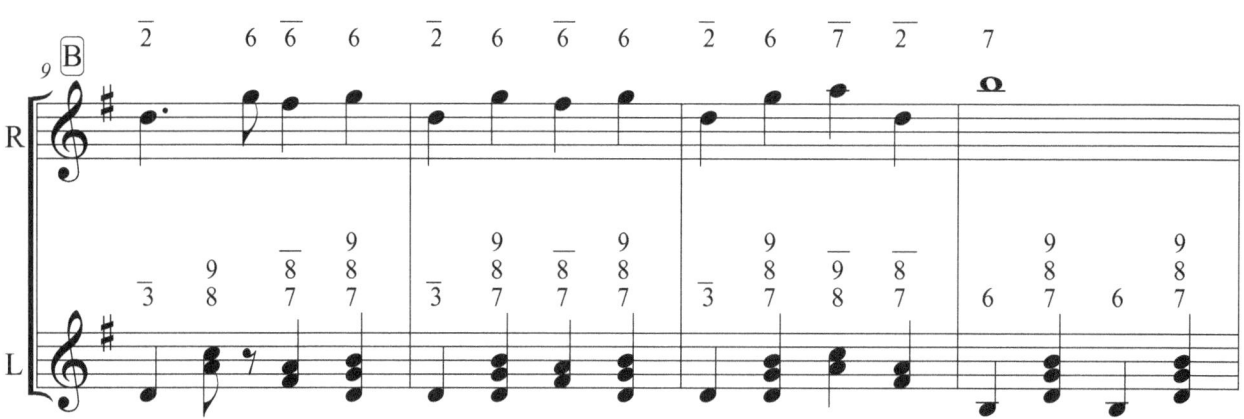

Double Lead Through

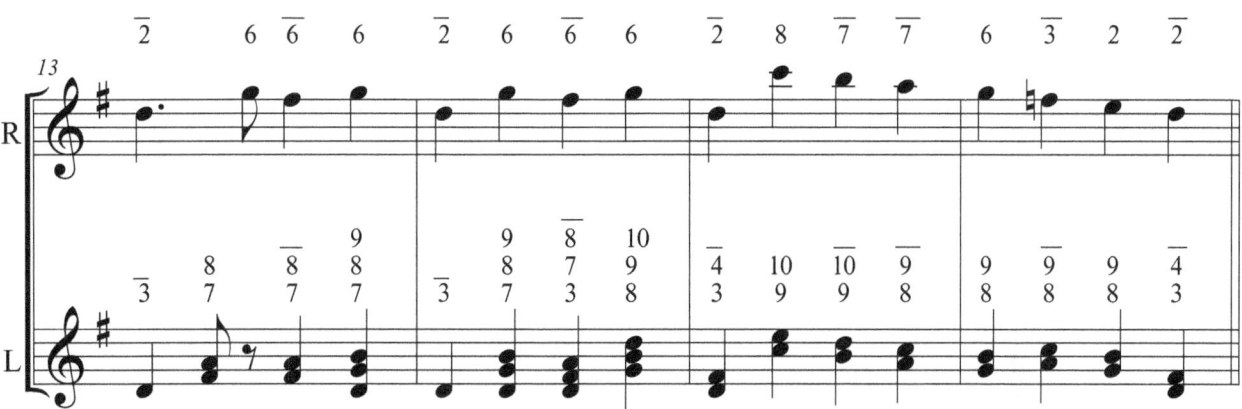

Double Lead Through

Four early two-row Anglo-German concertinas. Clockwise from upper left: Nickolds Crabb and Sons, circa early 1850s; Lachenal, ca 1862-1867; Jones, late 1850s; Jones made for Simpson, 1860s. All are from the collection of Stephen Chambers.

Hilly-go Filly-go
COUNTRY DANCE

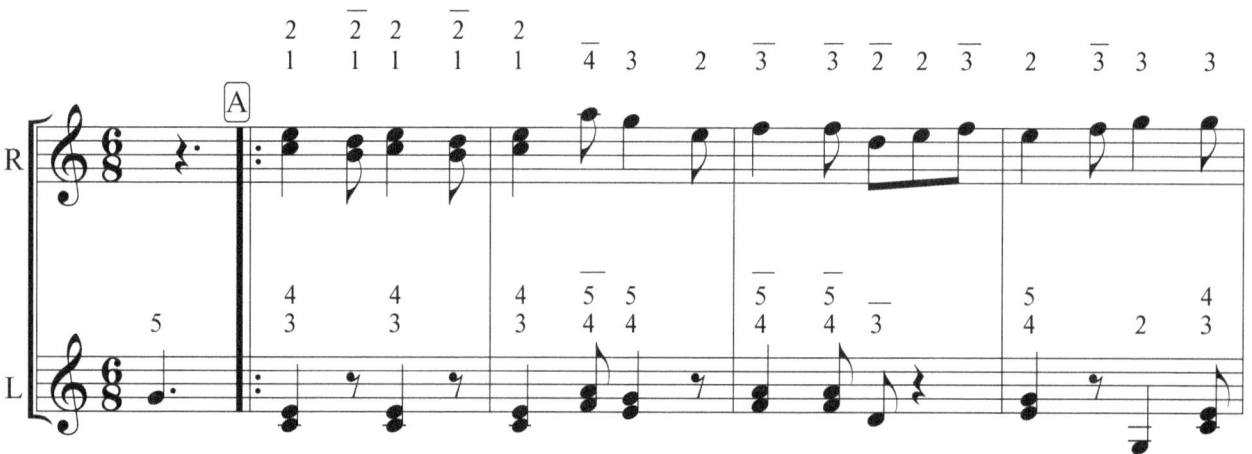

Hilly-go Filly-go

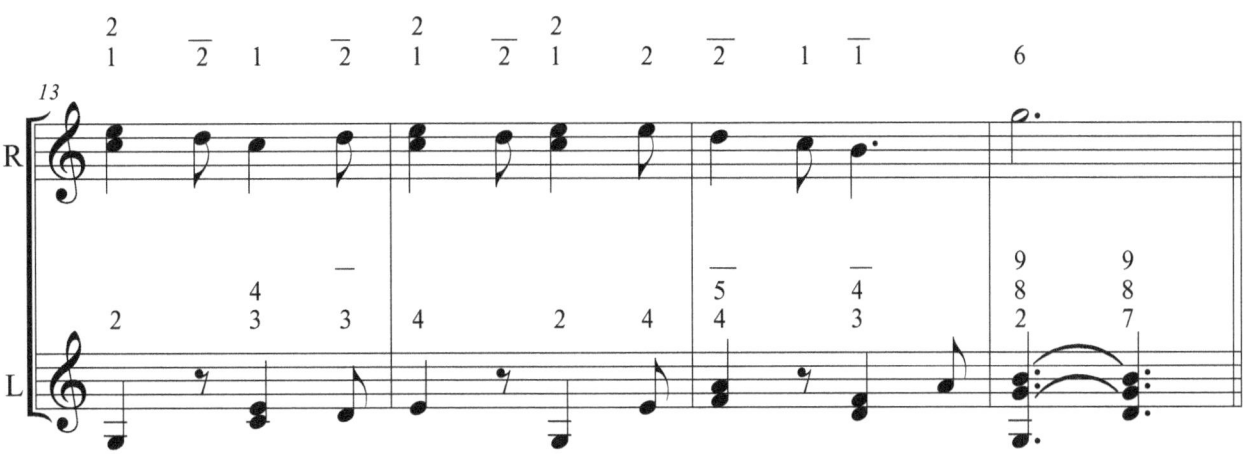
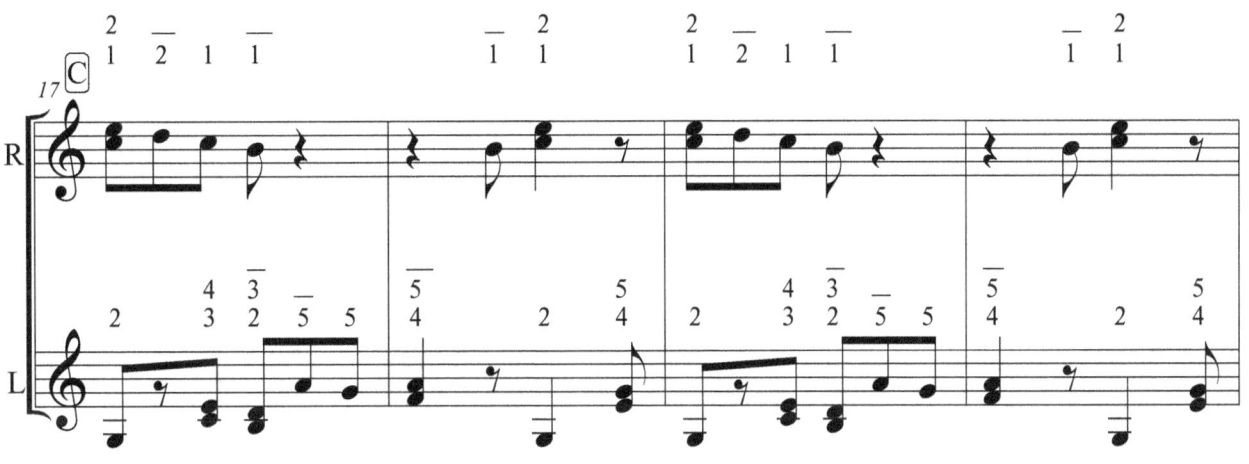

Off She Goes

COUNTRY DANCE

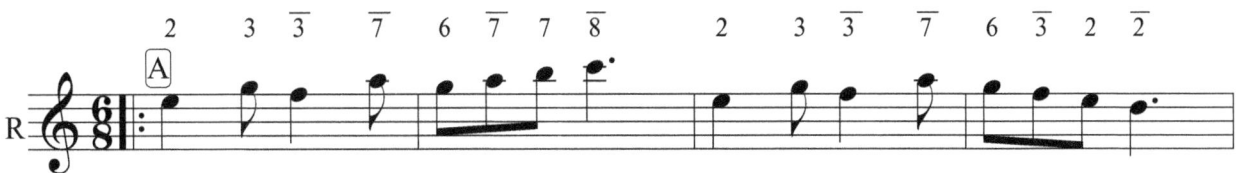
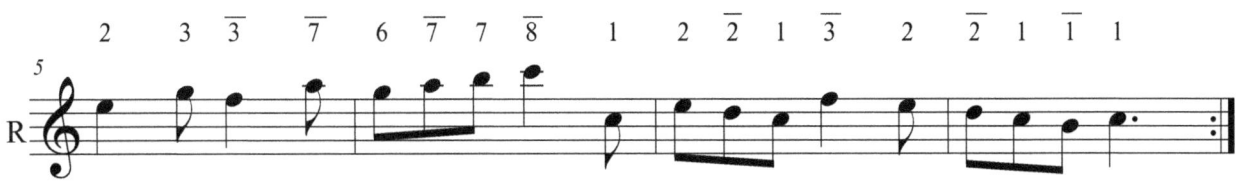
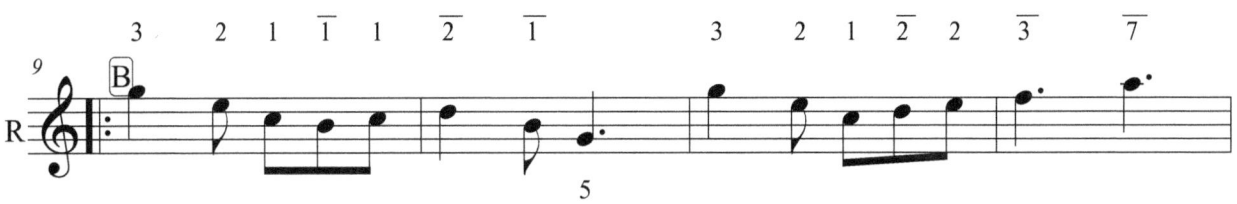
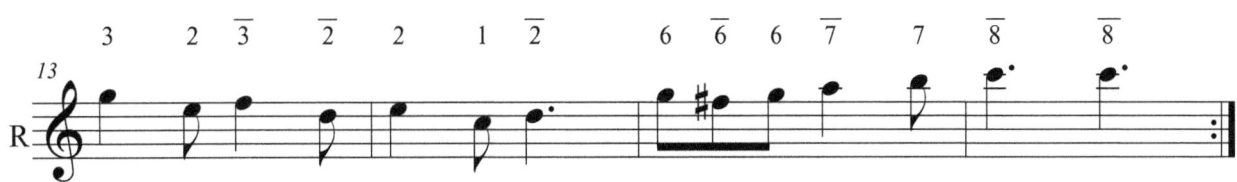

Pop Goes the Weasel

COUNTRY DANCE

Pop Goes the Weasel

Quaker's Wife

COUNTRY DANCE

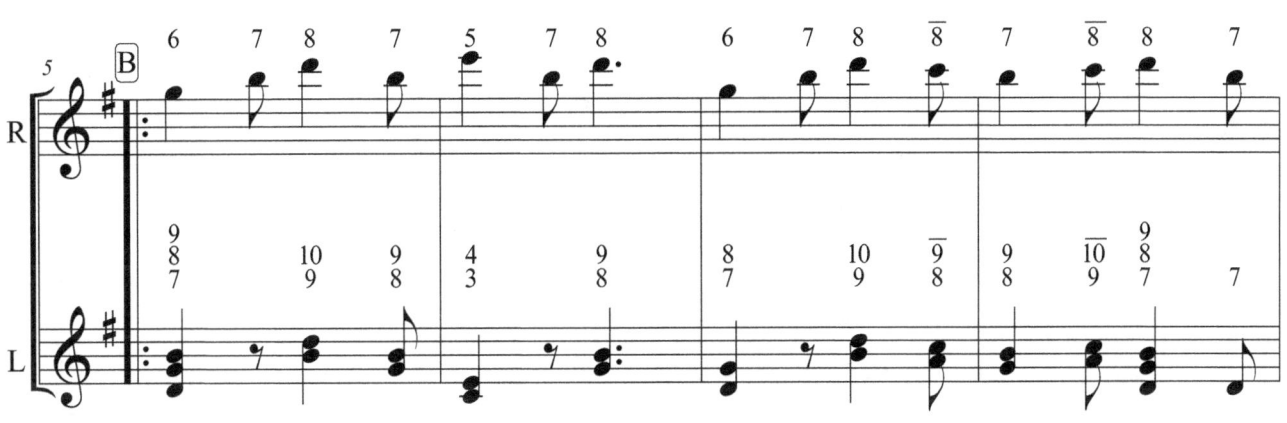

The Ribbon Dance

COUNTRY DANCE

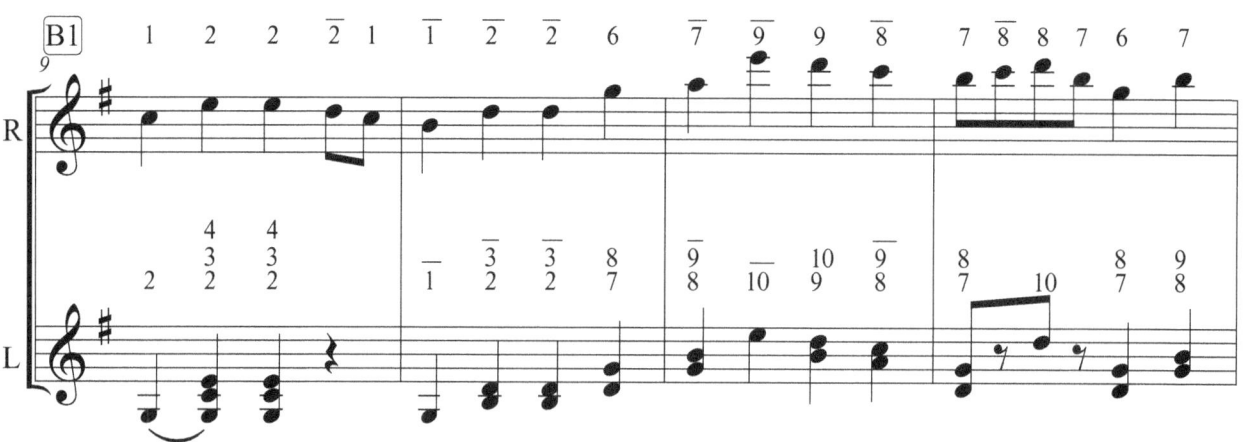

2 The Ribbon Dance

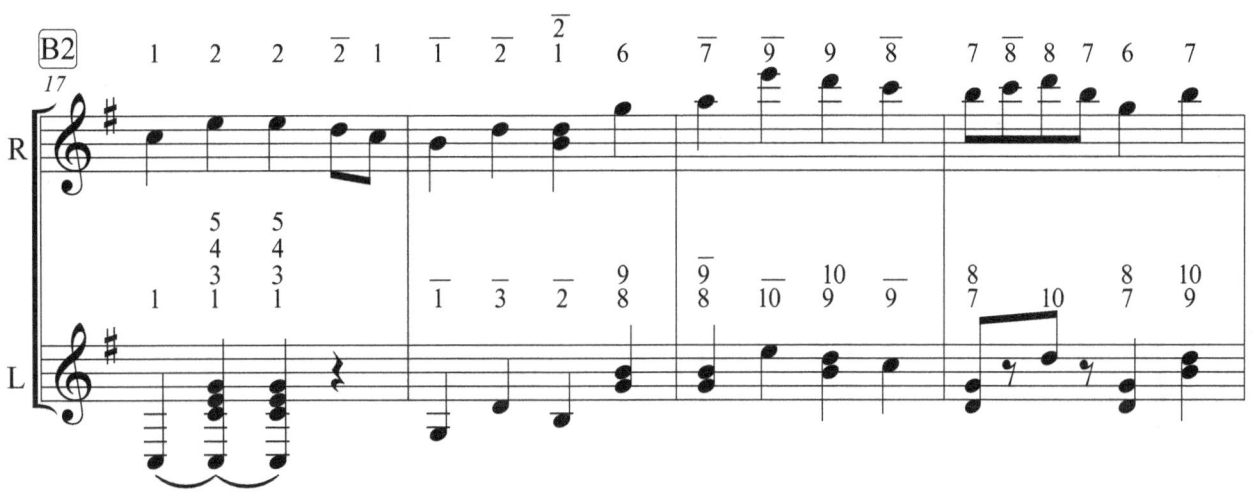

The Triumph
COUNTRY DANCE

The Triumph

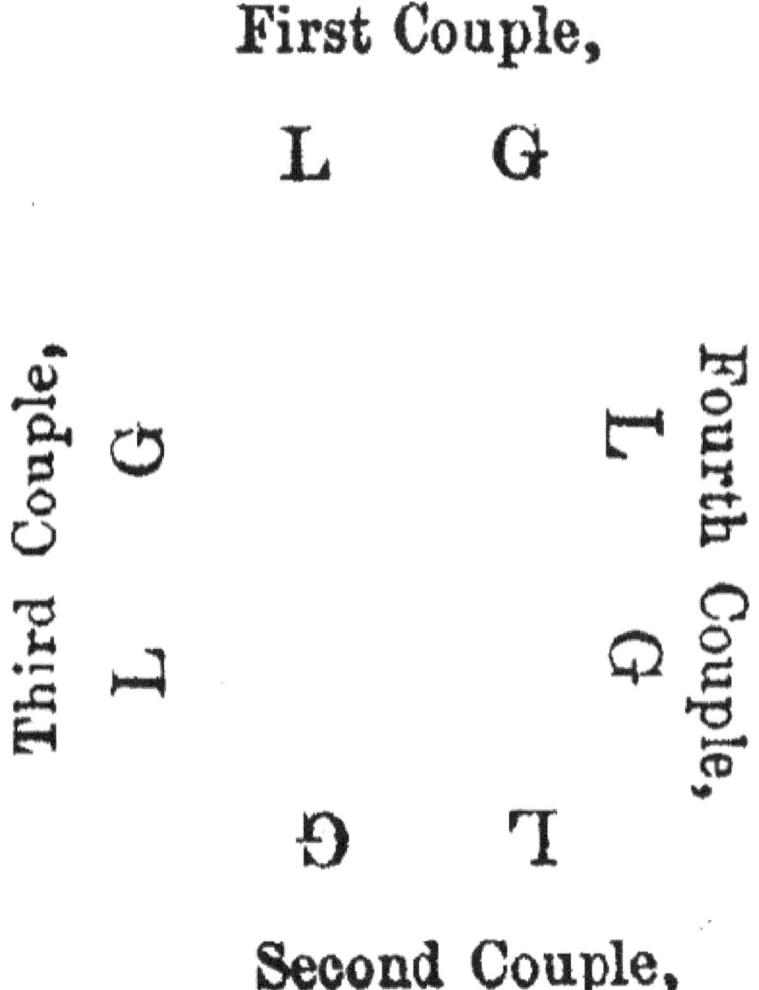

Figure 7.1. Starting positions for the Quadrille, from Elias Howe's *American Dancing Master and Ball-Room Prompter*, 1862

Chapter 7. Social Dance Part II: Quadrilles and Couples Dances

We are accustomed to thinking of Kimber in his famous role of playing for Morris dancers, and secondarily, in his later life, for playing country dances while at EFDSS festival events. As we've seen in the previous chapter, the country dances that he knew reflect more upon the time after he met Cecil Sharp than his time in the Quarry before Sharp. It is his repertoire of late nineteenth-century ballroom dances that gives us a glimpse of what the non-Morris side of his life as a village musician was like, in his younger years in the late nineteenth and earliest twentieth century. The term "ballroom" here refers to the popular dance forms of the nineteenth and earliest twentieth centuries, excluding the older country dances and of course Morris dance but including square forms like quadrilles, and couples dances like the waltz, polka, schottische, and galup, among others. The dances were introduced into upper-class ballrooms, but quickly trickled down the social ladder to dances at the rural village level, in houses or barns and outdoors. The following account of an 1877 dance, written by the local vicar's wife for a dance she and her husband sponsored for working-class villagers in Embleton, Northumberland, in 1877, is perhaps emblematic of the general situation in the English countryside that year, when Kimber was still a child:

> *Our guests arrived at 7; we were forty-four altogether. Our music was the only thing which was not altogether successful. The fiddler whom we had engaged had felt so bashful in coming to what he considered such a grand house that he cheered his spirits by a little whiskey first, and the whiskey seemed to have gone to his fingers and made his playing muddled. We*

varied his playing with quadrilles on the piano from me and polkas on the concertina from some of the young men. You would have been surprised to see the number of dances they performed. They did everything that is danced in the ordinary ballroom, though their valsing [waltzing] didn't come to much. Besides [that] they danced four or five kinds of country dances, schottische, reels, and polkas. Some of them danced extremely well, and it was amusing to watch the difference in their dancing to that of people of our position. They put their whole energy into their dancing and thought of nothing else. Conversation played no part in the proceeding, but the dancing was everything and had to be done as well as was possible. In fact, the faces of most of them were solemn all the time as if they were accomplishing an important task. At 1:30 they all went home and left us very tired.[1]

During the part of Kimber's lifetime when he played for village social dances, from roughly 1885 to World War I, the mix of popular dances continually changed. As mentioned earlier, the older country dances were rapidly on the way out, only to be rescued by Sharp and others in the early twentieth century. Quadrilles had seen a peak in popularity in the 1850s but were still very much a danced form in the last decades of the nineteenth century, judging from numbers of mentions in London publications (Figure 7.3). By Kimber's time there were several major varieties of quadrilles, including the Lancers, the Alberts, and the Caledonians, all of which Kimber knew and played tunes for. Polkas had arrived with a bang in the 1840s and were still extremely popular in Kimber's playing years. Waltzes, although present in England from the beginning of the nineteenth century, seem to have peaked in popularity in the Edwardian era. Other social dances that show up in Kimber's repertoire include the schottische (popular in England from the 1850s), the barn dance (or, as it was originally called, the Military Schottische), and the galup (which reached England in 1829).

At this time or slightly later in Horsted Keynes, Sussex, ninety miles southeast of the Quarry, contemporary Anglo concertina player Scan Tester (1887–1972) played a very similar mix of ballroom dance and step dance tunes to that of Kimber.[2] These

Figure 7.2. "Polkas, mazurkas, schottisches all follow each other in a breathless, enchanting haste." A village barn dance in Australia, 1889. Note the solo concertina player. From the *Illustrated Sydney News,* August 8, 1889.

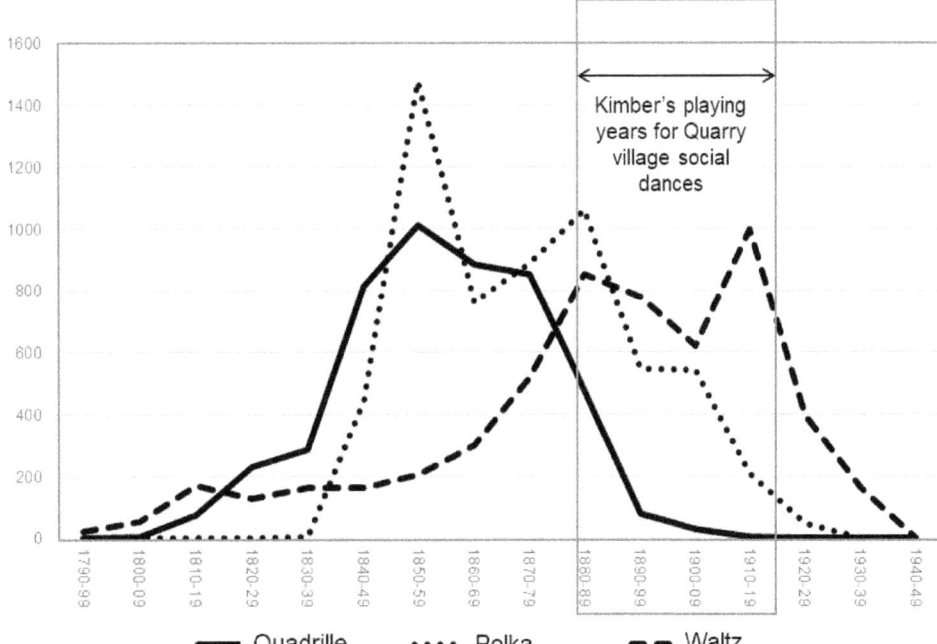

Figure 7.3. Numbers of observations of the words Quadrille, Polka, and Waltz in London publications, 1790–1940. Data from Bill Tuck, 2018, "Dancing in the Asylum," European Association for Digital Humanities Conference, London.

were the popular social dances of late Victorian and Edwardian times, not only in England but in Scotland, Ireland, Australia, New Zealand, North America, and British South Africa. Changing tastes after World War I plus the advent of the early jazz age caused all these dances to wane in the early twentieth century. The dancing of quadrilles, which required a community of dancers with a set of common skills—as opposed to a couples dance, requiring only two people—effectively disappeared across Britain by World War I, except for local dances for old folks.[3] On top of that, the suburbanization of Headington Quarry from a rural village to part of urban Oxford ripped the social fabric of the old village. There seems to be little indication that couples dances and quadrilles had much of a role in Kimber's public playing after the first decade of the twentieth century.

Kimber's ballroom dance repertoire

William Kimber's eleven recorded ballroom dance tunes, transcriptions for which are included at the end of this chapter, are second in number only to his Morris dance tunes. It is a bit odd in a way, because Cecil Sharp and the EFDSS at best ignored ballroom dances in Kimber's lifetime, and at worst were hostile toward them. All but two of his ballroom dance tunes were recorded in just one session, during a visit to Kimber's home by Peter Kennedy and Maud Karpeles on April 12, 1951—when Kimber was an advanced seventy-nine years of age. One gets the feeling while listening to the tapes that these recordings were merely the tip of the iceberg, and that Kimber could easily have recorded many more.

"Ballroom dance" is a type of social dancing where the emphasis is on couples dancing together, rather than on the group figure dancing of country dance—mostly comprising long lines or circles of people. These dances and their initial tunes exploded outward from Central Europe in the early nineteenth century, not coincidentally alongside the spread of new factory-made and inexpensive free-reed instruments manufactured in Germany, such as harmonicas, melodions, and concertinas. First to enter Britain was the waltz, which was reportedly danced by members of Wellington's officer corps after Waterloo and arrived in London the following year (1816).[4] It was at first considered scandalous, because of its close hold—something that did not occur in longways and circle country dances. It was the first of many so-called "couples" or "round" dances. "Couples" referred to the fact that one couple danced together for the whole piece (also at first considered scandalous), and "round" because all the dancers on the floor traced a circular pattern as they progressed around the dance floor. William Kimber recorded only one waltz (*Mayblossom*), but this may simply have been due to the fact that none of those recording him asked him to play more of such a common dance style.

Arriving at about the same time was the quadrille, which can perhaps be thought of evolutionarily as placed in between old-time country figure dances and the newer couples dances, because four couples arranged themselves into a square figure (hence the American term for quadrille: "square dance"). Quadrilles entered England in 1816 from France. The dances consisted of a sequence of sets of dance figures with successive tunes of varying rhythm (hence the Irish term for quadrilles: "set dances") that when taken together formed a complete quadrille. There were several popular quadrilles in England and its colonies, and Kimber was familiar with all of them in dances from his younger days during Whitsuntide:

> . . . *all the old-fashioned dancing; they'd know no other. I shall never forget . . . well we'd [done] one set of quadrilles . . . it was the Caledonians. . . . Quadrilles, you see there were three lots of quadrilles you see. Not Lancers; that's a separate thing with itself. There was the Caledonian Quadrilles, the Polka Quadrilles, and the Alberts.*[5]

The Lancers, Caledonians, Alberts and other quadrilles were originally introduced by musicians of military brass bands, and the dances came with specific associated tunes that the bands played. However, when the latest dances filtered down to English villages and to Irish country houses and to the Australian bush, enterprising musicians would substitute tunes of similar meter and rhythm taken from their own local repertoires. This was quite unlike the association of specific tunes with specific dances in English country dance, and it allowed musicians a great deal of freedom in how they used their repertoire. In County Clare, Ireland, the five sets of the Lancers are typically danced to reels, or a mixture of reels and polkas. In mid-nineteenth-century England, however, there was more variety in rhythm to the typical Lancers set as created by John Duval of 1817 Dublin.[6] Duval's set of "figures" (discrete dances that together comprise the Lancers quadrille) are listed here:

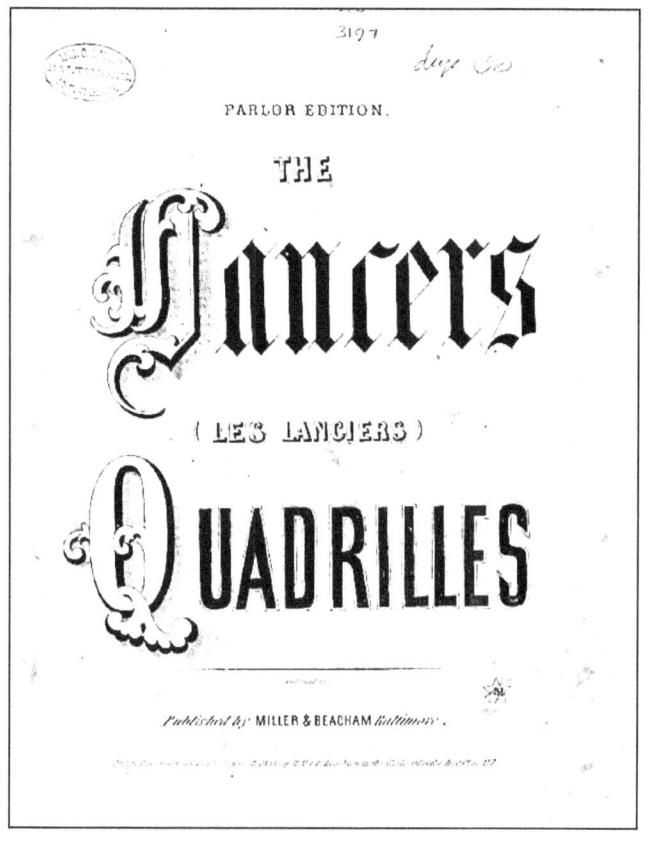

Figure 7.4. Cover for a version of the Lancers quadrilles published in Baltimore, 1858. The Lancers were perhaps the most globally popular of the quadrilles.

Figure 1: 3 strains of 16 beats each, usually in 6/8 meter.
Figure 2: 3 strains of 16 beats each, usually in 2/4 meter
Figure 3: 2 or 3 strains of 16 beats each, always in 6/8 meter
Figure 4: 3 strains of 16 beats each, usually in 6/8 meter.
Figure 5: chorus of 32 beats alternating with figure of 64 beats, usually in 4/4 meter.[7]

The authors have been unable to locate any village band tune set lists for late nineteenth- to early twentieth-century Lancers in rural England, but perhaps they weren't too different from their Australian bush band counterparts. The late Australian dance historian and musician Peter Ellis compiled dance lists from a number of early twentieth-century dance bands for the quadrilles and various couples dances. There the first two figures of the Lancers, with march-like vigor, could include tunes like *Redwing*, *Old Folks at Home*, *Silver Bell*, and *Red River Valley*, most of them pop tunes of that era. The jigs of the third figure might include *Garryowen* and *St. Patrick's Day*. The zippy fourth figure in Ellis's lists contained tunes like *The Girl I Left Behind Me*, known to Kimber as *Brighton Camp*, or perhaps *Golden Slippers*, or *Auntie Mary*, known to Kimber as *Cock o' the North*. The fifth figure might include *Scotland the Brave*, or even *All By Yourself in the Moonlight*.[8] All of these tunes would be admissible in a modern-day English traditional music session, and would have been known to village musicians a century and more ago. Daisy Bulwer (1892–1974), who along with her husband Walter Bulwer (1888–1968) played for quadrilles in their younger years in Shipdham, Norfolk, before those old country squares were finally displaced by tangos and foxtrots, remembered that they played mostly songs and march tunes for the Lancers, not unlike their Australian contemporaries.[9]

The Caledonian quadrille originated around 1823 using sets of figures—as in the Lancers—but danced to Scottish-themed reels and jigs.[10] Kimber knew several Scottish pieces that would work perfectly well in parts of the Caledonians, such as the *Highland Fling*, *Nae Good Luck about the Hoose*, and *Over the Hills to Glory* (originally a Scottish tune, *The Lass o' Gowrie*). According to Peter Ellis, several of these same schottische tunes were used in Australian bush dances for the Caledonian, along with reels and jigs.[11] In early to mid-twentieth-century County Clare, Ireland, the figures of the Caledonian were typically danced to a mixture of reels, jigs and hornpipes.[12]

The Alberts quadrille originated in England and was designed by a French dancing master, Charles d'Albert. It had a variety of rhythms in its figures, which d'Albert achieved by sequencing favorite figures from the First Set, Caledonians, Lancers and the Waltz Cotillion.[13] In its Australian bush dance form, it included reels or marches, polka mazurkas, and waltzes. A similar list of tunes to those mentioned for the Lancers could be used, with the addition in the final figure of waltzes like *Over the Waves* or *The Spanish Waltz*.[14] One of Kimber's schottisches, which he called *Kitty Come*, is a version of *The Kitty Schottische* composed by Charles d'Albert;[15] Kimber probably used it in playing for the Alberts quadrille.

Kimber was well equipped with tunes for playing for all sorts of quadrille dances, even though it is unrecorded which tunes he played for which quadrille. Galups and/or marchy jigs like *Bonny Dundee*, *Rigs o' Marlow* and *Cock o' the North* would work well in any 2/4 or 6/8 setting. Reels like *Soldier's Joy* or a vigorous tune like *Brighton Camp* would work for any required reel. And if polkas were used in the Alberts in village England, *Little Polly* and *I Love the Gal with the Blue Frock On* would be perfect.

Polkas originated in Bohemia in 1834 and arrived in London by 1844. They have a characteristic rhythm that combines an anacrusis on a rising step followed by three short steps and a hop, as in *a-one-two-three-hop, a-one-two-three-hop*. As noted in the preceding chapter, Kimber remembered them fondly and recorded three of them, all in a 1951 recording session with Peter Kennedy: *Donkey Cock Your Tail Up*, *I Love the Gal with the Blue Frock On*, and *Little Polly*. As mentioned earlier, they also could see service in a quadrille.

Schottisches, another central European import, arrived soon after the polka (a schottische was in the first known tutor for the German concertina, by Höselbarth, ca. 1838), and were in England by 1850. In the schottische the couple usually assumes a (closed) waltz position. In its simplest and earliest version, according to a Mrs. Nicholas Henderson of London in her mid-1850s dance manual:

Figure 7.5. The *Kitty Schottische* was written by Charles d'Albert for what became known as The Alberts Quadrilles. The tune was published around 1855. Kimber knew it as *Kitty Come*.

> It [has] a very elegant and withal a particularly pleasing movement, for it is a combination of two movements, a polka movement and a circular hop movement; and the two combined make up a most agreeable variety not to be found either in the Polka, the Deux Temps or Redowa.[16]

The tempo is variously 2/4 or 4/4 and is marked by a clear lengthening of the notes on the first and third beats (*Over the Hills to Glory* illustrates this rhythm nicely). In Scotland and Ireland, they are commonly known as flings or Highland flings. This dance did not ignite as large a craze as had the earlier polka and waltz, but it nonetheless had great staying power in many countries.[17] As mentioned, the tunes also saw service in quadrilles, and Kimber recorded several: *Keel Row/Highland Fling*, *Moonlight*, *Nae Good Luck about the Hoose*, *Kitty Come*, and *Over the Hills to Glory*.

The Barn Dance began as a late nineteenth-century American variation on the plain schottische that was originally called the "Military Schottische." It became popular in England when danced to the tune *Dancing in the Barn*, hence the title "Barn Dance."[18] Peter Kennedy listed Kimber's schottische tune *Kitty Come* as a "barn dance," and Kimber may have played it as such. As mentioned, that tune was originally composed by Charles d'Albert for his quadrilles.

Galups (also galops) originated in Hungary as a forerunner to the polka and reached England by about 1829. It was a popular kind of dance on which to end an evening's fun. The music for a galup is typically played in rapid 2/4 time. A couple in waltz position executes gliding steps that mimic a galloping horse, and the dance could also include smooth but rapid whirling waltz turn steps. It was one of the more exciting ballroom dances to execute, and yet one of the easiest to learn. Offenbach's

Can Can is a famous galup, as is the American tune *Ta Ra Ra Boom De Ay*, but Kimber's *Bonny Dundee* would make an excellent alternate.[19]

Other popular nineteenth- and early twentieth-century ballroom dance forms, such as the varsovianas, mazurkas, Valeta waltzes, and the waltz cotillon, are not found in Kimber's recordings, almost certainly because no one with a tape recorder asked him for them. They were present throughout the English countryside in the late nineteenth and early twentieth century and would have been in the Quarry alongside the quadrilles, schottisches and polkas.

Is this traditional music and dance?

As already observed, Cecil Sharp was not a fan of ballroom dances. He didn't mince words in the introduction to his 1909 collection of country dances:

> *The unlettered . . . have always sung the songs and dances of their forefathers, uninfluenced by, and in blissful ignorance of the habits and tastes of their more fashionable city neighbours. But this is, unhappily, no longer so. . . . In the village of today the polka, waltz, and quadrille are steadily displacing the old-time country dances and jigs, just as the tawdry ballads and strident street-songs of the towns are no less surely exterminating the folk-songs. . . . [The country dance is] the ordinary, everyday dance of the country-folk, performed not merely on festal days, but whenever opportunity offered and the spirit of merrymaking was abroad.*[20]

Sharp also decried the use in surviving country dances of polka, galup and waltz steps instead of the preferred springy walking step—a sure sign, to him, of degradation of the purer earlier forms of rural dance.[21] It is no surprise that Sharp's own notations of Kimber's tunes included hardly any ballroom dance tunes, and then only if it were used in a Morris dance. Luckily Peter Kennedy and Maud Karpeles in 1951, and later Theo Chaundy in 1956, tried to address part of that gaping hole in English traditional music, when they recorded a small sample of Kimber's ballroom dance tunes in Kimber's living room.

Figure 7.6. Dancing on the lawn, from an early twentieth-century English postcard. Is this scene portraying "traditional" dance and music? It didn't seem so at the time, when Sharp observed the disappearance of older country dances as popular culture moved toward the schottische and the waltz.

This image of what constituted pure folk dance and music in EFDSS activities continued well after Sharp's death. Village social dances—ballroom dances, for the most part—were overlooked in favor of rigidly defined "pure" English folk dance—the country dances.[22] At the same time in Ireland, clerics and the Gaelic League also rejected Victorian and Edwardian ballroom dances, and like the EFDSS, tried to interest the masses in "purer" ceilidh dances, themselves modern revisionist reintroductions of old country dances in Ireland.[23] In Australia there was no such ambivalence or opposition to the old ballroom dances, and they are celebrated even today as the backbone of the country's traditional folk culture.

In the early twentieth century, the old ballroom dances gave way everywhere to newer forms, especially the foxtrot and jazz dancing. After World War II in England there was an effort to revive the "old-time" ballroom couples dances—polkas, waltzes, barn dances and the like—as the "British Old Time Revival," but that revival occurred outside the EFDSS. Douglas Kennedy, then head of the EFDSS, tried to form more of an everyman image of the EFDSS and even incorporated a waltz in their Community Dance Manual of 1947. As dance historian Chloe Middleton-Metcalfe observed in her study of the clash between old-time dancing revival and the EFDSS in post-war Britain, it was a half-step at best, of which Reg Hall was to comment in 1988:

> *They [EFDSS] didn't want to know the couple dances, even though there was a popular tradition of couple dances all over England. Instead of building the folk dance revival, they ignored it and destroyed it. But the approach was illogical. It was all right to do the Waltz Country Dance but not the Valeta and the Barn Dance, even though the Valeta is danced as part of the Waltz Country Dance. As a couple dance it wasn't [considered] valid, although—perhaps because—it was in the popular tradition.*[24]

The old couples dances and quadrille tunes are now a part of the core repertoire of English traditional music (or "English Country Music") as played in pub sessions across Britain, a traditional music movement that is still somewhat separate from the "folk" dances of the EFDSS. In Ireland, quadrilles ("set dances") and most couples dances nearly died out in the mid-twentieth century after decades of suppression, but today "sets" are fully accepted by the traditional music and dance establishment there, and in fact have become the most popular traditional dance style in the country. Couples dance tunes such as barn dances, schottisches and polkas, once derided as foreign, are now completely acceptable in All Ireland instrumental competitions at the Fleadh Cheoil na hÉireann. In Australia by the late twentieth century, bush dancing and especially quadrilles were on the wane, but organizations like the Bush Dance and Music Club of Bendigo and District, as well as similar organizations across the country, have kept this music alive and linked to dance.

Two Music Collectors

Two men can be thanked for the vast majority of the songs and non-Morris tunes recorded from William Kimber, as well as for many of his stories.

Theodore William Chaundy (1889-1966) was born in Oxford of an old Oxford family; both he and his father, John Chaundy, were Freemen of the city. Chaundy read mathematics at Balliol College, Oxford on scholarship in 1906-1909, and became a lecturer in mathematics at Christ Church, Oxford in 1910. He was named to a university lectureship in 1927 in mathematics and a reader in 1947. Chaundy had an interest in Morris dance from his early university days and was one of those who started the dancing near Magdalen College on May morning. In 1926 he formed the Oxford University Men's Morris, and in 1938 formed the Oxford Morris Men (later, Oxford City Morris Men). Men in both of these groups were tutored by William Kimber in their early days. After Chaundy retired from teaching in 1956, he turned his attention back to the Morris, and in particular to his old friend Kimber, who was by then at the advanced age of 84. Chaundy and his wife Hilda Dott Chaundy (1890-1986) plus a few friends and family members visited Kimber at Merryville in 1956 and 1959, with a tape recorder. Chaundy asked Kimber the usual questions about the early days of Morris with Sharp, but also captured many non-Morris topics and tunes from Kimber. Those recordings are all available on an online website put together by Folk Arts Oxford, www.merryville.uk. Using the material from these sessions, Chaundy penned a substantial biography of Kimber in 1959.

Peter Kennedy (1922–2006) was a collector of folk music and songs in the 1950s and 1960s. In the 1940s his father Douglas Kennedy, then head of the EFDSS, helped make a set of studio recordings of William Kimber that concentrated on Kimber's Morris dance tunes. Peter Kennedy became interested in other aspects of Kimber's music that were not related strictly to the Morris, and while on the staff of the EFDSS he made a set of field recordings of Kimber in 1951 and 1956, containing many of Kimber's versions of country dance and ballroom dance tunes that would otherwise have been lost. He also recorded many other musicians across Britain and Ireland from the 1950s to the 2000s and hosted a radio series, *As I Roved Out*, on BBC in the 1950s. His voluminous musical collection was transferred after his death to Topic Records for archiving.

Theo Chaundy (front left) and others of the Oxford University Men's Morris, May morning 1929.

Theo Chaundy during his Oxford teaching days. This and the above image are courtesy of Chris Sheffield, Oxford City Morris Men.

Peter Kenned and family, ca. 1950s. Image courtesy of Vaughan Williams Memorial Library.

References:
Anon, n.d., "100 Years of Morris Dancing on May Morning in Oxford, online at www.folklore-society.com.
Theo Chaundy, 1959, "William Kimber: A Portrait by T. W. Chaundy," Journal of the EFDSS, vol. 8, no. 4, pp. 203–11.
Derek Schofield, 2006, "Peter Kennedy (Obituary)," Guardian, June 18, 2006. Also see the Peter Kennedy Archive, www.peterkennedy.org.

Tune sources and explanation

Bonny Dundee (p. 242) is a classic galup, recorded from Kimber's playing by Peter Kennedy and Maud Karpeles in 1951. It is derived from an old Scottish song, and its tune was published in Playford's *Dancing Master* of 1688. Sharp notated the tune from the Barrington Fiddlers in Somerset in 1903,[25] but did not include steps for it as a country dance in his books.[26] In Kimber's recording Kimber mentions it as a "galup," and it was perhaps more popular in his day as such. It was and is used as a galup by the Royal Horse Artillery.[27] A version was published in *Kerr's Merrie Melodies* of the 1880s as a reel. Accordionist Jimmy Shand played it as a waltz.

Bonnie Dundee: Digital audio of the transcription

Donkey Cock Your Tail Up (p. 245) was described as a march by Kimber when he recorded it in 1951, although it is rhythmically more like a schottische. It derives from a Scottish strathspey, *The Braes of Mar*, published in *Bremner's Reels* of 1758.[28] It is also known as an old Scottish song, *Some Say the Devil Is Dead*, and more recently was used by the Irish group De Danaan with the song *Love Will You Marry Me*. Kimber knew it alternatively as *Whoa, Jerusalem!*

Donkey Cock Your Tail Up: Digital audio of the transcription

Father O'Flynn (p. 246) is a 6/8 jig that was recorded from Kimber's playing by Peter Kennedy and Maud Karpeles in 1951. It appears in this chapter by process of elimination: it isn't a Morris dance tune, nor was it a country dance nor (apparently) a step dance tune, hence our guess that it may have been used in one of the jig-time figures in a quadrille. It is perhaps better known in Irish circles as the *Top of Cork Road*, a song of 1874 with lyrics by Alfred Percival Graves. The earliest known printed version is English, under the title *The Yorkshire Lasses* (1778), and it is in *Ryan's Mammoth Collection* of 1883.[29] Kimber plays this with only sparse left-hand accompaniment, as it is a sprightly jig played at a quick pace.

Father O'Flynn: Digital audio of the transcription

I Love the Gal with the Blue Frock On (p. 248), recorded by Kennedy from Kimber's playing in 1951, is a widely known polka among English and Irish musicians. It is also known as *The Girl with the Blue Dress On* or as *Babes in the Woods*. The title phrase is common in American minstrel sources, but the Traditional Tune Archive considers the A part of the tune as an adaptation of the Victorian era *The Kitty Schottische,* composed by Charles d'Albert (see *Kitty Come*, this chapter), and the B part as similar to the *Redowa Polka*.[30]

I Love the Gal with the Blue Frock On: Digital audio of the transcription

Keel Row: Digital audio of the transcription

Keel Row (p. 250) is a Highland fling/schottische that was recorded from Kimber's playing by Peter Kennedy and Maud Karpeles in 1951. It was reportedly contained in a Northumbrian tune collection by John Smith in 1752, now unfortunately lost, and in a Scottish tunebook of Neil Stewart in 1770, *A Collection of Favorite Scots' Tunes*.[31] In Kimber's recording he makes it clear that it was used in his time for a heel-and-toe polka dance; it is danced as a polka in Ireland as well.[32] He paired it on his recording with a similar schottische, *Nae Good Luck about the Hoose* (or, *There's nae luck about the House*).

Kitty Come: Digital audio of the transcription

Kitty Come (p. 252) is a schottische recorded from Kimber's playing by Peter Kennedy and Maud Karpeles in 1951. It is a version of *The Kitty Schottische*, composed by Charles d'Albert for what became known as the Alberts quadrilles. As mentioned earlier, Kimber recalled playing for Alberts in his younger years. Peter Kennedy listed it as a barn dance in the Folktrax CD of Kimber's recordings,[33] and indeed it could have been used for that.

Little Polly Polka: Digital audio of the transcription

Little Polly (p. 235) was recorded from Kimber's playing by Peter Kennedy and Maud Karpeles in 1951. It is essentially the same as the tune of that name in the ca. 1890 tune book of brickmaker George H. Watson (1859–1944) of Swanton Abbey, Norfolk.[34]

Mayblossom: Digital audio of the transcription

Mayblossom (p. 256) is Kimber's only recorded waltz, which was recorded from Kimber's playing by Peter Kennedy and Maud Karpeles in 1951. It was created by the American composer A. T. Cramer and published as the *May Blossoms Waltz* in 1885 in Cincinnati (Figure 7.7).[35] It is the only one of his recorded tunes where he utilizes the upper third row of keys on his thirty-button CG Jeffries concertina, to play the single note Bb. His arrangement sounds remarkably like the playing of a street organ or a park carousel, complete with a perfect oom-pah accompaniment that is highly unlike the rest of his repertoire. It may be that he was experimenting with recreating the sound of such a calliope or a street organ.

Moonlight (p. 260) is a schottische that was recorded from Kimber's playing by Peter Kennedy and Maud Karpeles in 1951. According to Kimber, it was danced as a "plain schottische; four right, four left, eight round." Its origin is unknown, at least to the authors.

Moonlight: Digital audio of the transcription

Nae Good Luck about the Hoose (or, *There's Nae Luck about the House*; p. 262) is another Highland fling/schottische that was recorded from Kimber's playing by Peter Kennedy and Maud Karpeles in 1951. He played it in a medley with *Keel Row*, both tunes were danced as a heel-and-toe polka, but in an unusual way that he said (in his interview with Theo Chaundy) was a Quarry practice. He played *Keel Row* once through (i.e., AABB), then *Nae Good Luck* once through, then *Keel Row* once through, and *Nae Good Luck* again once through. It is a well-known tune in the north of England. Its earliest manuscript form seems to be in the 1770s music book of Henry Livingston, a soldier in the American Revolution, but it is claimed to have been written in music and lyrics by Scottish poet Jean Adam as *The Mariner's Wife*, at some time before 1751.[36] It was used in the second figure of the Caledonians quadrille, as originally danced, and it seems likely that Kimber used it in this way as well.[37]

Nae Good Luck about the Hoose: Digital audio of the transcription

Figure 7.7. *The May Blossoms Waltz*, known to Kimber as the *Mayblossom*, was composed by American A. T. Cramer in 1885. Its presence in Kimber's repertoire underscores how dancers and musicians in late Victorian England—even in rural areas—kept up with the latest dance fashions.

William Kimber playing *Over the Hills to Glory* via His Master's Voice 1946

Over the Hills to Glory:: Digital audio of the transcription

Over the Hills to Glory (p. 264) was recorded by Kimber in a studio in 1946. The tune, a schottische, was originally a Scottish tune called *The Lass o' Gowrie* that was typically played as a march or a 2/4 reel. The 55th Foot Regiment of the British Army, raised in Stirling, marched to this tune in 1755, as did many later army units. Kimber's version is a schottische and has an English title; it is named for a group of women in southern England who were imprisoned in 1873 for their part in forming an agricultural workers' union, after which they were sent "over the hills to glory" [to prison]. They were later pardoned by Queen Victoria.[38] Sharp notated the melody from Kimber as a "country dance," but had no steps for it. A country dance from Northamptonshire was later named for it.[39]

The transcription includes two run-throughs of each of the A parts and B parts (i.e., no repeat signs) in order to display the subtle changes in the accompaniment on repeat playings of the parts. Playing like Kimber is not an exercise in memorizing specific accompaniment notes, but in remembering the various techniques he uses to craft an accompaniment from a starting point of simple octaves. These variations – the 'finishing touches' – can be called in at will whenever the player wishes.

[1] Louise Creighton, 1877, writing a letter that was quoted in James T. Covert, 2000, *A Victorian Marriage*, London: Continuum International Publishing Group, p. 115.

[2] Reg Hall, 1990, *I Never Played to Many Posh Dances: Scan Tester, Sussex Musician, 1887–1972*, Rochford, Essex: Musical Traditions, supplement 2, 147 pp.

[3] Hall, 1990, p. 82.

[4] Peter Eillis, 2005, *The Merrie Country Dance,* Bendigo, New South Wales, Australia: Bendigo Dance and Music Club, p. B103; Helen Brennan, 1999, *The Story of Irish Dance*, Dingle Ireland: Brandon Press, p. 99.

[5] William Kimber, as recorded by Peter Kennedy and Maud Karpeles, at Merryville, Headington Quarry, December 4, 1951, Folktrax 382, track 31. Folktrax materials are archived at www.folktrax-archive.org and administered by Loomis House Press.

[6] Traditional Tune Archive, www.tunearch.org, entry on Lancers Quadrille First Figure.

[7] Stockton California Folk Dance Camp, 2017, The Lancers Quadrille, 19th century ballroom. Manuscript notes.

[8] Ellis, 1987, *Collector's Choice*, volume 2, Melbourne: Victorian Folk Club of Australia, pp. 103–11.

[9] Hall, 1990, p. 82.

[10] Green Ginger, 2019, *The Caledonian Quadrilles*, liner notes to CD, Bandcamp.

[11] Peter Ellis, 1987, pp. 123–29.

[12] Larry Lynch, *Set Dances of Ireland: Tradition and Evolution,* San Francisco, California: Séadna Books, pp. 17, 27, 35, 43, 51.

[13] Dave Hunt, 2000, "Country dances, contradances, cotillons, and quadrilles: Musical Traditions reviews, February 8, 2000, https://www.mustrad.org.uk/reviews/quadrill.htm. [14]

Ellis, 1987, pp. 129–36; Mary Smith, Alberts Quadrille: YouTube, Nov. 12, 2011.

[15] A version of *The Kitty Schottische* was published in Sydney in the nineteenth century and can be found in the archives of the National Library of Australia.

[16] Henderson, Mrs Nicholas, n.d. (ca.1854), *Etiquette of the Ball-Room and Guide to All the New and Fashionable Dances.* 3rd ed., London. Also see Henderson, Mrs. Nicholas, n.d. (mid-1850s?), "Instructions for Dancing the Schottisch" on sheet music "The Hungarian Schottische," London. With thanks to www.kickery.com.

[17] See discussion in Dan Worrall, 2023, *House Dance: Dance Music Played on the Anglo-German Concertina by Musicians of the House Dance Era,* Honolulu: Rollston Press, pp. 53–56.

[18] Anonymous, n.d., "Military Schottische," Library of Congress, online at https://www.libraryofdance.org/dances/military-schottische/.

[19] Worrall, 2023, p. 57.
[20] Cecil Sharp, 1909, *The Country Dance Book*, pp. 7–8, 10, as quoted by Derek Schofield, n.d., Cecil Sharp and English Folk Song and Dance Before 1915: Country Dance and Song Society, www.cdss.org.
[21] *Ibid.*, p. 25.
[22] See Chloe Elizabeth Middleton-Metcalfe, 2022, "Couple Dances, Douglas Kennedy's English Folk Dance Society, and the British Old Time Dance Revival," CD-S Online, *The Scholarly Journal of the Country Dance and Song Society*, April 2022, pp. 17–23.
[23] Worrall, 2023, pp. 73–92.
[24] Reg Hall, as quoted by Derek Schofield, 1988, "The Dance Musician: One of the Catalysts of the Re-discovery of English Country Music was Reg Hall. Derek Schofield Tracks Him Down," 1988, *FRoots*, 9.10 no. 59, pp. 23–26. Also see Middleton-Metcalfe, 2022, pp. 19–20.
[25] Dave Townsend, 2021, *Complete Dance Music from the Sharp Collection*, volume 1, Serpent Music, p. 1.
[26] Chloe Elizabeth Middleton-Metcalfe, 2019, *An Introductory Bibliography of Traditional Social Folk Dance,* Vaughan Williams Memorial Library, EFDSS, Table 4.4, Dance List.
[27] A 1933 film of the Royal Horse Artillery parading with this tune is on YouTube at https://www.youtube.com/watch?v=1Tp3wOvSuoI.
[28] Leslie Nielson, n.d., "The Standard on the Braes of Mar," online on The Contemplator, https://www.contemplator.com/scotland/braesmar.
[29] Traditional Tune Archive, www.tunearch.org, entry for *Father O'Flynn*.
[30] Traditional Tune Archive, www.tunearch.org, entry for *Girl with the Blue Dress On*.
[31] Traditional Tune Archive, www.tunearch.org, entry for *Keel Row*.
[32] The Session, www.thesession.org, entry for *The Keel Row* polka.
[33] Liner notes to *William Kimber Anglo concertina*, Folktrax CD 382, track 36.
[34] Traditional Tune Archive, www.tunearch.org., entry for *Little Polly* polka. Also see East Anglian Traditional Music Trust, *George Watson's Swanton Abbott Tune Book*, www.eatmt.org.uk.
[35] *May Blossoms Waltz* by A. T. Cramer, US Library of Congress, control number 2023857032.
[36] Traditional Tune Archive, www.tunearch.org, entry for *There's Nae Luck About the House*.
[37] Ellis, 1987, p. 123.
[38] Traditional Tune Archive, www.tunearch.org, entries for *Over the Hills to Glory* and to *The Lass o' Gowrie*.
[39] *Journal of the EFDSS*, 1937, vol. 3, no. 2, pp. 135–37.

World War I Memorial, Holy Trinity Church, Headington Quarry, 2023.

Headington Quarry, from a ca. 1900 post card. Image courtesy of Stephanie Jenkins, Oxford History website, www.headington.org.uk.

Transcriptions:
Quadrilles and Couples Dances

Bonny Dundee

GALUP

Bonny Dundee

Bonny Dundee

Donkey Cock Your Tail Up

SCHOTTISCHE

Father O'Flynn's

IRISH JIG

Father O'Flynn's

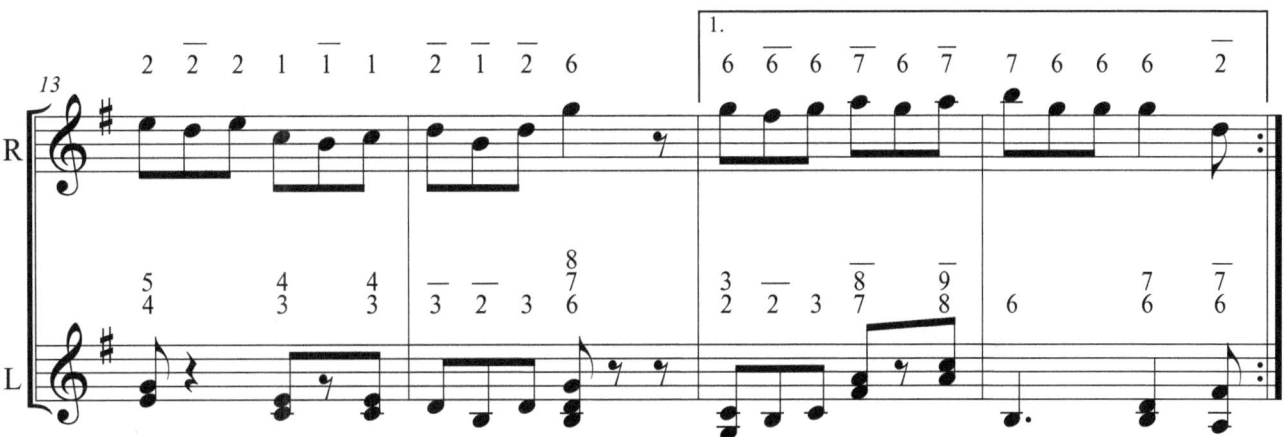

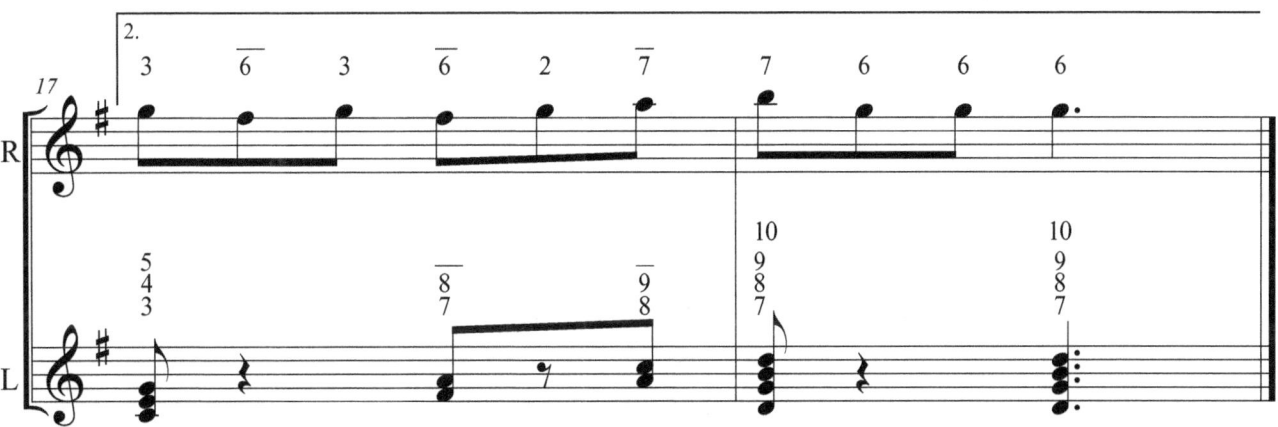

I Love the Gal with the Blue Frock On
POLKA

I Love the Gal with the Blue Frock On

Keel Row

HIGHLAND SCHOTTISCHE

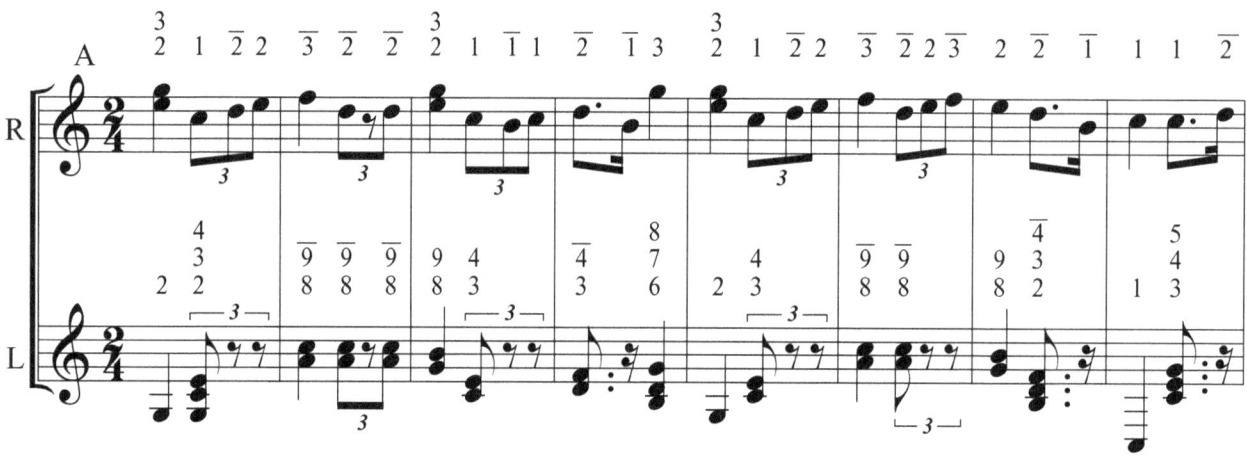
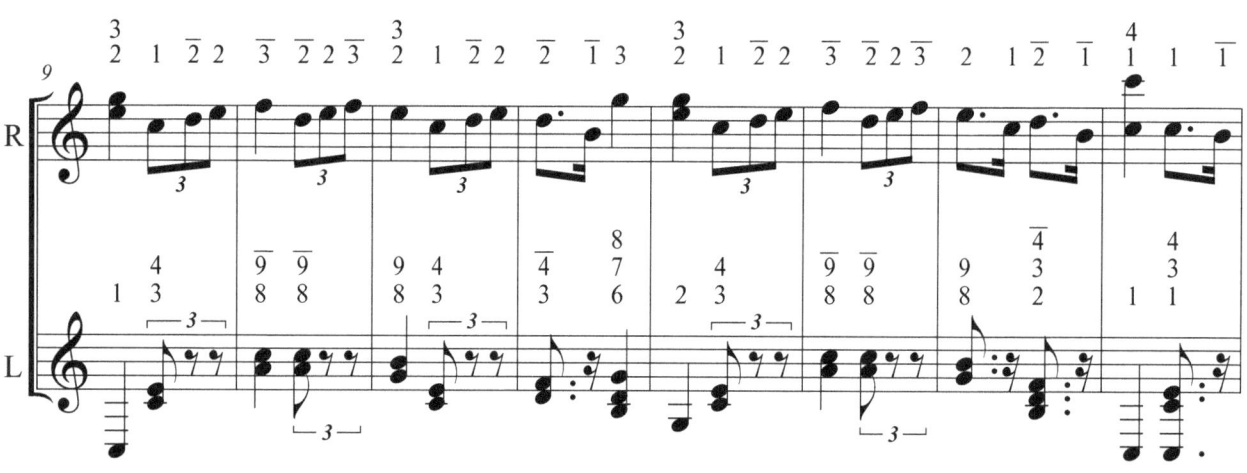
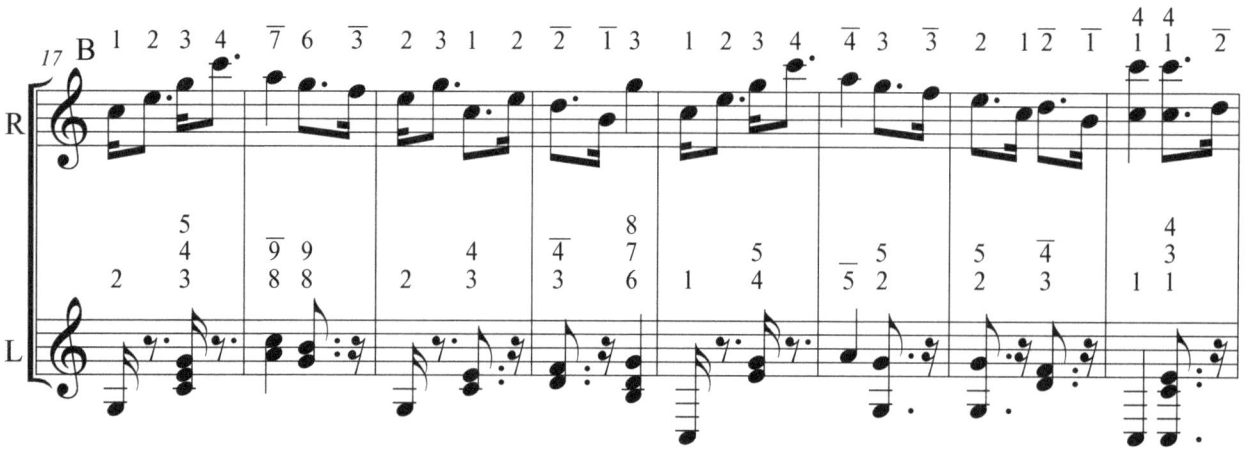

Keel Row

Kitty Come
SCHOTTISCHE

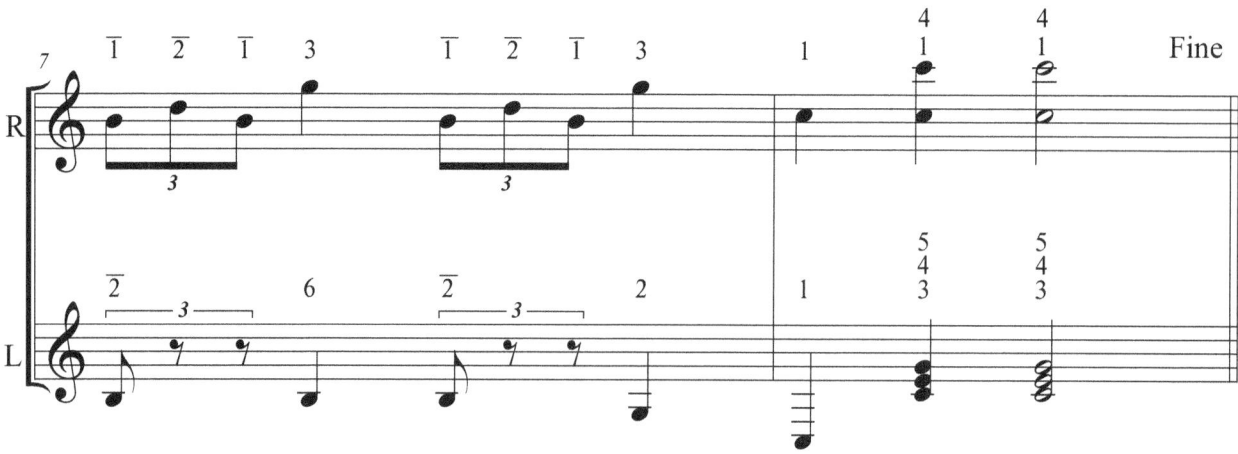

Kitty Come

D.C. al Fine

Little Polly
POLKA

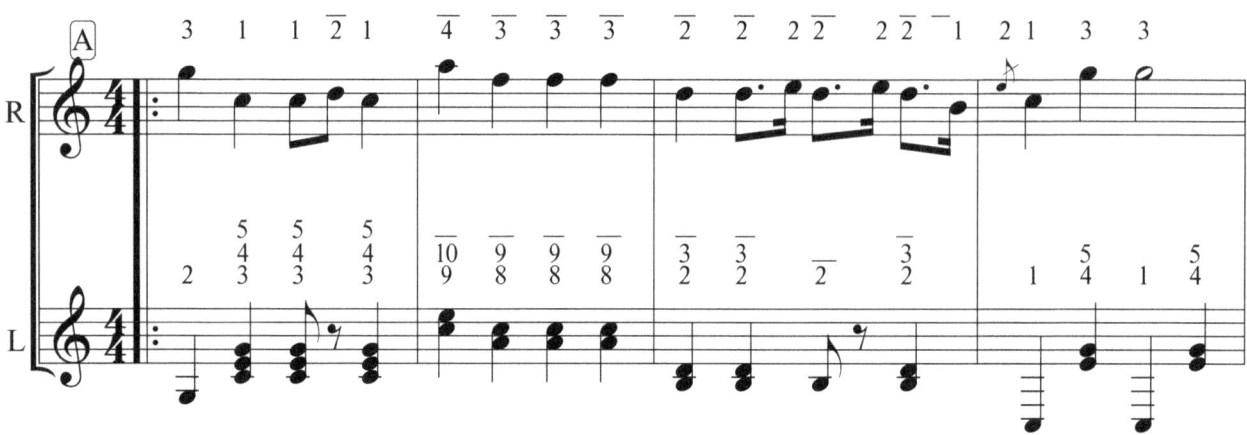

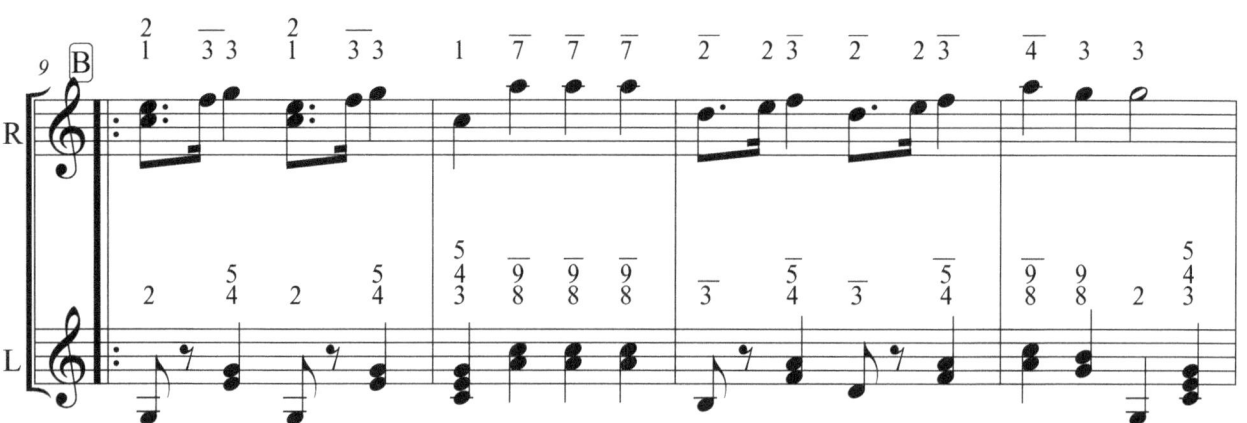

Little Polly

255

Mayblossom Waltz

WALTZ

Mayblossom Waltz

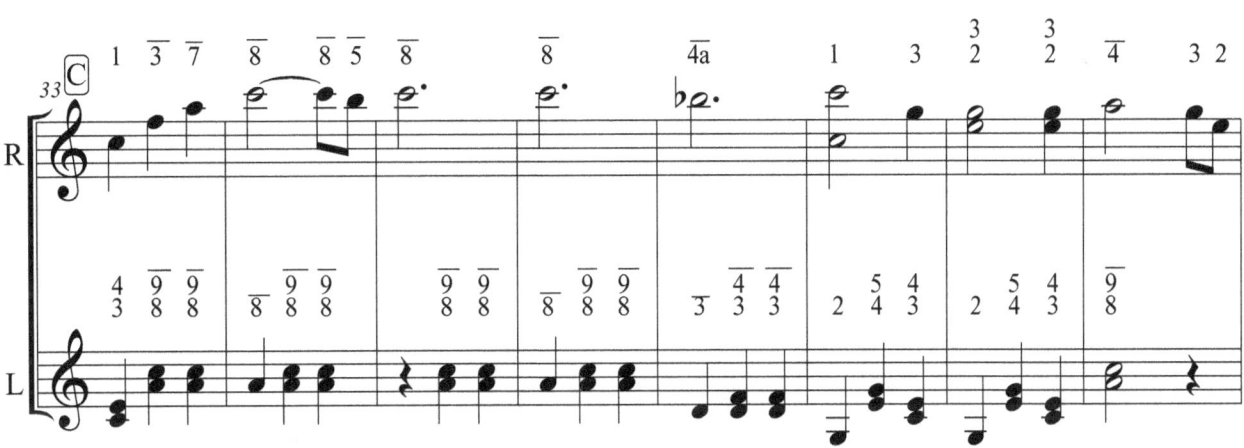
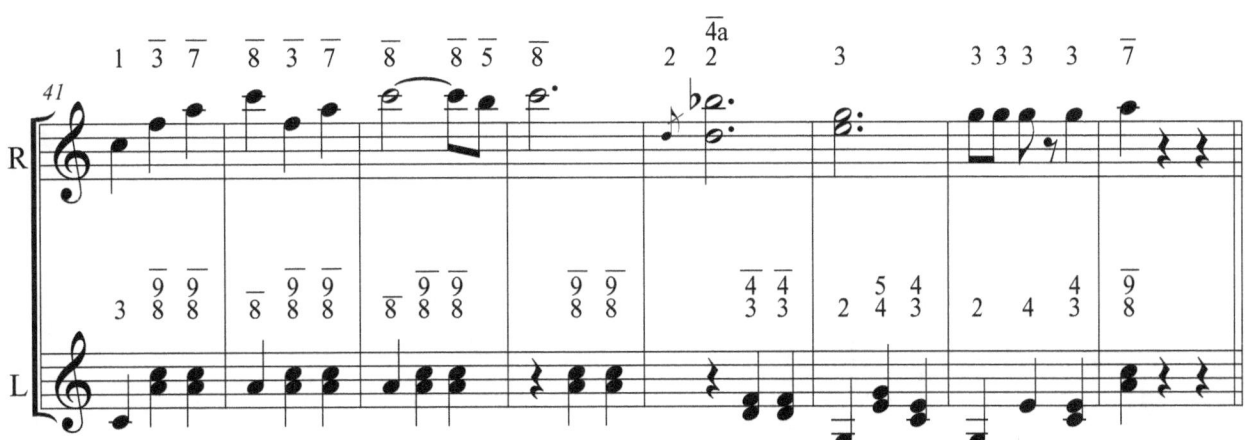

Mayblossom Waltz

Moonlight

SCHOTTISCHE

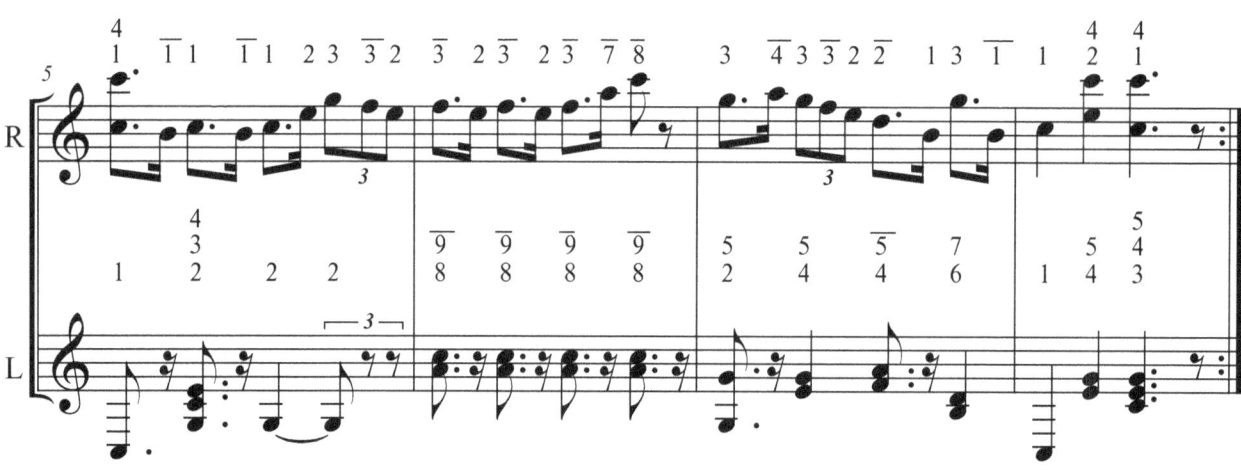

Nae Good Luck About the Hoose

HIGHLAND SCHOTTISCHE

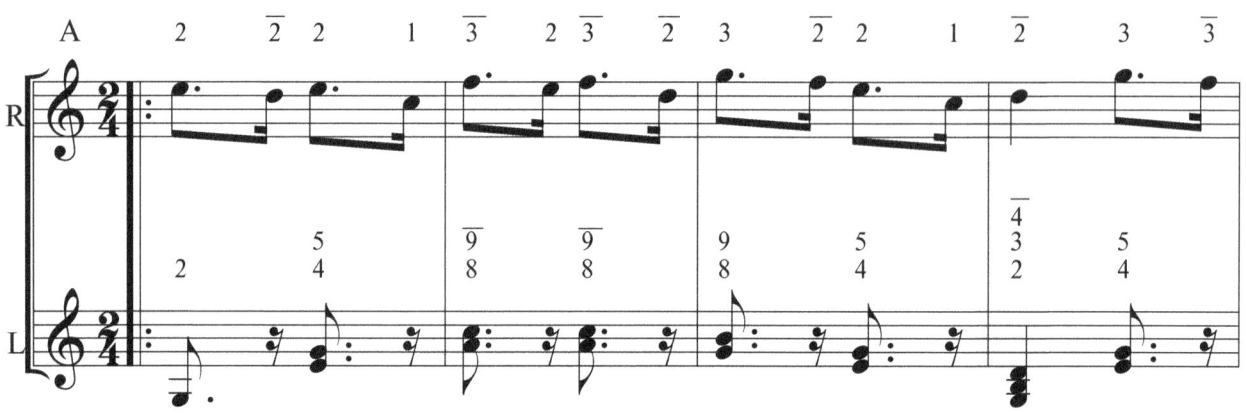

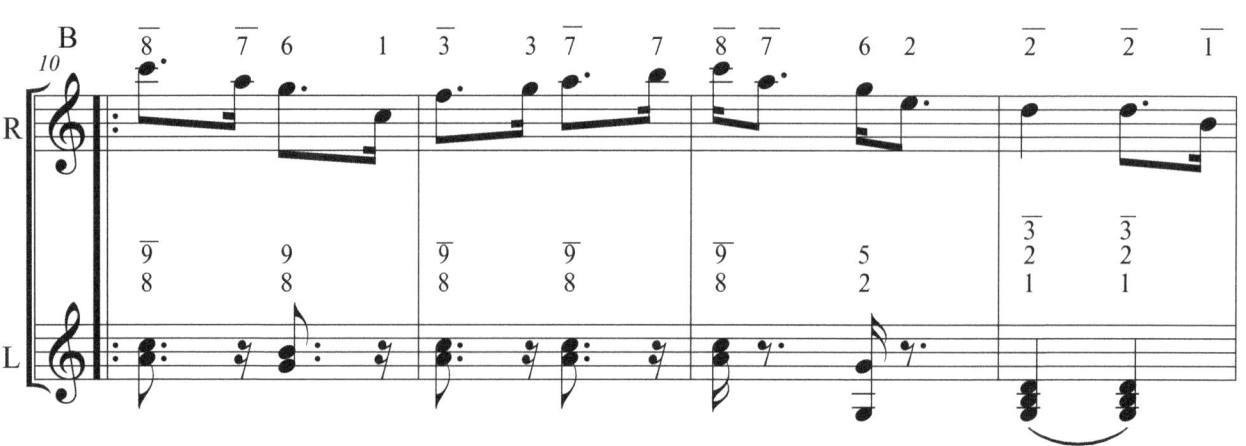

Nae Good Luck About the Hoose

263

Over the Hills to Glory

SCHOTTISCHE

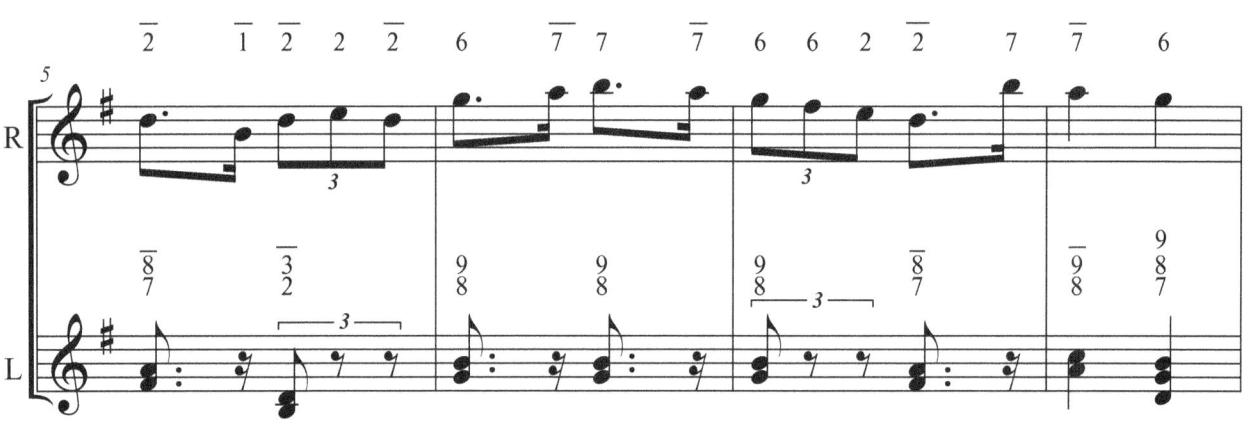

Over the Hills to Glory

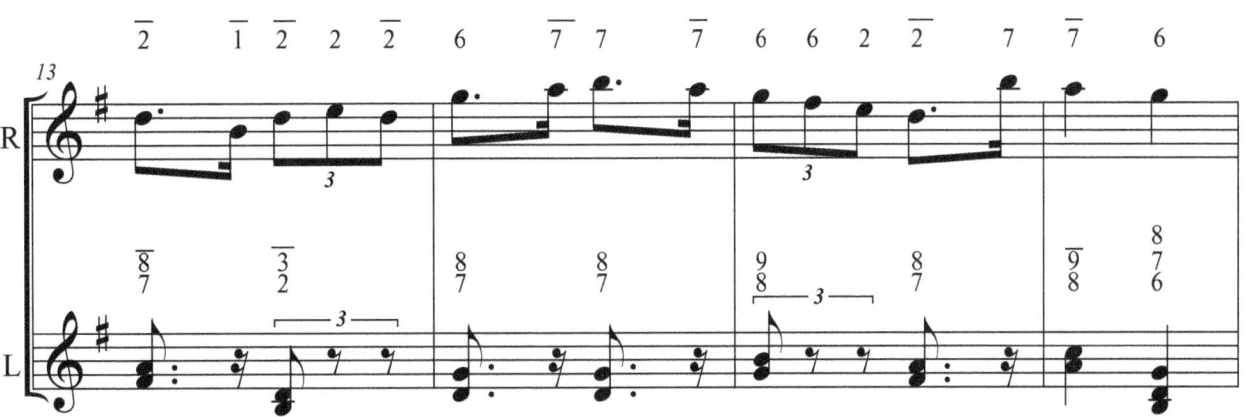
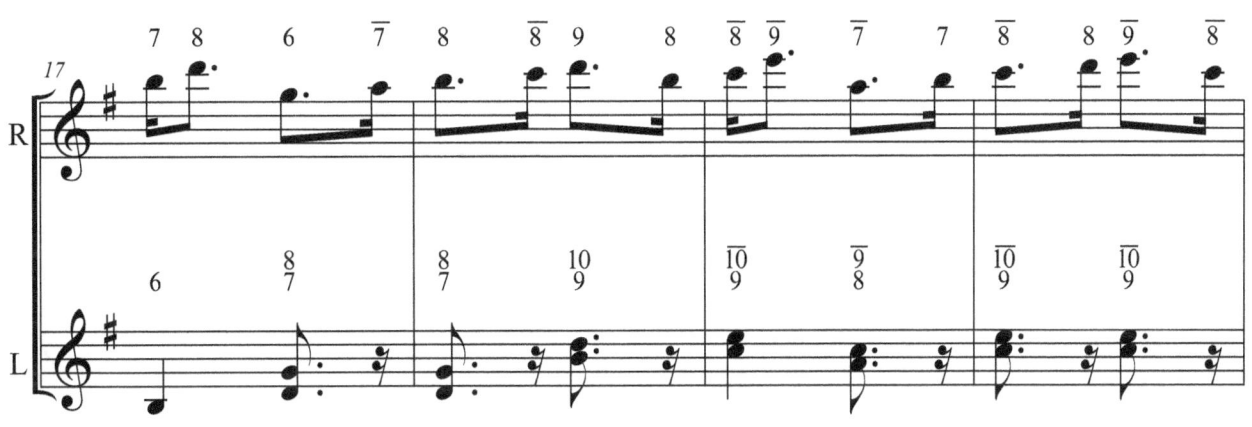

Over the Hills to Glory

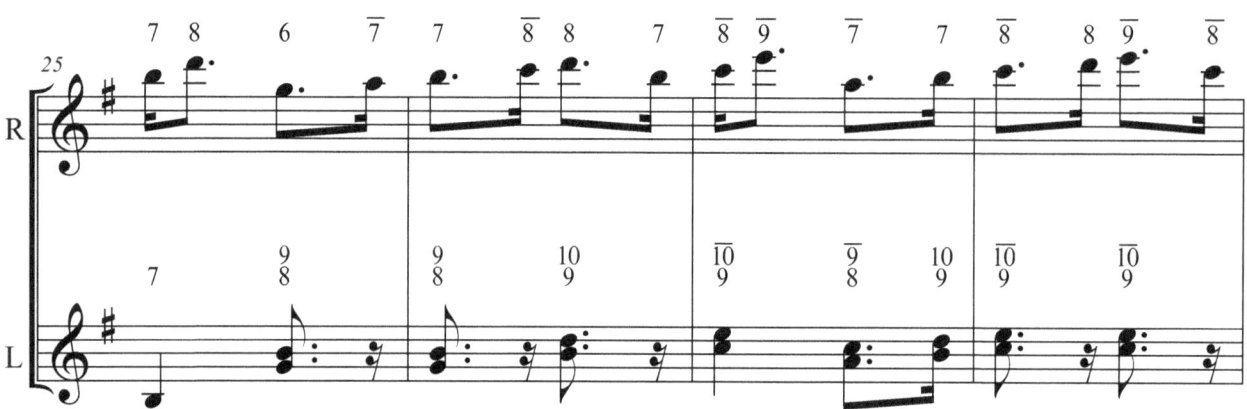

Figure 8.1. "Giving the boys a step." An evening in a California logger's hut, 1876. From *The Graphic*, 1876.

Chapter 8. In the Taproom: Step Dances and Songs

This chapter includes music played for amusement in the taproom of Quarry pubs. Such amusement could include playing for step dances, accompanying the singing of songs, and playing the occasional party piece.

Step Dances

Step dancing in rural southern England during William Kimber's early years was typically an all-male affair if danced in the taproom of village pubs. Step dancing was common at the time not only in England but in Ireland, Australia, North America, and elsewhere. Reg Hall described the basics of the genre as follows:

> *There has been a range of styles, but the common characteristics—the relaxed posture, the low centre of gravity, the loose swinging arms, the rhythmic beating and scuffling of the feet on the floor and the glazed facial expression—unite the diversity into one recognizable phenomenon. At its simplest, yet often most effective, the steps are little more than rhythmic battering and shuffling, picked up by watching others or invented by the dancer.*[1]

Scan Tester, a rural Sussex contemporary of Kimber's, described a situation that was perhaps not unlike that experienced by Kimber in Headington Quarry:

Course, they used to come in the pubs, you know, with their heavy boots on—the old pelted boots and all—and yorks and all on, and you see 'em out in the room that time of day doing the old stepdances, and they used to, if there was enough of 'em, they'd form a figure eight or form a four angles, you know, cross angles, and, you know, there was a lot of different ways they used to dance.

There used to be what we called a reel. It was ordinary four corners, four of them, and they used to step, and then the second part they change over and go in and form the figure eight. And really, it was old people that done it, mind you. The young ones, they used to join in. Get two in a set, see, and learn 'em.[2]

These were reels, but with steps. Kimber recalled that taproom step dancing was mostly reels:

Jack Hall from Horton . . . he used to come over and play a wooden whistle and his little dub. He'd sit with his old smock on and a high hat and dub away then. It was in the taproom, as you might say, it was six or seven of 'em a-reeling, dance a reel, mainly reels.

That's what they mainly danced.[3]

Figure 8.2. Dancing in the taproom of a Norfolk pub. From *The Graphic*, October 22, 1887, and from Reg Hall's *I Never Played to Many Posh Dances*, 1990.

Kimber described in some detail how the men fashioned reels in the pub:

Sometimes four, sometimes six. It's all the same method how you split up. . . . Say you was going to dance the Headington Reel. Put one three over there, one three over here. They can dance a three-handed reel that way. See, there's no crossing over. Well then, the dance for four . . . the two centers facing the two outsides, you see, for the B music, then they changes places, them two . . . that's all there is in that dance. That's the four-handed reel. So, not enough to make up six, they make up four. Not enough to make up four, they make up three, you see? But all the difference, one, two, three, four, you do the change as we used to call it, that's A music . . . then they "heel and toe." While that man is facing that man in the dance, he'd turn around, they'd both turn at the same time and face that man, and that man would come and face that man, and repeat that, then they'd go and [do] the chain again.

In the three handed reel . . . that middle man, he faced that man to dance after the B music, he'd turn around to face that [other] man to dance the other half of the B music. But they'd all keep heel and toeing, they didn't stop. Then go on with your chain. That's how you'd make the dance up. Till they got six, then they'd add the proper six-handed reel where they do the two chains, you see? Heel and toe for the first part, change over, that side would stop there for the remainder of the dance, then changeover again the next time, you see, bring them back to old position.

Figure 8.3. "The Gamekeeper's Party." A man and woman step dancing, London. From the *Illustrated London News*, March 6, 1886.

Women would dance a reel as well as the next, as long as she made a partner. But they could dance [too]. They'd have a go around, three or four sometimes, independent of the men, if we was outside at it. Oh, they didn't let the men have it all, don't think that! [4]

The reel *Soldier's Joy*, when danced outdoors as part of a Morris performance rather than indoors as a taproom amusement, was described by Sharp as being one of the Headington Quarry Morris dances. Step dances were danced by ladies and by couples as well, typically at parties or outdoor festivals, or outside pubs.[5]

Step dance tunes were typically in common time, as reels or hornpipes. *The Manchester Hornpipe*, which did double duty in some Morris sides as a solo Morris jig for the team's Fool (see Chapter 5), was a common pub stepdance tune. Another of Kimber's hornpipes, *The Wonder*, was used at the Quarry for a stepdance called the Lancashire Breakdown.[6]

There were also tunes and songs at the pub; not all of the night's musical entertainment was danced. Any of the Quarry Morris team's dance tunes could be played, as could nearly any tune known by musicians at the pub.

Song accompaniment

A part of any night in the taproom, or of a social dance, would include songs. William Kimber, like some of his contemporaries, knew many of them, but with all the attention going to his Morris dance activities, most of his songs were never recorded. Happily, Theo Chaundy and his wife Hilda Chaundy made a series of recordings of Kimber at the Chaundys' home in 1956 while doing research for a biography of Kimber that Theo published in 1959. They recorded Kimber singing all or part of the following songs: M*y Pretty Little Blue-eyed Maid, The Jolly Miller, Mary the Pride of the Dairy, Glorious Beer, Twankydillo, Up with the Lark in the Morning, Jones Ale,* and *John Blunt.* The details of most of these songs are beyond the scope of this book, but two are of particular interest due to the involvement of his concertina.

Figure 8.4. Singing in a Yorkshire pub during World War II. Illustration from the *BBC Radio Times,* May 4, 1940. With thanks to Katy Howson.

The existence of concertina song accompaniment was once a commonplace event as evidenced from records of Victorian and Edwardian era music hall entertainers, soldiers, and salvationists, but there are almost no recordings. In 1888 Herbert Booth, the son of Salvation Army founder William Booth, published a book of chords for accompanying Salvation Army songs, with the implication that concertinas would back up singers in choirs with the simple "three chord trick," playing chords only.[7] We can assume that polished music hall performers would do much more, but we have no recordings of them. Besides the two complete songs that Kimber accompanied on concertina, discussed later, we have only one other "old" recording of someone accompanying singing on a concertina—something that must once have been commonplace in music halls and taprooms in the nineteenth century.[8] That recording was of a Yorkshire bookmaker named Kit Jones (1869–1957), who recorded two songs for a

World War II era broadcast on BBC on June 4, 1940, as part of a series called "Thirsty Work" for soldiers abroad, in which the broadcasters tried to duplicate the sounds of a village pub for the benefit of homesick servicemen during a bitter part of the war. The recordings recently resurfaced and were researched and described by Katie Howson.[9] The accompanied singing of Jones, who was seventy-one at the time of the recording, hearkens back to a turn-of-the-century time, or so one assumes.

Figure 8.5. Image from a suffragette newspaper of 1915, *Votes for Women,* showing a woman sending away a concertina-playing street singer. From the collection of Stephen Chambers.

Which takes us back to Kimber's recordings of 1956, made by Theo Chaundy. There was no preparation beforehand, and there was no "performance." The group at Chaundy's home were trying to draw out songs that Kimber knew. He knew many, which they recorded. Kimber only partly remembered the song *The Jolly Miller*, and sang a bit of it *a capella*, but he used it as an occasion to discuss how he used the act of playing accompaniment to learn a tune:

> *It's called* The Jolly Miller. *[The song came from] An "old man" as we used to say— poor old Jack Dayko. All I used to care about was getting the accompaniment, you see? I could play [on the concertina] with him, or perhaps just the first line of the song, and that was it. The name of the song,* The Jolly Miller, *but I only knows the first start of it. As I was saying, all I used to trouble about was to be able to accompany him. That's how I got the tune, you see? And the chorus. It went something like this:*
>
> *On yonder hill there stands a mill as it did in my father's time . . .*

From this we can see that Kimber would accompany songs, but not sing along. That is the case with the two songs he accompanied that night: *The Fly Be on the Turmut* and *The Village Pump*.

Tune sources and explanation

Step Dances

The First of May: Digital audio of the transcription

The First of May (hornpipe, p. 283). The tune *The First of May* was notated by Sharp from Kimber at Chelsea in May 1909 as a Morris dance, but a half century later was unknown to the Headington dancers as a Morris dance, nor apparently have the Headington steps of Sharp's day been recorded. There is no extant audio recording, so only the melody line of Kimber's playing is known. The A part of the tune is a close version of the well-known fiddle tune *Fisher's Hornpipe*, which dates to tune collections of the late eighteenth century, but the B part differs. As Phil Heath-Coleman has described it,

> *Kimber's* The First of May *[the A part] is without a shred of doubt a simplified version of Fisher's Hornpipe, though for the first four bars of his second strain Kimber (or his source or his source's source . . .) "treads water," as was often the wont among traditional musicians in England who couldn't recall part of a tune (often repeating a simple phrase, as in this case).*[10]

The Wonder: Digital audio of the transcription

The Wonder (hornpipe, p. 284). Kimber was recorded playing this tune in 1951 by Peter Kennedy and Maud Karpeles. He described this tune as used for a clog dance (step dance) that they called the "Lancashire Breakdown." The tune is *The Wonder Hornpipe*, which was likely composed by fiddler James Hill (ca. 1811–1853) of Newcastle, Northumberland, an active player from the 1830s to 1850s. Scan Tester had a variant of this tune, which he called "No. 1 Stepdance."[11] *The Wonder* is widely known in England, Scotland and Ireland.

The Manchester Hornpipe (p. 288) was recorded in 1956 by Peter Kennedy from Kimber's playing. It was discussed in Chapter 5 as a Bampton Morris dance (*The Fool's Jig*), but it was also a widely known step dance tune, and is also known as *Rickett's Hornpipe*. It originated as a stage hornpipe with the London stage performer Robert Aldridge in 1781.[12] Early versions also include the ca. 1823 music manuscript of Joshua Gibbons of Lincolnshire, and *Kerr's Merrie Melodies* of 1880.[13]

The Manchester Hornpipe: Digital audio of the transcription

Soldier's Joy (Morris reel and step dance tune, p. 290) was transcribed from a 1948 studio recording by Kimber and was included as a Headington dance in Sharp's *Morris Book* volume 2 (see Chapter 4). In a pub setting it would be danced as a reel but with steps. An early version of that tune is contained in Rutherford's *Compleat Collection of Two Hundred of the Most Celebrated Country Dances, Both Old and New*, published in Scotland circa 1756.[14] It appears in Irish music collections by Levey in the 1830s, and by O'Neill in 1903. The tune remains internationally popular among fiddle players.

William Kimber playing *Soldier's Joy (Headington Morris Reel)* via His Master's Voice, 1948

Song accompaniment

The Fly Be on the Turmut (or *The Vly Be on the Turmut*, or *Turmut-hoeing*, p. 292) is a well-known song of uncertain origin. The earliest published version of the song seems to be that in Lucy Broadwood's and John Fuller-Maitland's 1893 *English County Songs*. According to Peter Kennedy, Broadwood got the song from a Buckinghamshire man. It has attached itself to Wiltshire, where it has become the unofficial song of that county and is one of the regimental marching songs of the Wiltshire Regiment.[15] "Turmut" is Wiltshire dialect for turnip, and various of the many versions of the song are sung with mock dialect words, possibly indicating a music hall origin.[16] In Kimber's recording, he accompanied the singing of another singer (name unknown). Kimber's playing is not unfamiliar: melody on the right, although restrained and with gaps left out for effect, with partial chords on the left. The lyrics as sung are:

Soldier's Joy: Digital audio of the transcription

> 'Twere on the jolly summer's morn, the twenty-ninth of May
> Giles Scroggins took his turmut hoe with which he trudged away.
> Now some folks they like hay-makin'. And some folks they likes mowin',
> But of all the jobs that I likes best, give I the turmut hoein.'

> Chorus:
> For the fly, the fly, the fly be on the turmut,
> And it's all me eye for I to try, to keep flies off the turmut.

> Now the first place as I went to work it were for farmer Towers
> He sweared and cursed and then declared I was a first-rate hoe-er.
> Now the next place as I went to work, I took it by the job,
> But if I'd a-knowed a little more, I'd sooner been in quod.

The Fly Be on the Turmut: Digital audio of the transcription

Chorus

Now when I was over at yonder farm, they sent for I a-mowin,
But I sent word back that I'd rather have the sack, than to lose my turmut hoein'.
Now all you jolly farmer lads, who sit at home so warm,
I now concludes my ditty with a wishin' you no harm.[17]

Chorus

The song was widely sung in folk clubs in the fifties and sixties,[18] so when Kimber learned this tune is not precisely known. But his steady hand on the concertina, for what was clearly an on-the-spot improvisation, shows that he was well-practiced at song accompaniment.

In the transcription of this and the following song, the top line of the three-line score is for the voice. In his playing with the singer, Kimber more or less follows the voice on his right hand, but an octave up from the singer. Kimber tends to leave out the voice's entry notes to help stay somewhat in the background, while adding chords on his left hand, played softly.

The Village Pump: Digital audio of the transcription

The Village Pump (p. 294). The second tune that Kimber accompanied in that informal session was *The Village Pump*, of English music hall origin. It was composed in 1907 by Archie Naish (1878–1923), who wrote songs and performed in the London halls between the late 1890s and his untimely death in the early 1920s. Like *The Fly Be on the Turmut*, it was widely revived during the 1950s and 1960s in folk clubs, so it is uncertain when Kimber would have learned it.

In the recording, Kimber started the tune in the key of C, but quickly realized that the pitch was too low for the singer, so he effortlessly moved it up to the key of G. From this we can see that his accompaniment was unplanned and unpracticed, and done in a way that was completely intuitive, like his approach to accompaniment of dance tunes. The lyrics are:

Figure 8.6. *The Village Pump* was written in 1907 and performed by Archie Naish (1878–1823), a comedian who appeared regularly in English music halls between the late 1890s and early 1920s. The song became a well-known standard for pub singers.

There's a quaint little village down our way,
Where they grows new potatoes, corn and hay,
There's a pretty little rill,
That works a little mill,
And the mill it keeps a-workin' all the day.
There's a lot of little 'ouses in a lump,
And a pub called the Magpie and Stump, But you make no mistake,
The thing that takes the cake,
Is the pride of all the place, the Village Pump.

Chorus:
The Village Pump, The Village Pump,
The Village P - U — M- P Pump,
The Village Pump, The Village Pump,
The Village P - U - M - P Pump.

Now t'other day the funniest chap you'd ever seen,
Come and give us a temperance lecture on our green,
'E said you fellers 'ere
You're much too fond of beer,
And 'e spouted like a penny Magazine.
'E runs down the Magpie and Stump,
Till he gives us all the bloomin' 'ump,
'E says "Water—that's for me."
So we says— "Right you be!"
And we took 'im and we ducked 'im at the Pump.

Chorus

Now our Squire 'e likes a bit of fun,
So when 'is lad was twenty-one
'E give us all a treat,
There was nuts and things to eat,
And the kids they had an orange and a bun.
There was games where you often skips and jumps,
And the kids all had candy peeled to scrump,
But to celebrate the day
In a sort of proper way,
We puts another 'andle on the Pump.

Chorus

Novelty piece

The Church Bells (p. 297). To conclude this review of William Kimber's taproom pieces, here is something that is neither a step dance tune nor a song accompaniment, but a popular Victorian-era concertina party piece. It was played widely by concertina players of that period. For example, at a minstrel entertainment in Oxford in 1895, a concertina player named Mr. Charles Bu Val "gave capital imitations of various instruments and church bells, &c."[19] Those imitations could be surprisingly realistic and memorable. Here is an account from the quarter-deck of a British Navy dreadnought in wartime and far from home, in 1915:

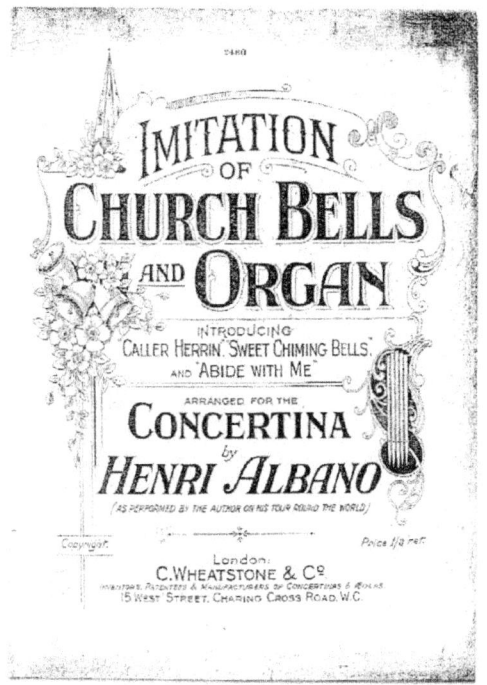

Figure 1. Henri Albano was the stage name of Henry Cumberbirch (1855-1922), one of several late Victorian and Edwardian concertinists to imitate church bells in their Music Hall acts.

They were there to witness an impromptu sing-song—a scratch affair organized at short notice to provide mirth and recreation for a ship's company badly in need of both. . . . Their lungs ached for a rousing, full throated chorus. . . . they were simply spoiling to be the most appreciative audience in the world.

A great burst of laughter and cheering broke out from the sailors, and redoubled as a private of Marines, holding a concertina in his gnarled fists, walked on the stage. . . . The whole audience, officers and men, were evidently reveling in some tremendous secret remembrance of this private of Marines. . . . Silence fell on the audience at length, and the concertina solo began. As has been indicated, Private Mason could play the concertina. In his rather tremulous hands it was no longer an affair of leather and wood (or of whatever material concertinas are constructed), but a living thing that laughed and sobbed and shook your soul like the Keening. It became a yearning, passionate, exultant daughter of Music that somehow wasn't quite respectable. And when he had finished, and passed his hand across his moist forehead preparatory to retiring from the stage, they shouted for more.

"Church bells, Nobby!" cried a hundred voices. "Garn, do the church bells!" so he did the church bells, as the wind brings the sound across the valley on a summer evening at home, wringing his shipmates' sentimental heartstrings to the limit of their enjoyment.

"Strewth," ejaculated a bearded member of the audience when the turn was over, relighting his pipe with a hand that shook. "I 'ear Nobby play that at the Canteen at Malta, time Commander-in-Chief and 'is staff was there—Commander-in-Chief, so 'elp me, 'e sob like a woman." The reminiscence may not have been in strict accordance with the truth, but, even considered in the light of fiction, it was a pretty testimony to Private Mason's art.[20]

Such was the power of this parlor trick. The imitation of the bells depended upon a sonic doppler effect imposed upon the concertina's sound that was achieved by waving the instrument at arm's length in a circular motion, like a windmill. Kimber taught it to his pupil Kenneth Loveless—who later recorded it in a characteristically bombastic version with variations[21]—but Kimber's own version is the essence of simplicity. He moved down the keys in a mimic of pealing church bells, overlapping the keys to mimic the long-ringing nature of each bell. This also required continual fingering across all three rows—something that was rare in his playing. It makes a lovely sound, regardless of the fact that he performed this rather strenuous arm-waving feat at the age of eighty-four.

Kimber was recorded playing it at Theo Chaundy's house in 1956. At a first visit to Chaundy's house, Kimber apologized for not remembering enough of it—he had forgotten the unusual fingering. But he visited the Chaundys again a few nights later and produced the full tune.

Except for the low G note, all of the notes that he played are on the pull. The long string of pull notes on the pull in measure 1 is played as the concertina is being brought rapidly down. We did not include a digital version – the digital audio doesn't even begin to capture the sound of the piece – so the reader is referred to the Chaundy collection audio tapes at www.merryville.uk.[22] There are fancier versions of this piece around online, especially by modern players (one by John Kirkpatrick is especially impressive, as is another by Australian player Peter Ellis).

---

[1] Reg Hall, 1990, *I Never Played to Many Posh Dances: Scan Tester, Sussex Musician, 1887–1972*, Rochford, Essex: Musical Traditions, Supplement no. 2, p. 72.

[2] Scan Tester, as quoted in Reg Hall, 1990, *I never played to many posh dances…, Scan Tester, Sussex musician*: Musical Traditions Supplement no. 2, Rochford, Essex, p. 77.

[3] William Kimber, 1956, as interviewed by Theo Chaundy and others, online at Merryville, the online home of William Kimber (www.Merryville.uk/collections), Tape 3, Whittle and Dub.

[4] William Kimber as recorded by Peter Kennedy, 1951, *William Kimber Talking*, an interview of William Kimber with Maud Karpeles at Kimber's home, December 4, 1951. Folktrax recording 383, track 42.

[5] William Kimber, as interviewed by Peter Kennedy and Maud Karpeles, 1951, *William Kimber* (CD), Folktrax 382, track 42.

[6] William Kimber, as interviewed by Peter Kennedy and Maud Karpeles, 1951: *William Kimber* (CD), Folktrax 382, track 42.

[7] Herbert E. Booth, 1888, *Instructions for the Salvation Army Concertina*, London: Salvation Army Bookstores. The book is available online at the Concertina Library, www.concertina.com.

[8] Roger Digby, personal communication, 2023.

[9] Katie Howson, 2021, "Thirsty Work: Part 2: The North—Singing from Ambleside, Redmire, and Harome," Unsung Histories website, www.unsunghistories.info.

[10] Phil Heath-Coleman, 2024, in a personal letter to Roger Digby.

[11] Traditional Tune Archive, www.tunearch.org, entry for *The Wonder Hornpipe*.

[12] Hall, 1990, p. 78.

[13] Traditional Tune Archive, www.tunearch.org, entry for *Manchester Hornpipe*.

[14] Traditional Tune Archive, www.tunearch.org, entry on *Soldier's Joy*.

[15] Wikipedia, entry for *The Vly Be on the Turmut*.

[16] Gwilym Davies, 2015, "The Fly Be on the Turmut," www.glostrad.com.

[17] William Kimber and others, 1956, *The Fly Be on the Turmut*, as recoded in 1956 by Theo Chaundy. Online website www,merryville.uk, Chaundy collection, tape 2.

[18] I'm grateful to Roger Digby for information about this song.

[19] *Jackson's Oxford Journal*, May 4, 1895.

[20] Bartimeus (pseudonym), 1915, *A Tall Ship on Other Occasions*. London: Cassell and Company, Chapter 8.

[21] Loveless's version of the church bells can be found on www.merryville.uk in the collection of Kenneth Loveless recordings.

[22] Tape 4 (1956), Theo Chaundy collection, www.merryville.uk.

William Kimber with his pupils, the Espérance girls, ca. 1906. The woman standing at left is probably Mary Neal. Image from the Vaughan Williams Memorial Library, EFDSS.

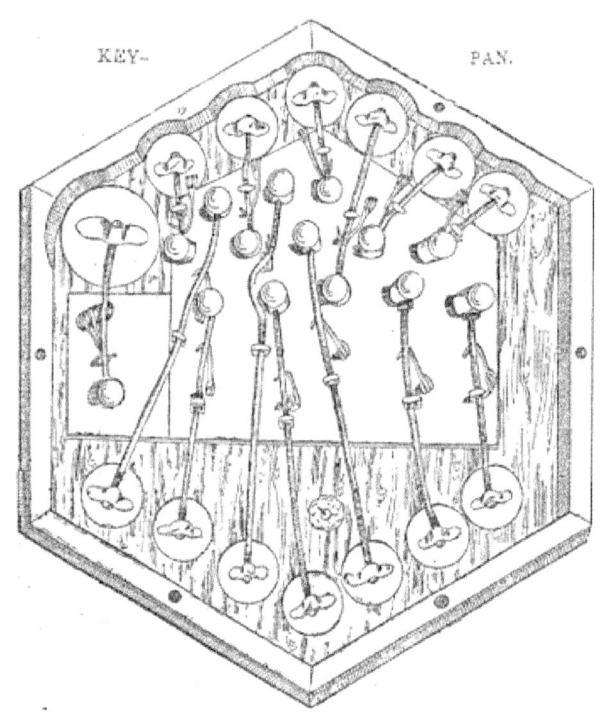

Transcriptions:
Stepdances, Songs, and a Novelty Piece

William Kimber, ca. 1950. Image courtesy of the
Vaughan Williams Memorial Library, EFDSS.

The First of May
STEP DANCE

The Wonder Hornpipe

STEP DANCE

The Wonder

The Wonder

The Manchester Hornpipe (Fool's Dance)
STEP DANCE AND BAMPTON MORRIS JIG

The Manchester Hornpipe (Fool's Dance)

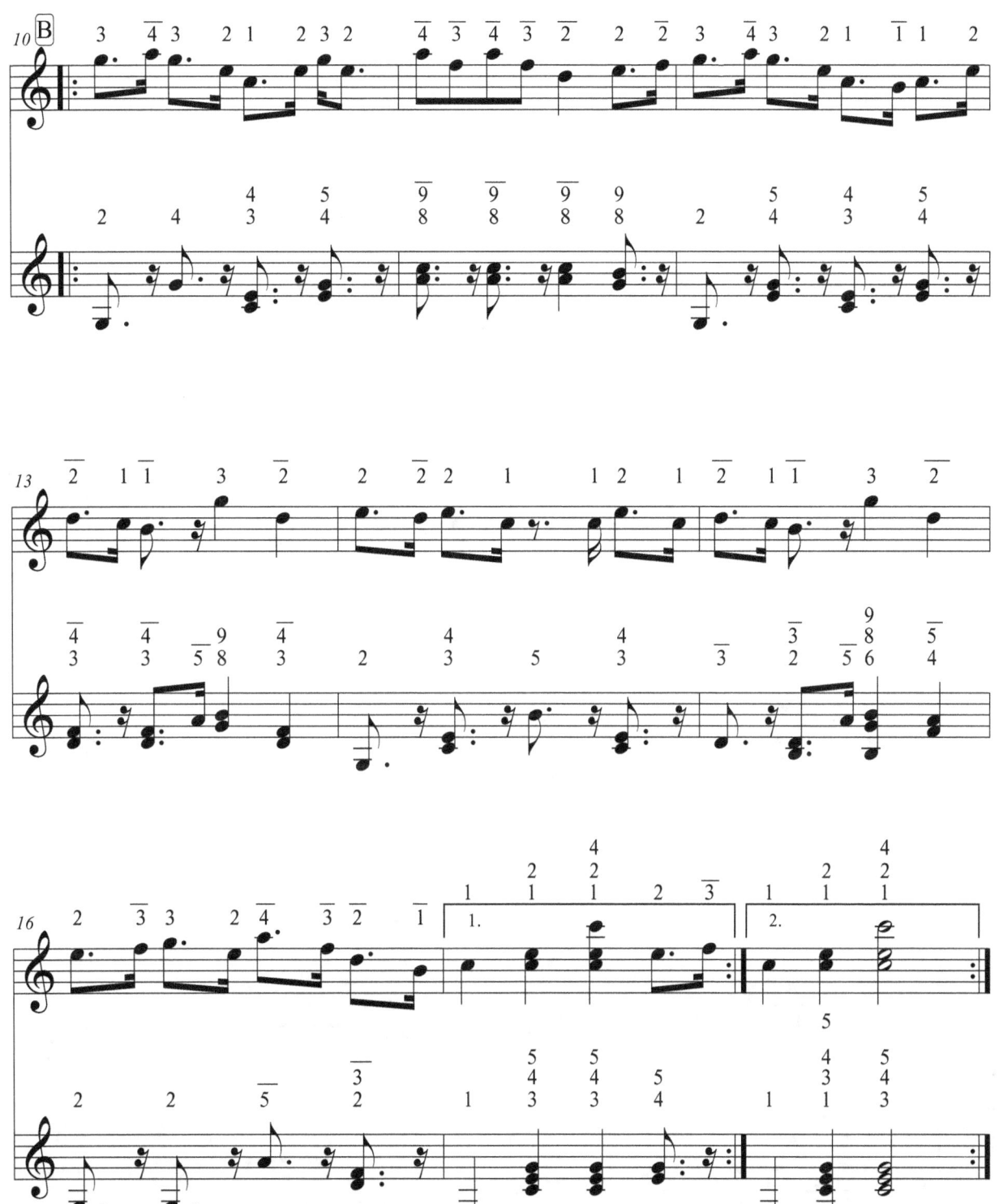

Soldier's Joy

HEADINGTON MORRIS REEL AND STEP DANCE

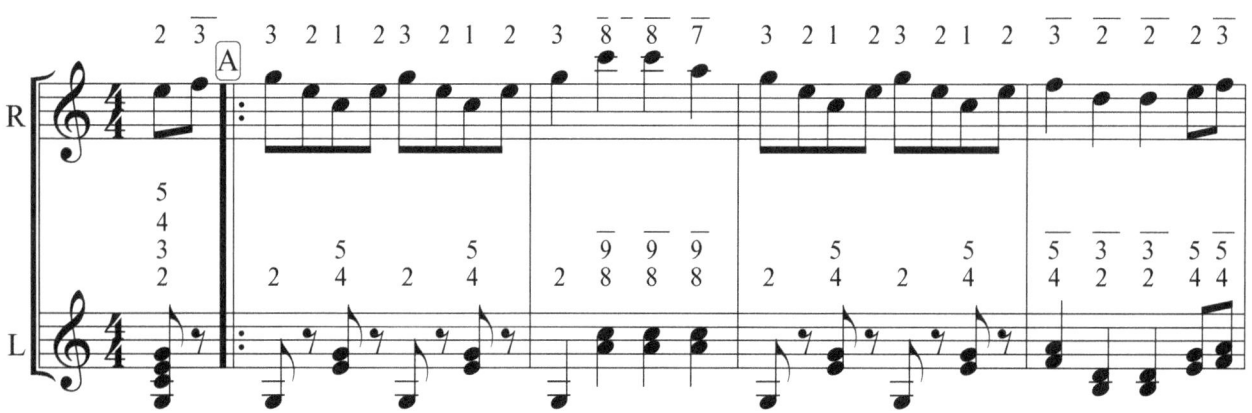
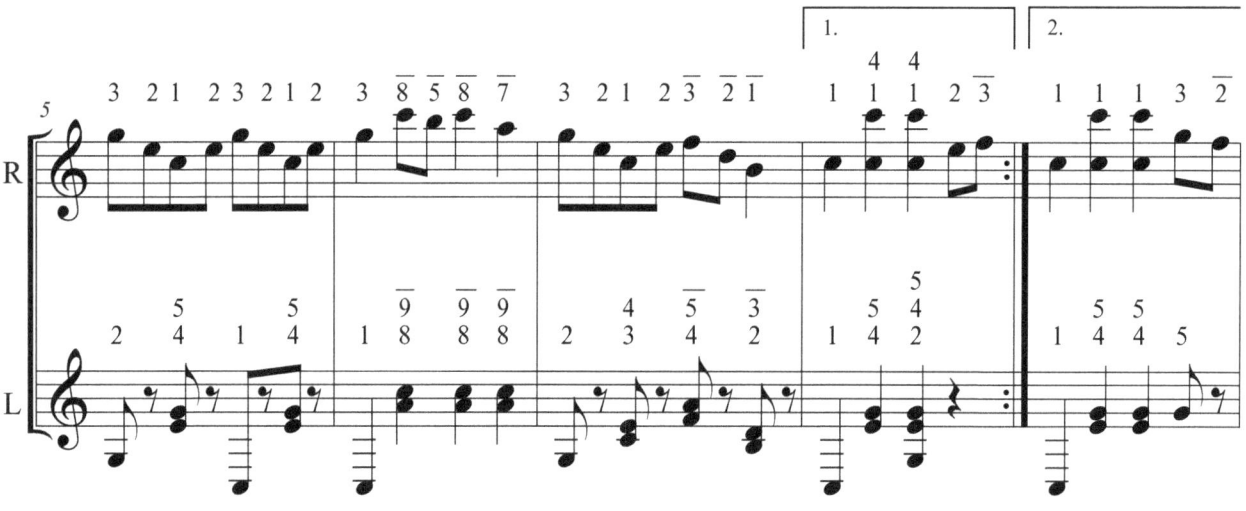
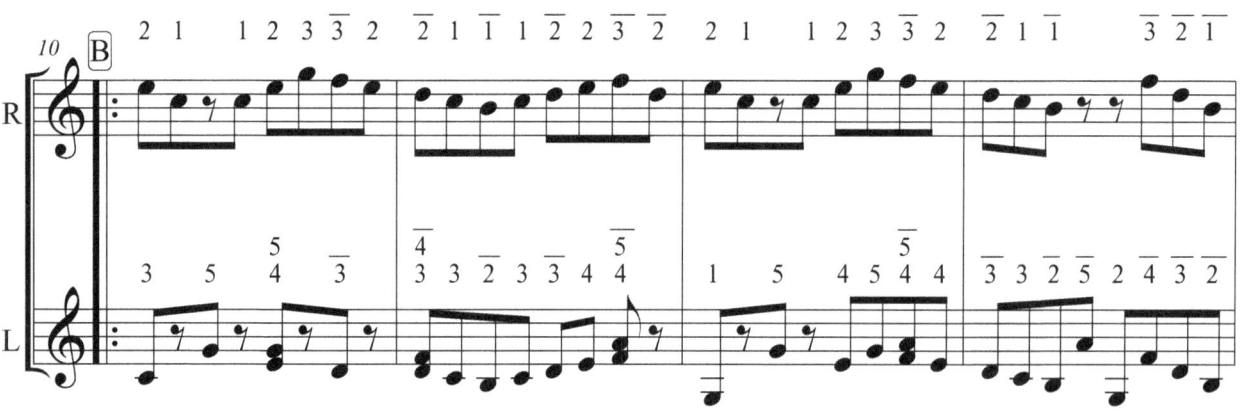

Soldier's Joy

The Fly Be On the Turmut

SONG ACCOMPANIMENT

The Fly Be On the Turmut

The Village Pump
SONG ACCOMPANIMENT

The Village Pump

Church Bells

NOVELTY PIECE

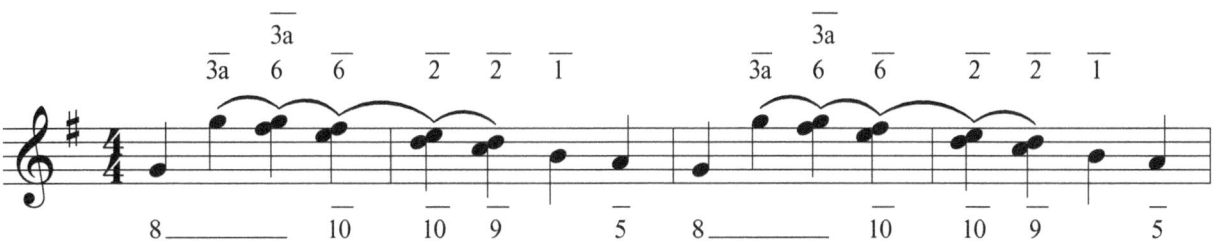
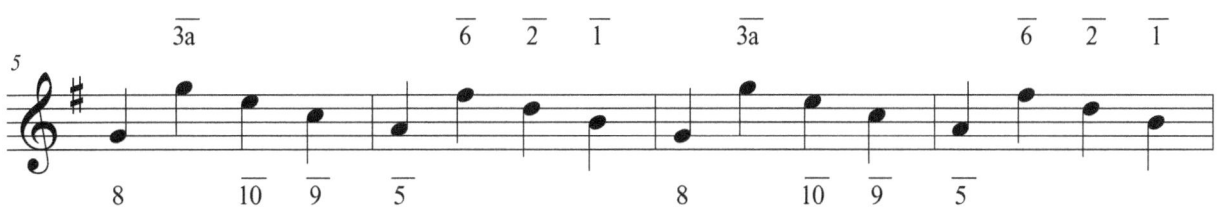
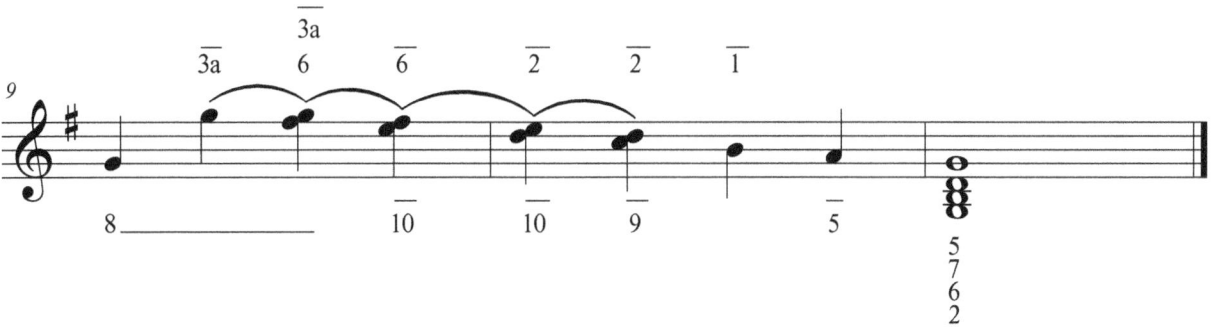

The Headington Quarry Morris side dancing *The Twenty-Ninth of May* to the Anglo concertina music of Andy Turner, outside of the Mason's Arms, Whitmonday, 29th May 2023.

Chapter 9. Epilogue

It has now been one hundred and twenty-five years since William Kimber and the Headington Quarry Morris side danced in the snow at Sandfield Cottage in the waning days of the nineteenth century. Much has happened since. The Quarry side of that meeting faded away, then a new one replaced it, only to be destroyed by a world war. Then another side, and another world war. Then in 1947 a new side developed that has stayed together continuously through the last half of the twentieth century and well into the twenty-first.

The Quarry village that Kimber knew was overwhelmed by urban growth, but the three Quarry pubs of Kimber's day still exist, and the Quarry side still dances in front of them on Whitmonday and on Boxing Day, with bells jingling, sticks cracking, and the treble voice of the Anglo concertina singing over it all.

78rpm gramophone recording of William Kimber playing *Rodney* and the *Rigs of Marlow*. Recorded and published by The Gramophone Company, Ltd. on the label His Master's Voice, 1947.

Chapter 10. Discography

1. **The Gramophone Co. Ltd**, on the label His Master's Voice (HMV), made a series of studio recordings in London in 1935, 1947, and 1948. These recordings were all later used in the creation of the 1974 Topic LP *The Art of William Kimber*.

Matrix number   Title   Issue number

Recorded 16 July 1935, Issued in Britain October 1935:

Matrix number	Title	Issue number
OEA 2166	Haste to the Wedding/Getting Upstairs	HMV B8368
OEA 2167	Over the Hills to Glory	HMV B8368

Recorded 31 October 1946, Issued in Britain August 1947:

Matrix number	Title	Issue number
OEA 11335-1	Haste to the Wedding	HMV B9579
OEA 11336-1	Getting Upstairs/Blue-Eyed Stranger	HMV B9578

OEA 11337-1	Rodney/Rigs o'Marlow	HMV B9520
OEA 11338-1	Double Set Back/Hunting the Squirrel	HMV B9578
OEA 11339-1	Double Lead Through	HMV B9519
OEA 11340-1	Over the Hills to Glory	HMV B9519
OEA 11341-3	Trunkles	HMV B9579
OEA 11342-2	Bean Setting/The 29th of May	HMV B9520

Recorded 1 June 1948, Issued in Britain August 1948:

OEA 13093-1	Laudnum Bunches	HMV B9670
OEA 13094-1	Constant Billy	HMV B9669
OEA 13095-1	Country Gardens	HMV B9669
OEA 13096-1	Shepherd's Hey	HMV B9670
OEA 13097-1	Headington Morris Reel – Soldier's Joy	HMV B9672
OEA 13098-1	Jockie to the Fair	HMV B9671
OEA 13099-1	Old Mother Oxford	HMV B9671
OEA 13100-1	Old Woman Tossed Up in a Blanket	unissued
OEA 13101-1	Bacca Pipes – Greensleeves	HMV B9672

2. **EFDSS LP 1001**, 1963, *William Kimber*, English Folk Dance and Song Society, London. The LP contains recordings made by Peter Kennedy in 1956, including Morris and country dance tunes and voice recordings of Kimber describing these dances. It is no longer in print, but a copy is in the archives of the Vaughan Williams Memorial Library.

Side I

Band 1. Morris On, Bean Setting, Constant Billy
Band 2. Jockie to the Fair, Shepherd's Hey, Bacca Pipes
Band 3. Rodney, Hunting the Squirrel, Rigs o'Marlow.
Band 4. Old Mother Oxford, Laudnum Bunches, Trunkles

Side II

Band 1. The Ribbon Dance, The Willow Tree, Old Woman Tossed Up in a Blanket
Band 2. Fools' Dance Bampton (Manchester Hornpipe), Four Hand Reel (Soldier's Joy)
Band 3. Step and Fetch Her, Pop Goes the Weasel, Over the Hills to Glory, Double Lead Through, The Quaker's Wife, Bonnets So Blue, Hilly-go Filly-go, Moonlight Schottische.
Band 4. Country Gardens, Blue-Eyed Stranger, Double Set Back, Haste to the Wedding, The Twenty-ninth of May, Getting Upstairs, Morris Off.

3. **Topic LP 12T249**, 1974, *The Art of William Kimber*, Topic Records, London. No longer in print, this album contains most of the Morris tunes included in the transcriptions of the present work. The recordings were made from original HMV 78 rpm records of the 1930s and 1940s. Most of this material has been reissued by the EFDSS (see below).

Side I
A1. Haste to the Wedding / Getting Upstairs
A2. Over the Hills to Glory
A3. Haste to the Wedding
A4. Getting Upstairs / Blue-Eyed Stranger
A5. Rodney / Rigs o'Marlow
A6. Double Set Back / Hunting the Squirrel
A7. Double Lead Through
A8. Over the Hills to Glory
A9. Trunkles

Side II
B1. Bean Setting / The Twenty-Ninth of May
B2. Laudnum Bunches
B3. Constant Billy
B4. Country Gardens
B5. Shepherd's Hey
B6. Headington Morris Reel – Soldier's Joy
B7. Jockie to the Fair
B8. Old Mother Oxford
B9. Bacca Pipes – Greensleeves

4. **EFDSS CD 03**, 1999, *Absolutely Classic: The Music of William Kimber*, English Folk Dance and Song Society, London. This CD includes 22 of the 28 tunes transcribed in this volume as well as an excellent biography of Kimber by Derek Schofield, archival photographs, and even some film footage. It should be considered an essential recording for anyone seriously interested in learning Kimber's tunes. Out of print for some time, it has recently been reissued by Talking Elephant Records.

1. Constant Billy
3. Bean Setting
5. Getting Upstairs
6. Rigs o'Marlow
8. The Twenty-Ninth of May
9. Country Garden
11. Trunkles
12. Bacca Pipes
13. The Willow Tree
15. Hunting the Squirrel
16. Jockie to the Fair
17. Rodney
19. Double Set Back
21. The Blue-Eyed Stranger
22. Over the Hills to Glory
23. The Morris Reel (Soldier's Joy)
25. Double Lead Through
26. Laudnum Bunches

27. Old Mother Oxford
28. Old Woman Tossed Up in A Blanket
29. The Rigs o'Marlow
30. Shepherd's Hey
31. Haste to the Wedding
32. Laudnum Bunches

5. **Folktrax CD 382**, 1980, *William Kimber (Anglo Concertina):* Folktrax International, Gloucester, England. This recording consists of studio and field recordings of Kimber that were made in the 1940s and 1950s by Douglas and Peter Kennedy and Maud Karpeles, as well as some voice recordings of Kimber. It is out of print. Upon Peter Kennedy's death in 2006, all Folktrax titles as well as most of Kennedy's recordings were moved to the care of Topic Records, Ltd.

Morris Dances recorded 31 October 1946:

1. Bean Setting
2. The Twenty-Ninth of May
3. Rodney
4. Rigs o'Marlow
5. Getting Upstairs
6. Blue-Eyed Stranger
7. Double Set Back
8. Hunting the Squirrel
9. Haste to the Wedding
10. Trunkles

Further Morris Dances recorded 6 January 1948:

11. Constant Billy
12. Country Gardens
13. Laudnum Bunches
14. Shepherd's Hey
15. Jockie to the Fair
16. Old Mother Oxford
17. Headington Morris Reel (Soldier's Joy)
18. Bacca Pipes

Two Country Dances recorded 31 October 1946

19. Double Lead Through
20. Over the Hills to Glory

Further Morris and Country Dances recorded 14 November 1956:

21. Morris On
22. The Willow Tree

23. Old Woman Tossed Up in a Blanket
24. The Fool's Dance (The Manchester Hornpipe)
25. Morris Off
26. Bonnets So Blue
27. The Four Hand Reel (Soldier's Joy)
28. The Quaker's Wife
29. The Ribbon Dance
30. The Triumph (Step and Fetch Her)

Other dances recorded by Peter Kennedy and Maud Karpeles, 4 December 1951:

31. I Love the Gal with the Blue Frock On
32. Pop Goes the Weasel
33. The Highland Fling (Keel Row) / Heel and Toe (Nae Good Luck about the Hoose)
34. Father O'Flynn (or The Rollicking Irishman)
35. The Moonlight (Plain Schottische)
36. Kitty Come (Barn Dance)
37. Little Polly (Polka)
38. Bonny Dundee (Galop)
39. The Mayblossom Waltz
40. Who Jerusalem (Kafoozalum / 'Donkey cock your tail up)
41. Bacca Pipes (Some say the devil's dead)
42. Lancashire step tune (The Wonder Hornpipe)

6. **Folktrax CD 383**, *William Kimber Talking*, Folktrax International, Gloucester, England. This CD consists of an interview with Kimber conducted by Maud Karpeles and Peter Kennedy at Kimber's home on December 4, 1951. Containing no tunes, it includes Kimber's descriptions of his experiences with Morris and country dancing. It is out of print. Upon Peter Kennedy's death in 2006, all Folktrax titles as well as most of Kennedy's recordings were moved to the care of Topic Records, Ltd.

7. **The Chaundy Collection** consists of tape recordings made by Theo W. Chaundy in 1956, 1957, and 1959. Available online through the www.merryville.uk website of Folk Arts Oxford. The recorded tunes include:

Tape 1, 1956:

The Quaker's Wife, Over the Hills to Glory, Country Gardens

Tape 2, 1956:

The Village Pump, The Fly Be on the Turmut, Getting Upstairs, Constant Billy, Christ Church Bells (incomplete)

Tape 3, 1956:

Princess Royal

Tape 4, 1956

Church Bells, Swaggering Boney

Tape 5, 10 June 1957:

Getting Upstairs, Shepherd's Hey, Laudnum Bunches, Jockie to the Fair, Young Collins, The Fool's Dance (Manchester Hornpipe), Brighton Camp / Cock o' the North, Bonny Green Garters.

Index

Page numbers in italic refer to illustrations and transcriptions. Entry names in italic are tunes.

A

Akenfeld 10
Alberts quadrilles 228-229

B

Bacca Pipes 51, 83-89, 113, *128*
Ballroom dance 227-232
Barn dance 230
Basic Template 81-86, 93
Bean Setting 114, *130*
Birch, Dora 28, 35
Blue-Eyed Stranger 115, *132*
Bonnets So Blue 199, *206*
Bonny Dundee 234, *242*
Bonny Green Garters 171, *178*
Booth, Herbert 272
Boxing Day 1899 24, 36-38
Branch, James Jarrett (about) 313
Brickmaking and bricklaying 12-13
Brighton Camp (Eynsham) 172, *180*
Britannia Public House 5-6, 25

C

Caledonian quadrille 229
Carey, Clive 53
Cecil Sharp House 62-63
Chapman, Dooley 77
Chaundy, Theodore 231, *233*, 272, 305
Chequers pub 5-6, 22, 25, *28, 31*
Chording and chord choices 78, 90-93
Church Bells, The 277, *297*
Cock o' the North 173, *182*
Constant Billy 38, 101-103, 115, *133*
Concertinas and playing them
    Arrival in London 32
    Arrival in Oxford 33, *34*
    Arrival in the Quarry 30-31
    Basic Template 81-86
    Chording and chord choices 78, 90-93
    Finishing Touches 87-88
    Keyboard basics 79
    Lesson from Kimber 99-100
    Modern playing styles 76
    Octave playing 76-77, 81-83, 95
    Playing to the step 78
    Song accompaniment 272-273
    Style on two-row Anglos 77, 79-80
    Use in Morris dancing 30-32, 77-78
Corn Exchange, Oxford 27-28
Country Gardens 93-94, 116, *134*
Coppock, George 55
Country Dances 195-199
Cox, Mark 27-28, 54-55
Cripps, Florence Mary 4, 35, 43
    Death 45, 58
Crown and Thistle pub 5-6
Cummings, Frank 24, 25, *26,* 77

D

Digby, Roger 75
Donkey Cock Your Tail Up 234, *245*
Double Lead Through 199, *208*
Double Set Back 116, *138*

E

East, Maurice 15-16
English Country Music 232
English Folk Dance Society *see* English Folk Dance and Song Society
English Folk Dance and Song Society 37, 62, 63, 65
    Position on traditional dance 231-232
English folk revival 45-52
Espérance Girls Club, 45-49

F

Father O'Flynn 234, *246*
Finishing Touches 87-88, 93
First of May, The 273, *283*
Fly Be on the Turmut, The 274, *292*
Fool's Jig, The 173, 274, *288*

G

Galup 230-231
Getting Upstairs 95-97, 117, *140*
Grainger, Percy 48, 64
Gramophone Company recordings, 301-302
Gypsies (Romany) 12, 22

H

Ham, Phil 75
Haste to the Wedding 118, *142*
Headington
    Ancient roots 1, 9-10
    Stone and quarrying 4-7
Headington mill, 2, 5-6
Headington Morris Reel 118, *274, 292*
Headington Roughs 12
Headington Quarry
    Brickmaking 12-13
    Economy 11, 13-15
    Gardening *8,* 14-15, 44-45
    Gypsies (Romany) 12, 22
    Headington Roughs 12, 16
    Laundries 14
    Music 34
    Magdalen Quarry 66
    Origin 1, 6-12
    Morris side *see* Morris Dancing
    Open village 10-11
    Pig raising 14-15
    Poaching 15-16
    Social customs 18-23
    Stone quarries 9
    Working life 13-17
Headington Quarry Morris Dancing
    At Chequers *31*
    At Sandfield 28
    Dance types 111-112
    Joins Morris Ring 65
    Today 299

Henry Taunt photos 28-31
Highland fling 230
Holy Trinity church 4, 5-6, 7, 17-18
   Churchyard 18
Hilly-go Filly-go 199, *212*
Horspath 2
Horwood, Saccy 22-23
How D'ye Do, Sir? 119, *145*
Huggins Cottage 3, 4, 5-6, *8*
Hunting the Squirrel 119, *146*

I

I Love the Gal with the Blue Frock On 234, *248*

J

Jockie to the Fair 120, *148*
Jones, Kit 272

K

Karpeles, Maud 57, 62-63, 227, 231
Keel Row 235, *250*
Kennedy, Douglas 63, 232
Kennedy, Peter 227, 231, *233*, 305
Kimber, Anthony 2, 9
Kimber, Job 2-3, 13, 24
Kimber, Sophia Ann, 2, *4*
Kimber, William junior
   Bacca Pipes dance 51
   Ballroom dance repertoire 227-232
   Birth 4
   Cornerstone for Sharp House 62-63
   Death 67-68
   Death of Sharp 62
   Early life 4, 18
   Early Morris dancing 18, 24-25, 27, 35
   Family life 35, 43-44
   "Father of the English Morris" 65
   Gardening 44
   Gold medal, EFDS 62
   Learns concertina 33
   Like a Greek statue 55-56
   Marriage to Florence Cripps 35
      Her death, 45, 58
   Marriage to Bessie Kethro, 60
   Meets Cecil Sharp 36-37

Missing the Corn Exchange 29-30
Money concerns 43, 60-61, 66
Morris demonstrations with Sharp, Neal 45-51, 55-57
   Morris Ring activity 65
   Oxford City Police Morris 61
   Pig raising 15
   Playing style 73-88
   Post WWI dancing 60-61
   Silver Jubilee Morris Ring 67
   Steinway Hall concertina presentation 50-51
   Teaching at Secondary School 65
   Work interruptions 51
   World War I 57-58
Kimber, William senior 2-4, *4*, 13
   Drinking problem and avoidance of Morris 29-30
   Morris dancing 24, 25, 27, 29
   Supporting son in conflict 54-55
Kimberlins 6
Kirkpatrick, John 75
Kirtlington Ale 24
Kitty Come 235, *252*

L

Lancers quadrilles 228
Laudnum Bunches 120, *152*
Levy, Bertram 101-103
Little Polly 235, *254*
Loveless, Rev. Kenneth 64-65, 68, 104

M

Macilwaine, Herbert 46
Manchester Hornpipe 173, 274, *288*
Manning, Percy 24, 27-29, 57
Mason's Arms pub 15, *16*
May Day 18-19
Mayblossom 235, *236, 256*
Merrie England Once More 48-49
Merryville 5-6, 12, 43-44, *44*, 64
Minstrel rhythm 95-96
Modern concertina styles 76
Moonlight 236, *260*
Morris dancing 23-30
   Headington Quarry side 3,4
   Early quarry dancers 25, *26*
Morris Motors Cowley 58-59

Morris Off 173, *186*
Morris On 173, *184*
Mummers 21-22

N

Nae Good Luck About the Hoose 236, *262*
Neal, Mary 46, 74
   Conflict with Sharp, 48-49, 52-57
   Espérance Girls Club, 45-49
   Leaves folk music and dance 57

O

Octave playing 76-77, 81-83, 95
Off She Goes 200, *215*
Old Mother Oxford 121, *154*
Old Woman Tossed Up in a Blanket 121, *158*
Open Magdalen 11-12
Over the Hills to Glory 98-99, 237, *264*
Oxford City Police Morris 61
Oxford suburbanization 58-59

P

Peeling horns 18-19, *19*
Pipe and tabor, *26*, 77-78
Polkas 226-227, 230
Pop Goes the Weasel 200, *216*
Princess Royal 99-100 174, *188*

Q

Quadrilles 226-228
Quaker's Wife, The 201, *219*

R

Recordings of Kimber 301-306
Reels, dance 26
Ribbon Dance, The 201, *220*
Rigs o' Marlow 122, *160*
Rodney 122, *161*
Rowley, Stephen 77

S

Sandfield Cottage 5-6, 24, 67

Schottische 226, 230
Sharp, Cecil
    Boxing Day 1899 36
    Biography 37
    Conflict with Neal, 48-49, 52-57
    Country dance 56-57
    Death, 62
    Lectures with Neal 45-47
    Demonstrations with Kimber 45-51
    Morris Book 47, 56
    Stratford upon Avon school 56-57
Sheep Roast 19-20, *20*
Shepherd's Hey 123, *163*
Shotover Hill 2
Six Bells pub 5-6, 22
Social dancing 22-23
Soldier's Joy 274, *290*
Song accompaniment 272-273
Smith, Sampson 12, 54
Stratford upon Avon school 56-57, 65, *194*
Swaggering Boney 174, *191*

T

Taproom amusement 269-273
Taunt, Henry photos 29, *31-32*
Tester, Scan 77, 226
Titup neighborhood 2, 5-6, *8,* 9
Trafford, Joseph 24, 25, *26,* 53-55, 97
Transcriptions, notes on 107-108
Triumph, The 201, *222*
Trunkles 123, *164*
Twenty-Ninth of May, The 124, *166*

V

Village Pump, The 275, *294*

W

Waltzes 226-227
Watcham, John, 75
Webb, Dusty 16-17
Wells, William "Jinky" 64, 65, *192*
Whitsuntide week 25, 27, 28
William Kimber Crescent 66
Willow Tree, The 124, *168*
Wonder, The 273, *28*
Worrall, Dan (about) 313

Y

Young Collins 175, *193*

Dan Worrall (top left), Jarrett Branch (bottom left), and both with Ann Droney Kirrane at Consairtín, at the launch of their book *Chris Droney of Bell Harbour and the Tradition of the Concertina in North Clare*, Ennis, County Clare Ireland, February 2023.

About the Authors

Dan Michael Worrall is one of a fifth generation of his family to live in the Houston, Texas area. Trained in regional geology, he enjoyed a career in petroleum exploration research and management. He holds a bachelor's degree from Rice University, a Master of Arts from the University of Wyoming, and a PhD from the University of Texas at Austin, all in geology.

Dan has played the concertina for almost 50 years and has published a number of works for that instrument, including a first edition of *The Anglo Concertina Music of William Kimber* (London: English Folk Dance and Song Society, 2005); *The Anglo-German Concertina: A Social History* (2 vols., Fulshear, Texas: Concertina Press, 2008); *Tripping to the Well: Six Clare Women and Mrs. O'Dwyer's Old German Concertina* (CD, Miltown Malbay, Ireland: Oidhreacht an Chláir, 2014), and most recently, with his co-author Jarrett Branch, *Chris Droney of Bell Harbour and the Tradition of the Concertina in North Clare* (Honolulu, Hawaii: Rollston Press, 2023). He also recently reissued a study that was originally published in 2012 by Musical Traditions, of the 19th century global house dance phenomenon and the concertina's connection to it: *House Dance: Dance Music Played on the Anglo-German Concertina by Musicians of the House Dance Era* (Rollston Press, 2022). He has been an editor of the online *Concertina Journal* since its inception in 2016 and has led an annual concertina workshop at the Palestine (Texas) Old Time Music Festival since 2004.

He is also an avid avocational historian, with two recent books on Texas history: *Pleasant Bend: Upper Buffalo Bayou and the San Felipe Trail* (2016) and *A Prehistory of Houston and Southeast Texas: Landscape and Culture* (2021). Dan and his wife Mary live on a farm in the lower Brazos valley just west of Fulshear, Texas. They have two grown children, Dan Jr. and Fiona, and three grandchildren, Teddy, Margaret, and Eleanor.

James Jarrett Branch is a native Texan who grew up in Pasadena, Texas, and currently lives in Friendswood, Texas with his wife Darby and daughter Maggie. James holds a bachelor's degree in computer science and mathematics from Sam Houston State University, and a master's degree in mathematics from the University of Houston. He has worked as a computer engineer since 2008.

James has studied music throughout his life by collecting and learning to play a variety of instruments, including drums, guitar, and highland bagpipes, and has performed music in different capacities through the years. James has always listened to Irish and English traditional music and wanted to play it with a small instrument that wasn't a whistle, which inspired him to pick up the concertina in 2018. Since then he has enjoyed focusing on learning the techniques and styles of Chris Droney and William Kimber, attending the Palestine (Texas) Old Time Music Festival, and becoming a part of the concertina community. The current work is his second; he co-authored with Dan Worrall *Chris Droney of Bell Harbour and the Tradition of the Concertina in North Clare* (Honolulu, Hawaii: Rollston Press, 2023).

www.ingramcontent.com/pod-product-compliance
Lightning Source LLC
Chambersburg PA
CBHW080542230426
43663CD00015D/2679